LITTLE KNOWN HISTORY OF THE TEXAS BIG BEND:

Documented Chronicles From Cabeza De Vaca to the Era of Pancho Villa

By Glenn Justice

Editors
Glenn P. Willeford
Dr. Dorothy P. Fuller
B. Tipton Chesney

Rimrock Press
P. O Box 13292
Odessa, Texas 79768
www.rimrockpress.com

First Edition

Manufactured in the United States of America

ISBN 0-9722083-0-5

For Boss

For Harry & Dora,
Hope you enjoy!
muchas gracias!
Glenn

CONTENTS

Acknowledgements

Little Known History of the Texas Big Bend is dedicated to Ronald Boyd Chambers of Presidio County, Texas. For more than twenty years, I had the great privilege of knowing Boyd and being his friend. He was a master storyteller and a walking encyclopedia of knowledge about horses, cattle, ranching, history, wildlife and the land. Boss was a man of his word and always the mediator on both sides of the border. With his passing, the Big Bend has lost one of its finest ambassadors.

I am indebted to historian Glenn P. Willieford of Ciudad Chihuahua for his insight and thoughtful editing. Also, thanks to Dr. Dorthy Fuller at Black Hills State University for graciously editing and proof reading the manuscript. My friend Tipton Chesney read and advised me about the manuscript from the earliest drafts. Thanks are due Melleta Bell and Gaylan Corbin for opening their fine collections in the Archives of the Big Bend at Sul Ross State University in Alpine. Wendy Lynn Wright contributed her talent and expertise by creating and designing the cover art and the photo section. I cannot forget to mention Marian Walker of Candelaria, granddaughter of J.J. Kilpatrick, who first inspired my interest in the wonderful history of the Texas Big Bend. Thanks is due as well to many others who shared their thoughts, family history, photographs, and allowed me to interview them over the years. Also, I wish to thank all of my friends in the Big Bend who over the years have helped with their ideas, encouragement and opened doors on so many occasions.

Preface

This book had its beginnings in 1977 when I made my first trip to the Big Bend and became fascinated with the region and its colorful past. Long obscured by myth, legend and time, the history of the Big Bend has not been fully written and that is why I wanted to write the book. I have tried to be as careful as possible and it has taken many years.

In my examination of the U. S. Army and the Texas Rangers and their clashes with Mexicans in the Big Bend during the revolution, I found a number of insightful sources, some of which had not been used previously. They include several collections of private papers, state and federal documents, unpublished manuscripts, and newspaper accounts. Some of the private collections are the papers of James Judson Kilpatrick 1857-1935, the correspondence of Robert F. Keil 1961-1969, and the Harry Warren Papers 1835-1935. These collections contain contemporary accounts and afterthoughts of individuals who had first hand knowledge of the events. Kilpatrick, Keil, and Warren are important because they bring to light an opposing view to that of the U. S. Army and the Texas Rangers which has dominated the historiography. Like any historical source each has their limitations.

Both Kilpatrick and Warren were very colorful and controversial individuals. J.J. Kilpatrick was a hard drinking but brilliant Georgia educator and cotton farmer who became known as the King of Candelaria because he ruled his town like a feudal baron. He refused to be intimated either by the violence in Mexico or the U. S. Army in Texas. Although the son of a prominent Baptist preacher in Georgia, Kilpatrick did not let his strict religious upbringing influence his enjoyment of strong drink. He frequently imbibed and at times proved himself to be quite a handful when he over indulged. Living on the border at Candelaria, he found sotol, the fiery Mexican liquor, in plentiful supply. Kilpatrick's drinking caused him innumerable problems. The fact that he was an alcoholic is evidenced in his writings, presenting the historical researcher with a considerable challenge. In spite of this, Kilpatrick's papers should not be dismissed as merely the ramblings of a drunk for they offer a unique insight. For this reason, every effort has been made to verify the Kilpatrick papers with other sources. Remarkably, many of Kilpatrick's accounts have proven to be accurate. The best two examples of the are the Porvenir massacre and his assessment of Albert B. Fall some twelve years before the senator went to prison for his involvement in the notorious Tea Pot Dome scandal.

Like Kilpatrick, Harry Warren had a college education and proved himself certainly not afraid to stay on the border when things got rough. Warren and Kilpatrick were very outspoken. The U. S. Army painted both men with a black brush because they tried to make public several incidents that embarrassed the military, including the massacre at Porvenir and the last American punitive expedition into Mexico in 1919. Harry Warren's efforts to bring the Porvenir murders to light lasted until the end of his life. Warren is more credible than Kilpatrick simply because the Porvenir school master had no axe to grind in spite of the fact that the U.S. Army did everything possible to ruin him because of his unceasing efforts to let the world know of the terrible events. His motives for doing this are above question. He suffered a great deal personally because of his outspokenness. Neither Kilpatrick nor Warren were present that terrible night in 1917 at Porvenir. Then Eighth Cavalry Corporal Robert F. Keil bears the burden of knowing about the Porvenir murders and keeping silent for more than forty years. Only Bob Keil knew his reasons for this. It was not until 1961 that he first put in writing his version of the massacre. Keil's writings are suspect because he is an apologist for the U. S. Army and others. Although present the night of the killings, Keil's commanding officer, Captain Henry H. Anderson, denied even the presence of U. S. troops at the massacre.

In addition to the Kilpatrick, Warren, and Keil accounts, I found a number of related state and federal documents in Austin at the Texas State Archives and the University of Texas. These include, *Proceedings of the Joint Committee of the Senate and the House in the Investigation of the Texas State Ranger Force*, January 13, 1919; *Biennial Reports of the Adjutant General of Texas* 1911-1918; *Governors' Papers, James E. Ferguson; Governors' Papers, William P. Hobby*, and *Texas Rangers Papers*. Federal Documents examined in Austin include, *Papers Relating to the Foreign Relations of the United States 1910-1920; Records of the Department of State Relating to the Infernal Affairs of Mexico 1910-1929; United States Senate Investigation of Mexican Affairs*, and the *Annual Reports of the War Department 1910-1920*. This wealth of information fills in many gaps in the story and points to other border topics needing further research.

Materials researched in the National Archives in Washington, D.C., include *The Records of United States Regular Army Mobile Units*, Record Group 391. These are divided into two groups, regimental records and troop records. They contain correspondence, general orders, special orders, and histories of officers, regimental scrapbooks, monthly returns, field returns, and registers of letters sent and received.

Also found in Washington are *Records of the United States Army Continental Commands, 1821-1920*, Record Group 393, including the records of the Big Bend District 1914-15 and 1917-20. RG 393 has general correspondence of the Big Bend district, 1918-1919, 1919-20, special orders 1917 and 1919-20; also, correspondence relating to U. S. Guards 1917-20, correspondence, telegrams, strength reports and reports of troop movement of U. S. Guards 1917-20, general correspondence of the intelligence officer 1917-21, correspondence relating to the Mexican revolution 1913-16, weekly reports relating to the conditions on the Mexican border, 1913-16, and general court martial orders 1913 and 1915-20. Record Group 393 contains the records of Fort D A. Russell, Texas, 1914-1946, with records of miscellaneous correspondence dealing with Mexican border troubles 1917-19. Record Group 407 of the Adjutant General's office has the monthly and semimonthly strength returns of the 5th Cavalry and the 8th Cavalry. There are records of events, troop assignments, troop strengths and locations, and officers present and absent and their assignments. These records were useful in tying the border raids to the Mexican revolution and understanding what was happening in Mexico.

Some of the newspapers researched are: *El Paso Times*, *El Paso Herald*, *New York Times*, *San Antonio Express*, and Mexico City *Excelsior*. A word of caution about the newspaper sources: frequently the American newspapers only printed the official U.S. Army version of the events since press blackouts were common and reporters were not allowed along the border.

"Being asked what route they took, having set out from the mines of Santa Barbola and the journey having been begun, and through what pueblos and provinces they passed, he replied that on the 6th of June of last year, 1581, he, his companions, and the religious set out from the valley of San Gregorio, of the jurisdiction of Santa Barbola, Nueva Vizcaya, and went down the same valley until they came to the river named Concha (Rio Concho), where they found a little settlement of wild Indians, who were naked and lived on roots and other things found in the fields; and following down the river, they came to another to which they gave the name of the Guadalquivir (Rio Grande), because it was large and carried an abundance of water. On this river they found other Indians of a different nation and tongue from those of the Concha, they too were naked. These and others received them peacefully, and willingly offered them what they had, and when inquiry was made of them as to whether there were more settlements beyond, they said yes, and that they were a people like themselves, and hostile to and at war with them."

From the Declaration of Pedro de Bustamente

Cabeza De Vaca and the People of the Cow Nation

Chapter One

To seventeenth century Spaniards familiar with the northern provinces of Mexico, the region containing the Texas Big Bend came to be known in their day as the *despoblado*. The *despoblado* included all of Trans-Pecos Texas and much of the present Mexican states of Chihuahua and Coahuila. In Spanish, *despoblado* means, "deserted spot, uninhabited place." One Spaniard wrote of the *despoblado* saying it, "contains steep places, dry places, few water holes, and great distances.... For this reason it cannot be inhabited nor populated by rational Christians." One Spanish governor recorded he saw no towns, birds, or animals in the *despoblado*. A´lvar Nu´ñez Cabeza De Vaca (1490-1556), a sixteenth century Spaniard but, more importantly, the first European to set foot in the Texas Big Bend, found the vast desert mountain valleys located between present day Presidio and El Paso to be inhabited by Native Americans who lived in mud houses, farmed, traded, and hunted buffalo. His journeys and writings became the first written account of the New World marking the important transition from prehistoric to historic times. De Vaca's writings ignited the flame of Spanish conquest in the American Southwest.[1]

In 1535, De Vaca and three companions arrived at the junction of the Rio Conchos and the Rio Grande not far upriver from present Presidio, Texas. De Vaca found his way to the mouth of the Rio Conchos after an extraordinary seven-year journey that began in February 1527. In that year the intrepid explorer received his appointment as treasurer of the ill-fated Pa´nfilio de Narvaez expedition. The expedition had been organized to colonize the coast of the Gulf of Mexico. Narvaez landed not far from present Tampa Bay, Florida in April 1528 and split his forces into two groups against the advice of De Vaca. De Vaca's band proceeded by a land route while the other group traveled by sea in the ships that transported them from Spain. Unfortunately, when the land party failed to meet at a prearranged time, the ships set sail for Spain leaving their companions marooned. Hoping to reach New Spain by crossing the Gulf of Mexico, Narvaez ordered the construction of crude boats. Then disaster struck. De Vaca's boat sank in a storm off Galveston Island. A second boat made it ashore not far away. Although some eighty men escaped drowning, only fifteen lived through the following winter. After being captured by Indians, De Vaca escaped and journeyed inland. The explorer lived for the coming years trading and traveling among the Indians of Texas.[2]

De Vaca's route to La Junta de los Ri´os is disputed. La Junta de los Ri´os is the name given to the area where Mexico's Rio Conchos flows into the Rio Grande a few miles upriver from present Presidio, Texas. Some scholars contend the Spanish explorer likely came to the river junction by traveling down Alamito Creek a few miles east of the Chinati Mountains in present Presidio County. More recent research points to De Vaca arriving in the river valley from the western bank of the Rio Grande. The precise route of Cabeza De Vaca across Texas or parts of Mexico before coming to the vicinity of La Junta de los Ri´os is a historical topic to be debated for years to come. However, when he departed La Junta de los Ri´os trekking upriver in the direction of present El Paso, his route was determined largely by the geography of the vast and rugged Rio Grande River valley. Bounded on the west by the Sierra Madre and on the east by the Sierra Vieja, De Vaca followed a trail through the mountains used for untold centuries by Native Americans. For more than two hundred years, other Spaniards followed the same Rio Grande River valley trail. It is along this river trail that De Vaca encountered the "Cow People", also known in later historical accounts as Jumano Indians. In later years, the fearless explorer penned an account of his adventures thus producing the first written record of the Jumano in Spanish records. De Vaca likely referred to the La Junta Jumanos as the "cow people" because they hunted buffalo which De Vaca called cows. First published in 1542, De Vaca's extraordinary narrative marks the greatly significant point of transition between prehistoric and historic times.[3]

De Vaca described his reception by the "cow people," "From now on, the natives, when apprised of our approach, did not throng out on the trail to welcome us as heretofore, but we found them (in an attitude of extreme dread and supplication) sitting in their houses facing the wall with bowed heads, their hair pulled down over their eyes, and all their possessions piled in the middle of the floor. Houses they had made to accommodate us stood ready. Our gifts, from the first place that received us like this on, included many skin blankets: but there was nothing they owned that they did not freely give us. They are the best looking people we saw, the strongest and most energetic, and who most readily understood us and answered our questions. We called them the 'Cow People,' because more cattle are killed in their vicinity than anywhere; for more than fifty leagues up that river they prey on the cows. They go as absolutely naked as the first Indians we encountered, the women of course wearing deerskins, as well as a few men, mostly those too old to fight anymore. The country is incredibly populous."[4]

De Vaca wrote, "We asked how it happened they did not plant corn. So they would not lose what they planted was their answer: no rain two years in a row; must have plenty rain before planting again. They begged us to tell the sky to rain; we promised we would pray. Where, we asked them, did they get the corn they had? From where the sun goes down; in that country it grew all over; the quickest way there was that path. They did not wish to go with us, so we asked them to be more explicit. They said to take the path along the northward; otherwise we would go seventeen *joradas* without finding anything to eat but *chacan* which, even after ground between stones, is hard to get down, being so woody and pungent and sure enough, when they showed us a sample we could not eat it. The people who lived along the river valley were enemies of the Cow People but spoke the same tongue; though they would nevertheless receive us hospitably and load us with cotton blankets, hides, etc., said our hosts who, however, advised against that route. Uncertain as to the better choice, we tarried another couple of days with these Indians, who plied us with beans and calabashes. Their method of cooking is so novel and strange, let me describe it. Not having discovered pots, they fill a medium-sized calabash (gourd) hull full of water and drop red-hot rocks in it with stick tongs until the water boils. Then for the whole while that whatever they put in to cook is cooking, they keep transferring more rocks from the fire and taking out the spent ones. They know which rocks take heat best, and the water boils on and on." De Vaca concluded his narrative of the "people of the cows," by saying, "After two days of indecision, we concluded that our destiny lay towards the sunset and so took the trail north only as far as we had to....[5]

De Vaca's "cow people" were more than likely the same Native Americans described by later Spanish explorers as Jumano Indians. But there are many problems with the term Jumano. The designation is vague and elusive at best since it is a broadly used label given these Indians by the Spanish. Jumano is a Spanish name widely and sometimes carelessly applied to many different Indian groups. Also, written accounts of the Jumanos end by about 1700. The Spanish referred to the name Jumano to mean *rayado* or "striped Indian" referring to their practice of painting or tattooing their bodies. Spanish documents reflect a number of variations of the name including Jumano, Jumanas, Humanas, Humanes, Umana, Xumanas, Choma, and Choman. The French called them Chouman. As many as nine different Indian groups occupied the Texas Big Bend according to Spanish accounts. These include the Jumanos, Julimes, Rayados, Oposmes, Polumes, Polulanas, Polaques, Cibilos, and Patarabueyes. The Jumanos, the Cibilos, and the Apache are identified as having lived at one time or the other in the Texas Big Bend. Of some nine Indian groups, early historical documents deal primarily with the Jumanos, Cibilos, Patarabueyes, and the Apache. Some Jumanos were buffalo hunters who followed the bison herds across the plains of West Texas during the hunting season, spending the winter in the warmer climate of La Junta. In their travels, they traded bison hides and buckskin among the Native American tribes with whom they enjoyed friendly relations.[6]

The Jumanos have been historically described as, "aggressive traders of the highest order." In addition to trade in hides, the Jumanos exchanged meat and salt and likely engaged in slave trading. They also may have exchanged East Texas Osage orange wood, used in making bows and arrows. Some evidence indicates the Jumanos carried on trade as far east as the Gulf Coast of present Texas. Karankawa Indians of the Texas Gulf Coast are also thought to have used the Toyah arrow point as did the Patarabueyes. The Jumanos may have introduced the sinew-backed bow into central and southern Texas in their trading activities. Cabeza De Vaca noted that the bow and arrow was in wide spread use across Texas, and he observed that most tribes obtained the bow and arrow through trade. It is interesting to note that a great deal of Jumano barter took place in prehistoric times before the introduction of the horse by the Spanish. Also noteworthy is the fact that the La Junta Jumanos lived in a location that permitted trade with East Texas tribes as well as Southwestern and Mexican Indian groups. From the Patarabueyes to the west, the Jumano acquired turquoise, cotton cloth, copper bells, and probably sinew-backed bows as well as arrows. From the south, they obtained maize, hides, and flint.[7] It is known that by 1683, the Jumanos carried on trade with more than thirty-six Indian groups. They have been described as having been friends and allies of the Patarabueyes and the Cibolos. In addition, the Jumano enjoyed friendly trade with the Tejas, the Red River Caddo, the Tompirio of Gran Quivira, the Iapes, the Xabatoas, and the *jediondos* among many others. Early on, the Jumanos enjoyed good relations with the Spanish and the French. After 1700, the Jumanos settled their differences with the Apache, who had been bitter enemies in earlier times. The Jumanos proved themselves to be assertive warriors and counted among their enemies the Chisos, Cuitoas, Escanjaques, Aijados, and in the eighteenth century, the Comanche and Wichita. The Jumanos lived in various camps, rock shelters, and *rancherias* usually situated near springs, creeks, or rivers. Some lived in buffalo skin tepees. Little is known about the physical characteristics of the Jumano although they have been as being "flat headed." They decorated themselves with tattoos and paint. Probably the hair and dress styles were similar to the Patarabueye whose men wore scalp locks beautified with feathers. The Jumanos made long bone beads worn in the hair. In addition to hunting, the Jumano fished, gathered mesquite beans, calabashes or gourds, and prickly pear. Jumano villages appear to have been of varying sizes. As many as two thousand Jumanos lived in one *rancheria* although other tribes may have been included in the number. Another Jumano *rancheria* was located near La Junta in 1716.[8]

The Patarabueye of Spanish accounts are sometimes confused with the Jumanos although some research shows the two groups to be separate. The Patarabueyes, like the Jumanos, were known by many different names and may have also been De Vaca's "cow people". Archaeological evidence indicates the Patarabueyes may have been more of a farming culture. There existed among the Patarabueyes several different bands or tribes, with the more prominent being the Julimes, Conchos, and Cibolos. Patarabueyes lived along the Rio Conchos from Julimes to La Junta, and near the Rio Grande from about present Redford upriver roughly north of Candelaria and in "immediately adjacent areas." The Cibolos Indians lived in a pueblo in the Chinati Mountains near Cibolo Creek, which probably got its name from these Indians. Cibolos or Sibolos as they were called by the Spanish, means "bison" and the Cibolos, like the Jumanos also hunted buffalo. The Patarabueyes had friendly relations with the Conchos, Sumas, Jumanos, and usually the Spanish. They counted as their enemies the Chisos, Apache, and depending upon occasion the Spanish.[9]

Spaniards describe the Patarabueye to be tall and clean with the men being handsome and the women, beautiful. They adorned their, "faces, arms and bodies striped with pleasing lines." The men usually went naked but when necessary covered themselves with tanned buffalo hides. The males of the Tanpachoas decorated their penises with colored cotton ribbons. Patarabueye men had short hair on the sides leaving the hair in the middle of their head longer. They painted their hair in a way that made it appear to be a skullcap and wore scalp locks beautified with the feathers of "geese, cranes, and sparrow hawks." The women had long hair usually worn tied. Patarabueye were fond of jewelry and ornaments fashioning such embellishments from turquoise, shells, and polished pebbles. They used hematite to produce red colored body paint. One Patarabueye male was observed wearing a piece of copper tied "about his neck with some cotton threads." Like the Jumanos, the Patarabueye hunted buffalo, deer, and other game, but they were mainly farmers growing corn, beans, squash, wheat, watermelons, pumpkins, and tobacco. Early Spanish reports describe Patarabueye farmers flooding their fields as a means of irrigation. Apparently, early in the eighteenth century, they used ditch irrigation methods. In addition to farming, the Patarabueye gathered mesquite beans, mescal, prickly pear fruit, and other wild plants. The Patarabueye fished the Rio Grande and Rio Conchos with nets.[10]

The housing of the Patarabueye also seems to identify them as a distinct group separate from the Jumanos. The Jumanos lived in tepees, pitched in nomadic camps, and are known to have occupied rock shelters. Patarabueye dwellings, however, were much more permanent. The Patarabueye lived in pit houses constructed "half under and half above the ground." The framework of the houses consisted of cottonwood uprights and beams, some as large as a man's thigh. They probably constructed the walls by cutting *ocotillo* stalks, attaching them to the beams and covered the wall with mud. Some of the houses were quite large, providing shelter to several families. Patarabueye are known to have constructed ceremonial houses containing altars made of adobe. Other structures built by the Patarabueye include storage buildings described as "granaries built of willow after the fashion of the Mexicans, where they keep their provisions and their harvest of mesquite and other things." In many cases, Patarabueye villages were built on high ground and contained "neatly kept" *plazas*. At least one such village is known to have been surrounded by a wall, probably built for protection. The villages were of varying size and population ranging from as few as 80 residents to more than 500 with scattered estimates running higher.[11]

Patarabueye Indians fashioned a large number of different tools and pottery. These Indians processed buffalo hides by using stone scrapers and softened the skins by beating them with stones. The Patarabueye cut the hide with stone knives and used various awls and drills. Patarabueye archaeological sites reveal large numbers of *metates* that were used in conjunction with oval shaped bowls to grind foodstuffs. They made pottery in the form of bowls, jars, and trays by the coiling method decorated their work with red paint. Several types of pottery have been identified as being of Patarabueye manufacture including Chinati, Capote, Paloma, and Conchos. They also made stone pipes and ceremonial drums resembling tambourines that are mentioned in Spanish accounts. Patarabueye warriors used sinew-backed bows and defended themselves with shields made of buffalo skin, and in at least one instance of warfare utilized "bludgeons half a yard in length made of *tornillo* wood."[12]

Following his adventures in Texas, Cabeza De Vaca made his way to Mexico City in 1536 bringing with him tales of fantastic wealth and riches in the northern provinces. Relating the stories told him by Naive Americans, De Vaca described large populated cities containing great riches in the north. Viceroy Antonio de Mendoza received De Vaca's report favorably thereby beginning an era of Spanish exploration. Although the original reports that the intrepid explorer gave to the viceroy have been lost, De Vaca wrote in later years, "Throughout this region, wherever we encountered mountains, we saw undeniable indications of gold, antimony, iron, copper, and other metals." He said the Jumanos and other tribes he encountered "regard gold and silver with indifference, seeing no use for either." As a result of De Vaca's glowing accounts, the viceroy sent Fray Marcos De Niza, a Franciscan friar, to verify De Vaca's claims. Friar Marcos set out in 1539 from Culiacan and later returned to further excite the Spanish saying he had seen the fabulous seven cities of Cibola. Actually, Friar Marcos probably only saw some Zuni pueblos from a distance and felt compelled to exaggerate his experience.[13]

Fueled by a desire to conquer the riches of the northern provinces, Spanish exploration continued for more than two hundred years. Almost half a century after De Vaca recorded his account of the '"cow people," the Chamuscado-Rodriguez *entrada* passed through the La Junta region and recorded observations of the Jumanos living there. Led by a Catholic priest, the *entrada* originated in the mining town of Santa Barabra near the headwaters of the Rio Conchos in southern Chihuahua. Santa Barabra was a rich mining district lacking only in a supply of slave labor to operate the mines. Although illegal, the use of slaves was practiced during that time with some slave hunting expeditions going into the country north of the Rio Grande. It is for this reason that many of the Indians feared the Spanish and hid from them when they approached. In traveling along the Rio Conchos, the *entrada* passed by Pazaguantes and Conchos Indians before reaching La Junta. On July 6, 1581 the *entrada* came to a point on the Rio Grande about five or six leagues (approximately thirteen to sixteen miles) above the mouth of the Rio Conchos near the Chinati Mountains. During this time, the valley of the Rio Grande near La Junta was known to the Spanish as Valle de Concepti´on.[14]

The *entrada* stayed in Valle de Concepti´on for only few days. They saw many Jumano Indians and placed crosses in several of their *rancherias*. The chronicler of the expedition, Hernando Gallegos, noted that the Jumanos in the valley spoke a different language than the other tribes he saw living along the Rio Conchos, but the two groups could understand each other. He also described the Jumanos by saying, "The men are very handsome and the women beautiful." The Jumanos wore stripes on their faces and lived in mud houses subsisting on pumpkins, beans, and corn. The community was situated, "in a beautiful valley, filled with large trees," and the soil looked suitable for cultivation. One pueblo was occupied by a "great number" of Indians, and the Spaniards noted that these were the first "fixed residences" they had seen in their journey up the Rio Conchos. The Indians received the *entrada* with "respect and homage" which the Spaniards attributed to Cabeza De Vaca's "miracles." The Otomacos told the Spaniards stories of seeing four men with beards many years ago thus leading the members of the *entrada* to believe that this was in reference to Cabeza De Vaca's party. The Indians also related that "clothed people with large pueblos" lived not far upriver. This information caused the *entrada* to move in that direction. As many as 300 Indians accompanied the party. After traveling some 45 leagues or about 118 miles, the *entrada* arrived at an Otomaco village of Magdalena on the western bank of the Rio Grande. The place marked the northern boundary of the La Junta Jumano community. During the next few months, Father August´in and the Spaniards continued their journey up the Rio Grande traveling into the vicinity of Santa Fe exploring many of the pueblos of the upper Rio Grande. Early in 1582, Father August´in and another friar resolved to remain among the Indians, and the *entrada* departed. A short time later, Indians murdered the two priests.[15]

The *entrada* reached Santa Barbara in April 1582, unaware of the fate of the two priests. A second expedition headed by Antonio de Espejo set out from Santa Barbara in November 1582 to rescue the priests. Espejo, a native of Spain where he had been a successful cattle rancher, came to Mexico as an officer of the Inquisition after he had been involved in the murder of a *vaquero*. Hoping to gain clemency from the royal Spanish crown, he traveled to the northern provinces heading the expedition to rescue the two priests. Espejo's *entrada* consisted of two Franciscans and fifteen soldiers each of whom supplied their own arms and provisions. A small number of Indian servants and interpreters joined the expedition. Following a route up the Rio Conchos similar to the one taken by Father August´in, Espejo reached La

Junta in twenty-six days.[16]

In a chronicle of his expedition, Espejo described his stay among the La Junta Jumano, "... we came to another (nation) who call themselves the Jumanos, and whom the Spaniards call, for another name, Patarabueyes. This nation appeared to be very numerous, and had large permanent pueblos. In it we saw five pueblos with more than ten thousand Indians, and flat-roofed houses, low and well arranged into pueblos. The people of this nation have their faces streaked, and are large; they have maize, gourds, beans, game of foot and wing, and fish of many kinds from two rivers that carry much water. One of them, which must be about half the size of the Guadalquivir (Rio Grande), flows directly from the north and empties into the Rio Concho. The Conchos, which must be about the size of the Guadalquivir, flows into the North Sea. They have *salines* consisting of lagoons of salt water, which at certain times of the year solidifies and forms salt like that of the sea. The first night, when we pitched camp near a small pueblo of the nation, they killed five of our horses with arrows and wounded as many more, not withstanding the fact that watch was kept. They retired to a mountain range, where six of us went next morning with Pedro, the interpreter, a native of their nation, and found them, quieted them, made peace with them, and took them to their own pueblo. We told them what we had told the others, and that they should inform the people of their nation not to flee nor hide, but to come out to see us. To some of the *caciques* I gave beads, hats, and other things, so that they would bring them in peace, which they did; and from these pueblos they accompanied us, informing one another that we came as friends and not to injure them; and thus great numbers of them went with us and showed us a river from the north, which has been mentioned above."[17]

Espejo continued, "On the banks of this river Indians of this nation are settled for a distance of twelve days journey. Some of them have flat roofed houses, and others have grass huts. The *caciques* came out to receive us, each with his people, without bows or arrows, giving us portions of their food, while some gave us *gamuzas* (buck skins) and buffalo hides, very well tanned. The *gamuzas* made of the hides of deer; they also are tanned, as it is done in Flanders. The hides are from the humpbacked cows which they call *civola* and whose hair is like that of the cows of Ireland. The natives dress the hides of these cows as hides are dressed in Flanders, and make shoes of them. Others they dress in different ways some of the natives using them for clothes. These Indians appear to have some knowledge of our holy Catholic faith, because they point to God our Lord, looking up to the heavens. They call him Apalitoi in their tougue, and say it is He whom they recognize as their Lord and who gives them what they have. Many of them, men, women, and children, came to have the religious and we Spaniards bless them, which made them appear very happy. They told us and gave us to understand through interpreters that three Christians and a negro had passed through there, and by the indications they gave they appeared to have been Cabeza De Vaca, Dorantes Castillo Maldonado, and a negro, who had all escaped from the fleet with which Panfilio Narvaez entered Florida. They were left friendly and very peaceful and satisfied, and some of them went with us up the Rio del Norte, serving and accompanying us." Espejo traveled into the provinces of New Mexico as far north as Taos before returning to Mexico by way of West Texas along the Pecos River. Jumano guides led Espejo from the Pecos River near Toyah Creek across the Davis Mountains back to the Rio Grande in the vicinity of present day Candelaria. The expedition was the first to explore the Pecos River to any extent and, like the Chamuscado-Rodriguez *entrada* and the Coronado expedition, increased Spanish desire to conquer this new found land.[18]

While a great deal of Jumano history is shrouded by the passage of time, it is known that both the Jumanos and Patarabueyes had strong political leaders who their people held in apparently well deserved esteem. These chieftains wielded a great deal of power, ruling with considerable authority over a number of Native American groups. The chiefs conducted war, directed hunting and trading activities, and some possessed remarkable political talents as evidenced by their dealings with the Spanish. One example of such leadership took place in the summer of 1629 when a Jumano chieftain known only as "One Eye" arrived at the Mission San Antonio at Ysleta located not far from present Albuquerque, New Mexico. "One Eye" came to the mission accompanied by twelve other chiefs said to be members of other tribes and about fifty Indians. The presence of "One Eye" and his followers at the mission was not an unusual occurrence; for each summer for six years these Indians had camped in the vicinity of the mission for a few weeks visiting Fray Juan de Salas. They asked for baptism, requested that the Spaniards send missionaries to their homelands, and personally invited Father Salas to live among them. Apparently, no priests had been sent in earlier years because none were available, and Father Salas could not leave his post.[19]

During his talks with the padre that summer of 1629 "One Eye"and his followers related a wondrous account of a miraculous vision witnessed by his people. The Jumano said a mysterious Franciscan nun preaching in their native language appeared among them. The "Lady in Blue," so described because of her gray habit worn under a blue cloak, told the Indians of the Christian religion and admonished them to receive baptism. The Indians related that the "holy woman" had appeared to them where they hunted buffalo in the Texas Panhandle or on the plains of West Texas. The location of the reported visions cannot be pinpointed, but it is safe to say that the vision appeared in a very unlikely place for a Franciscan nun. The Indians said they recognized a painting of Mother Luisa de Carrion, another nun of the Franciscan Order and said that the apparition had been dressed like the nun in the painting but had the face of a beautiful young girl. The Indians said the vision told them to, "summon the Fathers to instruct and baptize them, and that they should not be slothful about it."[20]

A demonic spirit then entered the story chronicled by Alonso de Benavides, a Spanish church official who rose to be an officer of the Inquisition, hoping to convert both the Apache and the Jumano. Benavides desired to become the Bishop of New Mexico, and his ambitions colored his accounts of the mysterious demon. According to Benavides, following the appearances of the "Lady in Blue," a demon feared that the Jumano might be delivered, so the spirit, "dried up the lagoons of water that they drank" and scattered the "great herd of bison which were there, by which all these nations sustain themselves." The demon then used Indian shaman to spread the word that the Jumano should leave the buffalo hunting grounds and "change their location to seek food." The following day at dawn, the "Lady in Blue" again appeared to the Indians and told them that they should not go, and soon afterward, a party of priests arrived. According to Benavides the "Miraculous Conversion of the Xumana Nation" then took place when probably exaggerated numbers of Jumanos took baptism.[21]

A little more than half a century later, another Jumano chief related to the Spanish a remarkably similar account of a supernatural vision that resulted in a miracle. In the fall of 1683, Chief Juan Sabeata journeyed to El Paso del Norte, the present location of Juarez, Chihuahua, leading a delegation of his followers. Sabeata is the best known of the Jumano chieftains, who led the Jumano in the closing years of the seventeenth century. Sabeata was also the last prominent Jumano leader recorded in Spanish accounts before the tribe vanished into obscurity. Little about Sabeata as a youth is known; although, he was said to have been born in Mexico and received baptism at San José Parral in present Chihuahua. One source noted that Sabeata was a "Tawaehash chief from the mouth of the Rio Conchos." At El Paso del Norte, the cunning chieftain approached Spanish authorities asking Governor Cruzate to establish missions among the Jumano. To entice the Spanish, Chief Sabeata told the governor that thirty-three Indian nations, including the Jumano, eagerly awaited baptism. According to the chief, the reason for this outbreak of religious fervor among the Indians was the result of a miracle that changed the course of a fierce battle with the Apache. The Apache greatly outnumbered the Jumano. Sabeata said the Jumano and their allies were few, "while their enemies numbered more than thirty-thousand." Just when it looked as if the Jumano were going to be defeated, a cross mysteriously appeared in the sky allowing Sabeata's followers to win a "bloodless victory" over their enemies.[22]

Juan Sabeata like his predecessor "One Eye", did not make such a startling revelation known to the Spanish simply for religious reasons. In fact, the chief's story about the appearance of the cross during the battle was pure fabrication. A Tejas Indian who traveled with Sabeata apparently conceived the story. The chief later admitted the story of the miracle as being untrue, but he used it because the Jumanos faced a desperate situation, one, which eventually led to their demise. For better than a century, the "cow people" had been engaged in a war with the Apache who by late in the seventeenth century had almost driven the Jumano from their source of livelihood, the buffalo hunting grounds of West Texas. Apache raiders struck deep into Jumano territory. They terrorized villagers along the Rio Grande, at La Junta, and in the Chinati Mountains. In addition, the Jumano needed protection from the slave hunters who were always on the lookout for Indians to work the mines of Chihuahua. Sabeata proved himself a pragmatic, resourceful headman who knew that if the Spanish authorities sent priests to live among his people also would come soldiers who the chief hoped would provide a defense against Apache raiders and Spanish slave hunters. The grand chief knew the Spanish well and had no small amount of knowledge about the Catholic religion. As earlier noted, he received baptism as a youth at San José Parral where the priests gave him the Christian name Juan. While the chief professed a deep religious faith, the plight of his people motivated his actions. The chief has been described as, "a master at frontier intrigue." Sabeata's ruse apparently worked. At the very least, if the chief was not directly responsible for the establishment of missions at La Junta, his actions at least prodded the Church and Spanish military into action. Governor Cruzate reacted positively to Sabeata's petition and ordered Lieutenant General Juan Dominguez de Mendoza to assemble an expedition to the Jumano country. Mendoza was a capable military man with more than thirty years experience serving the Spanish military in present West Texas and New Mexico. To minister to the religious requests of the Jumano, Fray Nicolas Lopez, an official of the Franciscan Order, approved the building of several missions near La Junta and made arrangements to personally join the expedition. Following his petition to the governor, Juan Sabeata journeyed to La Junta in advance of the expedition but returned to El Paso del Norte a short time later to serve as an escort and guide for the priests. Within a few months of Chief Sabeata's petition, the Mendoza expedition set out for La Junta.[23]

The priests led the way down river to the Jumano country. On December 1, 1683 Fray Lopez and a party of church officials left Paso del Norte and headed south down the Rio Grande in advance of Mendoza and the soldiers. Two weeks later, Mendoza and the main body of the expedition followed. Along the way to La Junta, Mendoza passed through many Indian villages and the Indians made the Spaniards welcome. A short distance below Paso del Norte the expedition was welcomed by the chiefs of the Zuma Indians. Mendoza observed that the Zuma were a poor people who subsisted by eating, "mescal which is baked palms." Mendoza noted that not only the Jumano had been threatened by the Apache, "All these *rancherias* asked of me aid and help against the common enemy, the Hapaches [sic] nation, alleging generally that most of them were already disposed to becoming Christians. In fact a considerable portion of them were already reducing themselves to settlements and alleging that the Apache did not allow them in their lands."[24]

The expedition made its way downstream from Paso del Norte on the western side of the Rio Grande. Mendoza forded the river entering present Texas a few miles from a place Mendoza called Senora del Rosario. Some evidence suggests the crossing took place in the vicinity of the present Ruidosa, Texas. On December 29, the expedition came to a Julime village near the river a few miles southwest of the Chinati Mountains. Mendoza called the place La Navidad en las Cruces Chief Sabeata had told the Spanish that the cross appeared in the sky near La Junta and the Spanish called the place La Navidad en las Cruces. At the village, Fray Lopez awaited Mendoza. Mendoza described the place. "These *rancherias* are the people of the Julimes nation; they are versed in the Mexican language, and all sow maize and wheat. Here we overtook the reverend fathers, Fray Nicolas Lopes, custodian and ordinary judge of the provinces of New Mexico, Fray Juan de Sabaleata, commissary of the Holy Office, and Fray Antonio de Asebedo. Generally all these Indians asked for the water of baptism, and more than one hundred persons were baptized. All the meadows of the river are very spacious, and have good lands, good climate, and abundant pasturage and wood." At this settlement the Spanish must have been surprised to find that the Indians had constructed, "a good-sized church, built of reeds, with an altar the size of that in the "church in El Paso."[25]

While it is not possible to pinpoint the exact location of the place Mendoza called Navidad en las Cruces, it likely was situated at or near the abandoned community of Ochoa located some nine miles northwest of Presidio on F.M. 170. Historian Carlos E. Castaneda wrote of the place, "the settlement or pueblos of the Julimes must have been slightly above present day Presidio and Ojinaga." According to a State of Texas historical marker placed at Ochoa in 1936, Fray Lopez established the Mission San Francisco De Los Julimes at Ochoa in 1683-1684. Little is known of the mission for it remained in operation for less than a year. In later times, the Ochoa community grew around the site and a church was built there. Today the place is once again abandoned although descendents of the Julimes are still said to live just across the river in Chihuahua.[26]

The Mendoza expedition remained at Navidad en las Cruces for several days to allow time for the men and horses to rest. The priests ministered to the Indians in several nearby by *rancherias*. Father Antonio de Acevedo elected to remain at the mission to, minister to the Indians. Guided by Juan Sabeata, the expedition set out again on December 29 traveling 7 leagues or about 19 miles to a place Mendoza called Apostol Santiago (the Apostle

Saint James) This location is thought to be at or near Fort Leaton about a mile southeast of present Presidio on F.M. 170. Again the Spaniards found another church the Indians had prepared for them. This church was described as being, "larger and more carefully made, and a dwelling made for the priests." Here the Fray Lopez established the Mission Del Apostol Santiago near the mouth of Alamito Creek. Like the Mission San Francisco De Los Julimes, the mission only remained in operation for a short time before the priests were forced to flee for their lives.[27]

Juan Sabeata guided Mendoza up Alamito Creek passing east of the Chinati Mountains. They crossed the Pecos River probably not far from Horsehead Crossing and a little later encountered several Buffalo herds that provided the expedition with meat. On January 17, 1684 the expedition came upon a *jediondo* (ill-smelling) Indian village and made a remarkable discovery. Mendoza wrote of the encounter, "Their chiefs and other people came out to received us with much rejoicing, most of them on foot, others on horseback, carrying a holy cross very well made, which apparently must be two and a half long, of somewhat heavy timber, painted red and yellow, and fastened with a nail which they call. The holy cross 'showed that they had made it some time before. They also brought forth a banner of white taffeta, a little less than a long; in the middle of the banner were two successive crosses of blue taffeta, very well made. At the time of meeting us they fired several shots, Don Juan Sabeata firing with a fuse a *harquebus* barrel without a lock; and I ordered the salute returned on our part with two volleys."[28]

The white taffeta banner Mendoza described was a French flag. Although he made no mention of his reaction, the Spaniard could hardly have been pleased with such a discovery. The flag was unsettling evidence of French intrusion into territory the Spanish claimed as their own. Where the flag came from or how the sacquired it remains a mystery since it happened a year before the French are known to have been in Texas. In 1684, the intrepid French explorer Rene Robert Cavelier Sieur de la Salle set out from France intending to colonize the mouth of the Mississippi River. La Salle landed not at the mouth of the Mississippi but on the coast of Texas in the area of Matagorda Bay. There he established Fort Saint Louis in February 1685. He then began a series of expeditions. On his first expedition, La Salle travelled west trying to determine the eastern limits of New Spain. Little is known of this expedition. After finding the French flag, the Mendoza expedition remained at the village for seven days. The Indians did their best to make their guests comfortable. Mendoza wrote, "All of the Chiefs and other people wished to give us lodging and entertainment in their own *rancheria* in some huts of tule which they had made for us, but I did not consent to it, because of the evil results which might follow, excusing myself with good reasons." During this time, Juan Sabeata and the other chiefs asked Mendoza if he would hold a council with them and he agreed. Mendoza ordered all of his ranking soldiers and the chiefs to assemble. At the council Mendoza called upon Juan Sabeata and the chiefs to speak their mind and heard a plea that had become familiar. Sabeata and the other chiefs implored Mendoza to make war on the Apache saying that the Apache were enemies of both the Spanish and the Jumano. The chiefs requested that Mendoza take them with the expedition indicating their fear of a possible immediate attack. Mendoza assured those in attendance that he would make war on the Apache and recalled that the chiefs seemed pleased with this announcement. To show his appreciation, Juan Sabeata brought the Spaniards sixteen deerskins that he divided among the officers and soldiers. While at the place, the Spaniards killed twenty-seven buffalo providing the expedition with a good quantity of meat.[29]

So it seemed Chief Sabeata received what he wanted with Mendoza's promise. In addition, Fray Lopez had committed to the missions among the Jumanos. A few weeks after eliciting the pledge of war on the Apache things began to turn sour for Sabeata when Mendoza accused the chief of making false reports about the Apache being nearby. Mendoza ordered Sabeata and several Jumano scouts to leave the expedition and replaced him with another guide, "because of the frauds in which he had been caught." Although Sabeata had fallen out of favor with Mendoza, the chief continued to manipulate Spanish authorities with political intrigues for years.[30]

While it is not clear how long Juan Sabeata reigned as chief of the Jumano, his actions as an influential leader are recorded in both Spanish and French records from 1683 to 1692. During this time, the chief made at least eight journeys across present Texas as well as traveling into Chihuahua. He spread news of French colonial activities among the Spanish. While Sabeata's travels definitely had political motivation, they usually were timed by a seasonal cycle that Native Americans had followed for centuries---the annual migration of the Great Plains buffalo herds. It has been estimated that as many as thirty million buffalo once lived on the grasslands of the Great Plains of North America. They ranged from the Rocky Mountains to the Mississippi River. Each year the herds migrated south into West Texas to escape the harsh winter and to graze in prairie grass renewed most years by increased rainfall in August, September, and October. The Jumano converged on the hunting grounds each autumn. In addition to hunting, the Jumano brought with them trade goods and participated in trade fairs with other tribes on the High Plains of the Texas Panhandle. Juan Sabeata's people excelled at trading, bringing many goods such as mineral pigments, turquoise, cotton, salt, bows and (arrows as well as agricultural staples. Following the hunt they traded in pelts, meat and other buffalo products. During the winters, they came back to their homes, the Jumanos to La Junta, the Cibolos to the Chinati Mountains.[31]

Shortly after being expelled from the expedition, Chief Sabeata returned to La Junta. Mendoza arrived at La Junta a few months later. Probably as a result of Sabeata's influence, Mendoza found the friendly attitude of the Jumanos living along the Rio Grande changed considerably. Also, an Indian revolt that would cause the Spanish considerable trouble was spreading. Mendoza wrote that Sebeata fled La Junta because the chief, "...had plotted with some nations to kill us, and then found out we had learned it..." Mendoza learned the tribes of the Zuma nation located on the Rio Grande just north of the Jumano country were rebelling against the Spanish. Seizing the opportunity to cause trouble for the Spanish, the Apache encouraged the revolt, which soon spread to several tribes in Chihuahua including some Julimes. Fearing reprisals, Mendoza returned to Paso Del Norte avoiding the Zuma villages. When the Spanish reacted by executing eighteen Julimes Indians San José Parral, the peaceful tribes of La Junta joined the revolt. In the summer of 1684, Fathers Acevedo and Zavaleta abandoned the two missions at La Junta and escaped to the safety of Parral.[32]

Two years later, a group of Sabeata's followers were sighted by the French in east Texas at a Tejas Indian village. The Jumanos told the French that the Jumanos had been at war with the Spanish and that a group of *Tejas* Indians had joined them in fighting the Spanish. Some months later, a party of Cibolos and Jumanos approached Fray August´in de Colina with troubling news. The Indians told Father Colina that they had heard of strangers among the *Tejas* who "went about in plate armor carrying on trade with the *Tejas* giving them axes and clothing in exchange for "horses and the fruits of the land." The Indians said that these strangers slept at night on the water in wooden houses and that one of their houses had sunk. Presumably the Indians were talking about the French. The Frenchmen told the *Tejas* of their plans to penetrate the rich Spanish mining district along the Rio del Parral in wagons.[33]

In early 1689, the Spanish deemed it necessary to investigate the reports of French intrusion by dispatching Captain Juan de Rentana and a contingent of soldiers to La Junta. When Chief Sabeata learned of the expedition, he arranged a meeting with the Captain. When the two met, the chief gave Rentana a full report of French activities and presented the Spaniard with "some papers and a ship painted on a parchment written by hand in the French language." Sabeata explained that the documents had been taken from a party of Frenchmen that had been killed by Indians. Rentana regarded the information given him to be of sufficient value that he sent Sabeata to his superiors to tell them what he knew. The chief seized the opportunity to regain the confidence of the Spanish. He and several of his followers reported that they had seen a party of Frenchmen "wearing doublets of steel" not far from La Junta. According to the Indians, they saw the French soldiers traveling up the Rio Grande in canoes. Sabeata confirmed the worst fears of the Spanish when he told them that the French soldiers had inquired about the distance to Spanish settlements and appeared most interested to learn where the Spanish silver mines were located. Although it may never be known with any certainty, French soldiers described by Juan Sabeata may have been part of La Salle's expedition to establish a fort on the Rio Grande. Although Juan Sabeata made an admirable attempt to gain the support of the Spanish, his efforts finally ended in failure. The chief disappeared from the pages of history not long after his meeting with Rentana. While the reports of French intrusions caused a considerable stir among the Spanish, the threat was more perceived than real. La Salle only ventured west of Fort St. Louis once before being murdered in 1687.[34]

The eighteenth century was a transitional period for Juan Sabeata's followers as well as the Apache. During this time the Apache emerged as the dominant Native American group in the Big Bend and De Vaca's "cow people" began to disappear from written records. Much of this had to do with the Spanish introduction of the horse into the Southwest. Although it is not clear exactly when Native Americans first obtained horses, several plains tribes had considerable numbers by the end of the seventeenth century. The Apache acquired horses about 1660. As a result hunting and warfare changed profoundly. Horses gave the Indians great mobility allowing them to hunt and raid over wide areas. It revolutionized the hunting of buffalo making the hunt much more efficient and less time consuming. In addition, the Spanish unwittingly placed a powerful new weapon in the hands of Indian warriors. Mounted warriors could raid and escape while covering vast distances. When Indians were able to obtain firearms, the Spanish soldier had met his equal. Early in the eighteenth century the Comanches began to move into the South Plains. As the Comanche moved southward, they forced the Apache into the mountains of New Mexico and into the area now known as the Texas Big Bend. The Apache were also drawn to the Spanish frontier because of the availability of horses. The Big Bend has been described as "the ideal Apache habitat" because of its remote location and rugged terrain. Four Apache groups are said to have frequented the region, the Mescaleros, Faraones, Llaneros, and Lipanes. The Mescaleros and Faraones, who frequented the western mountains of the region, knew the Chinati Mountains well.[35]

The relationship between the Jumanos and the Apache in the late seventeenth and early eighteenth centuries underwent a curious change. For most of the 1600's, the Jumanos and Apache remained fierce enemies. They fought for control of the buffalo hunting grounds on the Plains of West Texas. Apache raiders terrorized the Jumano villages along the Rio Grande and in the Chinati Mountains. In the early eighteenth century, however, the Apache became the dominant tribe and eventually many Jumanos became part of the Apache culture. There are numerous references in Spanish documents referring to Indians they called Jumano-Apache. Although the Spanish had many problems with Apache raiders, there are also quite a number of instances of friendly relationships between the two cultures greatly depending on circumstance. One solution the Spanish initiated in order to deal with the Apache problem was the paying of bounties for Apache scalps. The policy had its beginnings when the Spanish offered bounties to friendly Indians who killed those Indians the Spanish deemed to be their enemies. Such payment required proof in the form of a war trophy. Initially this usually meant that trophy hunters brought proof of a kill in the form of heads and ears. This practice evolved into the taking of scalps. One Pima Indian presented for payment of the bounty the scalps of 54 individuals he claimed had been taken from 31 Apache men and 23 Apache women. Of course there was no way to prove such scalps came from Apache heads. Bounties ranged from 20 to 100 pesos for scalps or heads taken from Apache warriors.[36]

Largely because of Apache raiding, the missions of La Junta remained abandoned for thirty years. In 1715, the Spanish renewed their efforts to maintain missions around La Junta. Captain Juan Antonio Transvina Retis headed a large *entrada* that came to La Junta with orders to re-establish missions in the region. The *entrada* was well supplied bringing lard, meat, flour, soap, tobacco, writing paper and wine for the priests who took up residence in three new missions along the Rio Grande not far from present Presidio. They named the two new missions San Jose Antonio de Padua and San Cristobal. About this time, the Spanish founded a mission in the Chinati Mountains near the Cibolo pueblo. Very little is known about this mission, even the name is unclear. It may have been called Mission San Pedro Alcantara but is mostly referred to as the "Mission of the Cibolos". It is perhaps the least known of the La Junta missions. Seven priests, including Father Gregorio Osorio who lived at the Cibolo mission in the Chinati Mountains operated the La Junta missions. The priests stayed at the missions until about 1726 when they were forced again to flee the missions because of hostile attacks by Native Americans.[37]

At some point early in the 1700's the Apaches drove the Cibolos from their pueblo in the Chinati Mountains. Comanche raiders also caused considerable trouble as raiding parties struck Spanish outposts to steal horses. In 1747, the Spanish sent an expedition headed by Captain Commander Don Joseph de Ydoiaga to La Junta to explore the region and investigate the feasibility of establishing a presidio to guard against Indian attacks. Ydoiaga made careful and detailed written observations of the places and people he saw. His writings offer the single best source of knowledge about the Cibolo Indians and their pueblo in the Chinati Mountains. When the Ydoiaga expedition explored the Cibolo pueblo, the site and the mission had been abandoned for a number of years. Ydoiaga began his march into the Chinati Mountains on December 4, 1747.[38]

In his report to the Viceroy of New Spain, Ydoiaga described his march. The expedition, escorted by a contingent of militia, traveled up Cibolo Creek into the mountains. Six Indian guides accompanied Ydoiaga as well as an unnamed Cibolo chief. It may have been Francisco Palacios who was listed as the "General" of the Cibolos on a Spanish census recorded in November 1747. On the first day, the expedition traveled nine leagues, approximately twenty-three miles, "in the direction of the north." Ydoiaga wrote, "The greater part of the route was rocky and with much *lechugilla.* At sunset, the expedition set up camp, "in a ravine upon some good pastures but without water and little firewood." The *entrada* camped within a few miles of the present site of Shafter.[39]

The following morning the expedition covered about three leagues or some eight miles when they found an arroyo "that flows from north to south, boxed in by rugged mountain ridges." He wrote of a *bosque de palizada* growing in the *arroyo* perhaps referring to thick stands possibly composed of seepwillow or burrowbrush. Ydoiaga knew that the Cibolo pueblo lay near a large spring, so he continued upstream following a flow of water he described as being "equivalent to that of three and a half furrows." The walls of the *arroyo* became quite steep and the going rough because of the heavy growth of the *palizada.* Ydoiaga asked his guides if they knew of a trail that would take them to the springs around the *arroyo* , and they told him, there was no other route except though the *arroyo* itself. Leaving their horses behind, the expedition continued through the thick brush approximately one league or about two or three miles before reaching the source of the water. Leaving their horses behind, the expedition continued through the thick brush before reaching the source of the water.[40]

Ydoiaga described the place. "It was at the foot of a high mountain that is seen to the northeast; and said spring, forming the *arroyo* downstream, results from two good springs that join together from two cattail ponds, or marshes. And it may be seen that less water comes from them than is evident downstream the reason being that other different small springs can join said arroyo so it may abound and become larger." He continued, "Nearby, a small rocky hill divides an *ancon* of land which is where there are some old walls of a few of the houses of the *rancheria* of said Sibolos. And where, likewise there are vestiges or signs that they cultivated the lands of said *ancon* taking the water out of the *arroyo,* but only in small quantity due to the difficulty of getting it out to the top. And as far as could be judged about said the taking of the water for its irrigation, the planting of two and a half *fanegas* with the necessary irrigation would not be so bad."[41]

Ydoiaga's writings provide only tantalizing clues to the location of the Cibolo pueblo in the Chinati Mountains. It may have been located near the headwaters of Cibolo or Oso Creek. At least one researcher has suggested that the Cibolo village may have been located in the vicinity of Shafter. It is important to consider however, that the distances recorded by Ydoiaga were anything but precise. They were simply estimations made by a Spaniard completely unfamiliar with the countryside more than two hundred years ago. Rough terrain could have easily caused Ydoiaga to overestimate the stretch he traveled as it befuddles Big Bend visitors today.[42]

The Cibolos apparently never re-occupied their pueblo in the Chinatis. After leaving the mountains, the Cibolos occupied a pueblo known that became known as Nuestra Senora de Guadalupe. This pueblo, situated on a high gravel mesa within the present town of Ojinaga, Chihuahua was the largest of the eight La Junta pueblos occupied by as many as 550 residents. The Cibolos shared Guadalupe with the Polacmes Indians, each tribe living in a separate section of the pueblo. The pueblo has been described as being well built, containing two plazas, one for each nation. Captain Ydoiaga visited Guadalupe in late November 1747 and wrote, "I found the Indians to appear to be contented, restored from the rebellion, and united in said pueblo." Ydoiaga appears to present the last known account of the Cibolos. He recorded ninety-three Cibolos Indians living at Guadalupe. In 1760, Rubin Ode Celis established a *presidio* near the pueblo to guard against Indian attacks. While no documentary evidence offers any details of the Cibolos after Ydoiaga took a census of them, they likely intermixed with the Polacme, the Apache, and the Spaniards. Many eighteenth century records carry petitions from Spanish soldiers stationed at the *presidio* asking to marry, "women of the town." Probably some numbers of people living today in modern Ojinaga are descendents of the Cibolos.[43]

"We reached Faver country three days after leaving Marfa. We proceeded to headquarters, Rancho Cibolo, one of the earliest ranches in the Big Bend. We pitched camp near a splendid orchard, which was irrigated from the most beautiful spring that I had ever seen. The house was a large adobe structure. The walls appeared to be about three feet thick, the roof was made of cottonwood poles, over which was a layer of sotol poles. There was an overall covering of mud, set with broken, jagged bottles to prevent Indians scaling the house top, nor did I know for what purpose the bottles had been placed on the house top nor did I know that on two previous occasions the Indians had raided the house and had stolen most of the livestock--cattle, horses, and mules. I was soon to learn that the house and all the corrals were stockaded (sic). Port holes enabled the defenders to shoot from the inside. Faver had come from old Mexico and had brought Mexican cattle, goats, and peons with him. After dinner, my father told me to go to headquarters and tell Mr. Faver that he would like to have an interview with him. I was quaking in my boots as I approached the house."

William Burton Mitchell, 1885[44]

Peach Brandy, Starve Outs, and a Wolf at the Door

Chapter 2

When William Mitchell first saw Cibolo Springs in the summer of 1885, he was but fifteen years of age. The young man and his father came to the Chinati Mountains from a drought stricken ranch south of San Angelo, Texas, hoping to find open range land and, more importantly, a place with good water. Young Mitchell's initial encounter with Milton Faver proved so profound that it remained permanently etched in his memory. Mitchell, like other men who crossed Faver's ranch, regarded the old cattle baron with considerable respect and no small amount of fear. Perhaps, this came as a result of Faver's regal bearing or simply from Faver's undoubted reputation as a man not to be trifled with. Mitchell recalled Milton Faver as being a "rather hump shouldered" old fellow with a long white beard that reached his waistline. The story persists to this day that Don Milton, as his *peons* addressed him, surprised and shot more than one unworthy character with a small pistol which he kept tucked in his waistband, well hidden from sight beneath the long beard. Supposedly, Faver tricked these unfortunates by stroking his whiskers as a distraction while drawing his gun with his other hand. The old rancher was a crack shot and seldom went anywhere without a large caliber octagon-barreled rifle that he wielded with commanding accuracy. William Mitchell thought Faver to be about 75 years of age in 1885 although, in reality, Don Milton was probably 65 in that year. Mitchell's account is one of the few surviving first person narratives describing Milton Faver, who is credited with being the first Texas cattle baron west of the Pecos River.[45]

Much about Milton Faver is obscure and contradictory. The man and his myth are almost inseparable, so much so, that Don Milton has frequently been labeled the "mystery man of the Big Bend." Even today, he continues to be exactly that--a mystery, an enigma. Most of his story originated in the oral tradition and has been altered over the years by the frailty of memory and kindly interpretation. Little is clearly established about Faver's formative years before he carved out his kingdom in the Chinati Mountains. The birth place of one "Melton Flavers" is listed on the Fort Leaton 1860 Census as being in Missouri while the 1870 and 1880 Census indicate he may have been born in Virginia. He was probably born in 1821. There is some other evidence that Faver lived, at least for a time, in Independence, Missouri. His good friend, John Pool, who started a ranch in the Chinati Mountains in 1885, insisted until his death that he knew Faver when the two men lived in Independence. According to Pool, Milton Faver got into a political quarrel, and the confrontation turned violent. Faver shot a man, and assuming he had killed him, fled Missouri before eventually coming to Texas. In those years, the initials, "GTT" referred to those individuals who had "Gone to Texas" usually to escape punishment for a wide variety of crimes. For a time, Faver may have lived in California, but this cannot be substantiated. Then he went to Mexico before coming to Texas. There are many conflicting stories. Years passed, and when John Pool encountered Faver in the Big Bend, he told the bearded fugitive that the fellow he had shot in Missouri did not die. According to Pool, Faver seemed somewhat surprised and greatly relieved by the revelation.[46]

Another account states that Faver, as a young man, lived in New York City, where he fell ill with tuberculosis. Doctors advised Milton that he only had a short time to live and that he should move west. Apparently, according to the story, Faver had purchased a sizeable amount of life insurance, and the insurance companies, convinced that his death was eminent, offered a substantial settlement to release them from their contractual obligations. Faver is said to have accepted the offer and to have moved to the Big Bend where his health returned. He used the money to begin ranching.[47] Milton Faver may have participated in the Mexican War of 1846 as an officer in the United States Army. After the war, it is said he went to Chihuahua where he found employment in a Meoque flour mill owned by Francisco De Leon. At Meoque, Faver met, courted, and took Francisca Ramirez as his wife. Not long after the marriage, Faver left his job at the flourmill and took up freight hauling between Meoque and Ojinaga. It was a profitable business, and before long, Faver's freight wagons transported goods as far as Santa Fe. In 1857, Milton and Francisca moved to Ojinaga where he owned a general merchandise store.[48]

The Faver store did a fair amount of trade with Indians who exchanged livestock, hides, and skins for merchandise. The Indians particularly liked the ornate Mexican bridles and silver spurs that the store offered for sale. Although the establishment did a good business, Faver did not remain long in Ojinaga. He purchased a cattle ranch and moved with Francisa to Cibolo Springs in the Chinati Mountains. It was here that Milton Faver established his ranch headquarters about 1859. Not long after, Faver expanded to Cienega Springs located some five miles east of present Shafter. Over the years, Faver's largest cattle operation centered at Cienega although the headquarters of the ranch remained at Cibolo Springs. Later, Don Milton expanded his operation to a third ranch at La Morita located a few miles from Cienega. Faver stocked La Morita with sheep and, before long, accumulated the largest sheep herd in the Big Bend. But Milton Faver is mostly remembered as a cattle rancher. He evidently obtained his first cows from Indians in San Pablo, Chihuahua, about 1849 by bartering brown sugar and sweet potatoes. His herds have been described as being "of every color and mixture that can be imagined, and as wild as deer." In his first years, Faver learned ranching from his foreman, Carman Ramirez, who "knew how to handle *peons* as well as sheep and cattle." Ramarez proved to be invaluable in Faver's operations until a band of Apache raiders killed him.[49]

Perhaps Milton Faver is best known for building two forts: one at Cibolo Springs and another at Cienega to fend off Indian attacks.

Although Don Milton had amicable relations with Indians who traded in his store in Ojinaga, almost the opposite was true in his encounters with the Apache after he moved to the Chinatis. From almost the first moment he set foot north of the Rio Grande, he faced continual problems with the Apache who raided his ranch, stole livestock, and raided Faver's freight wagons. In one fight, Don Milton almost lost his life, but he survived and recovered from his wounds. Yet, by 1857, Faver had managed to build his cattle herd to about 300 head. Then the Apache struck again and made off with practically the entire herd leaving behind only thirty milk cows. Determined not to be driven out, the cattle baron built his famous forts. The strongholds were imposing, heavily fortified structures made of adobe with walls eleven feet high and three feet thick. Don Milton erected twenty-foot tall lookout towers at each corner of the stronghold and positioned gun slits throughout the walls. A sallyport large enough to permit the passage of a team and wagon furnished the only entrance. The U. S. Army provided Faver at least one small cannon at Cibolo Springs since the fortress afforded travelers the only refuge from Indian attack between Fort Davis and Presidio.[50]

Once, when an Apache war party raided Cibolo Springs, the Indians launched "great showers of arrows" at the fort, but the arrows inflicted little damage and bounced harmlessly off the adobe walls. After this tactic failed, some of the warriors tried to dig a tunnel under the walls of the fort to gain entrance. Faver and his men waited patiently pretending not to take notice of the digging. Finally when an Apache poked his head through the end of the tunnel inside the fort, one of Faver's men killed the Indian by driving a sword though him thereby pinning the dead warrior to the earthen floor. When his companions tried to pull the impaled body back out of the tunnel, they couldn't understand why it couldn't be removed. Not all the attacks, however, were so easily repulsed. About 1870, Apache marauders struck at La Morita where Carmen Ramirez lived with his family. Unlike Cibolo and Cienega, La Morita did not have a fort. The Indians plundered La Morita and took the foreman and his family captive. The next day after the raid, the foreman's brother, Pancho Ramirez, rode from Cibolo to La Morita and discovered what had happened. He spread the alarm and led a group of armed men on the trail left by the Apache. About two miles from La Morita, the pursuers found Carmen Ramirez's mutilated body stuffed in a rock crevice. They continued on and came upon several pieces of a woman's dress that was thought to have belonged to the foreman's wife. Apparently, in an attempt to mark the way for her rescuers, Senora Ramirez tore pieces from her dress and secretly dropped the torn cloth along the trail. When the pursuers came upon a creek bed filled with running water, numerous fresh tracks in the mud indicated that the Apache were very near. Fearing an ambush by a large war party, Pancho's men refused to go any farther. They retreated and buried the bodies. No rescue came for the captives. No direct word of their fate ever came although years later, rumors did circulate that the Ramirez children had been seen alive in the Indian Territory.[51]

Milton Faver was a tough, determined cattleman who carved out a huge beef empire in the face of great adversity. Faver's cattle herd has been estimated to be as large as between ten and twenty thousand head. These numbers, however, are not well documented. It is said that most Faver cattle were never branded because of the ruggedness of the Chinati Mountain terrain and the fact that Don Melton had so many cattle that he could never count them all. Presidio County Tax Assessor's records between 1876 and 1889 document that Faver officially declared ownership of no more than three thousand head. This figure is not surprising since ranchers frequently claimed they owned fewer cattle than they actually did to avoid the payment of taxes. In addition to cattle, Milton Faver raised a considerable number of sheep and goats. In 1883, 1884, and 1885 Don Milton had in excess of 5,000 sheep and 1,500 goats. Such a large amount of livestock required a considerable amount of land. Although Faver ran his cattle, sheep, and goats over a vast area in the Chinatis, he actually owned less than 2,300 deeded acres including 640 acres at Cibolo Springs and 640 acres at Cienega. This was possible because most of the land in Presidio County in those years was open rangeland "asking for someone to claim it" as one writer put it. And claim it Don Milton did. He once bragged, "I am monarch of all I survey. My rights there are none to dispute." At the dedication of a Texas Historical Commission Official Marker in Shafter, a speaker said of Faver, "From the peaks of the Chinati Mountains in Presidio County--north, south, east, west--as far as the eye could see, the herds were his own."[52]

Faver became absolute monarch of the Chinatis and remained so for more than thirty years. On the ranch, Faver enforced his own law. He built a large whipping post of cottonwood, and according to one source, "a thief was in hard luck when Don Milton got a hold of him." But he was also said to be, "kind and helpful to all that came his way if, in his eyes, they merited such treatment." Milton Faver and Francesca Ramarez had only one male child, Juan. Don Milton gave the boy every educational advantage wealth could provide. He sent Juan away to school first in San Antonio, Texas, and later in England, France, and Germany. The youth spent most of his formative years away from the Chinati Mountains and his father. Once when he returned home after being absent for several years, Juan attempted to play a joke on his father. Juan traveled to Cibolo Springs with a group of freight wagons. When the wagons neared his father's ranch, Juan borrowed a mule from one of the freighters and rode ahead to meet his father. When he arrived at the fort, Don Milton came out and greeted his son. Juan replied in German, saying, "I came to tell you that your son is with a train of freight wagons that will soon be here." Faver intently studied the young stranger before replying, "I think you are my son." The two were then reunited, and a small celebration took place.[53]

About the time of the Civil War, Juan met and married Gavina Ramirez, "a very attractive woman, not related to his mother." This union fell apart when Juan found his beautiful wife in the arms of a Captain Mose Kelly, who was in charge of the Presidio Customs House. The dashing Captain Kelly had something of a reputation as a "Border Don Juan," and when the jealous husband learned of the affair, he set in motion a plan to catch the two lovers. At the time, Juan and Gavina lived in Ojinaga. Juan told his wife he was leaving on an extended journey and would be away for some time. Gavina wept, telling her husband, "I shall be so lonely until you return." Juan pretended to leave but hid in the house. A short time later, Captain Kelly came to the house to see Gavina. Juan surprised the lovers, drew his gun and killed Kelly. After the shooting, Juan crossed the river to Presidio and hid in the home of his friend Richard Daly. When Don Milton learned of the shooting, he reacted by demanding to know why Juan had not killed his wife instead of her lover. In a clear demonstration of his authoritarianism, Favor turned his son over to the Mexican police. One wonders if Don Milton would have done the same if Juan had shot his wife instead of Captain Kelly. At any rate, Juan spent as long as a year in the Ojinaga jail for the killing. Don Milton "almost banished the son from his fireside after this event." Another version of the same story states that after Juan spent some time in the Ojinaga jail, Don Milton had a change of heart and paid the enormous sum of $100,000 to secure his release. Several years after this episode, Juan married Gomesinda Zubia who bore him several daughters. Gavina continued to live in Ojinaga until her death in 1933.[54]

While some writers have labeled Milton Faver as a recluse, he carried on a wide number of varied business activities and evidently had a good education. Don Milton "fluently" spoke English, Spanish, French, and German. Faver also maintained long-term friendly relations with the U. S. Army by keeping forage and military stores at Cibolo Springs for the cavalry supply wagons that came his way. In fact, Cibolo Springs, like Fort Leaton, became an unofficial military outpost in the absence of any other established government facility. Finding Don Milton's cooperation to its advantage, the U.S. Army reciprocated by providing at least one cannon for Faver's use at Cibolo Springs. Don Milton's achievements are more than significant for his time. He possessed a keen business sense and perhaps more importantly the ability to recognize and take advantage of opportunities that surfaced. This is demonstrated during his earliest years when he foresaw opportunities brought about by Chihuahua Trail trade. Later, he prospered as a merchant and rancher. His considerable success in ranching speaks for itself. No small part of this feat came from his ability to find prime locations for his ranching operations located near some of the best springs in the area. By the time most Anglo ranchers began to hear of the Chinatis in the 1880's, Don Milton had already established an empire of land, cattle and sheep.[55]

Milton Faver became quite well known for the peach brandy he distilled at the ranch. The brandy proved to be exceedingly popular with soldiers, cowboys, and Indians alike. And Don Milton greatly enjoyed sipping his concoction. Before the coming of the railroad, the army provided a steady market for Faver beef as well as his brandy. On his ranch, Don Milton built stone fences to enclose horse, cattle, and pig pens, garden plots, and a peach orchard irrigated by the abundant spring water. The place proved to be a near perfect location for a peach orchard because of the good water and mild winters. When and where he obtained his first peach trees is not known, but he had a two hundred-gallon still manufactured in Cuidad Chihuahua and delivered to the Chinati Mountains by mule train. The soldiers and townsfolk of Fort Davis consumed quite a bit of the brandy which was described as "better than good" by Nick Mersfelder, Justice of the Peace in Fort Davis, who readily admitted to having "tasted the stuff" on several occasions. Another Fort Davis resident remarked that the brandy was the "smoothest likker [sic] that ever slid down his gullet." The brandy business became so satisfactory that Faver had to deliver his product to Fort Davis by the keg. Although the army frowned on soldiers drinking in the bar rooms and brothels in operation near the fort, Don Milton's product was readily available. In addition to the brandy, Faver sold "peaches to the soldiers and civilians at Fort Davis on many occasions."[56]

Faver sometimes traded his brandy to friendly Indians and gave drinks to cowboys and soldiers who passed by the ranch. Don Milton enforced two rules when he provided brandy to the Indians. First, no Indian was allowed within two hundred yards of Faver's ranch house, and once they received the liquor, they had to leave immediately before imbibing. Faver also made it plain to Indians "that if they were hungry they could come to him and he would help them. But if they stole from him, the penalty would be death." In 1886, Bill Jones and Jesse Merrill recalled crossing Faver's ranch on a cattle drive along with about seventy-five cowboys and owners. When they entered Don Milton's country, the old cattle baron showed up every evening of the trail drive in his buggy with a keg a brandy, which he freely dispensed to any cowboy with a cup. While most of the cowboys thought Faver to be simply a generous old man, Jones and Merill observed that they really thought he intended "to keep a shrewd eye out that careless riders did not include any of his F-branded cattle with the brands of the other owners." Although Don Milton was well known for his brandy, it should be said that he was not the only producer of the drink in the Chinati country. In 1870, "Uncle John" Davis began ranching on Alamito Creek, a few miles east of Cibolo, where he too grew peaches and made brandy.[57]

Milton Faver also kept a close eye on his cattle when it came time to sell them. He had a somewhat peculiar, but never the less, practical method of collecting money at the time of sale. As each cow passed through the tally point, Don Milton insisted the buyer pay for the cow in cash before another could be counted or sold. He insisted this method prevented arguments about the count and the money involved. In addition to the cattle drives to Fort Davis, Faver also conducted trail drives to Abilene, Hays, and Dodge City, Kansas, between 1868 and 1884. Faver cowboys made "one bit" or 12 and 1/2 cents per day plus food, clothing, and a place to sleep. Faver's method of collecting money was certainly not his only eccentricity. Don Milton's daughter-in-law recalled that the cattle baron only ate vegetables grown in his own garden although he sometimes ate white meat or rare beef. He liked the tender white meat of rattlesnake but also was known to eat the breast meat of quail or chicken which he "washed down by draughts" of peach brandy. Don Milton's choice of aristocratic clothing was also noteworthy for he wore the latest European style custom tailored for him in Cuidad Chihuahua.[58]

In 1881, Don Milton Faver entered the closing years of his life with his sixtieth birthday. By this point he had become quite wealthy. And his cattle ranch was the largest west of the Pecos River. The amount of Faver's wealth will probably never be known since he apparently distrusted banks and preferred to deal in "hard money" or gold. More than one story says that Faver kept a fortune hidden in a strong box buried at his Cibolo Ranch headquarters. Long after his death, treasure hunters persisted to no avail in trying to find the strong box.[59] The 1880's proved to be a time of transition and change in Chinati Mountains when two important events set in motion the end of the Faver era. In August 1880, the final chapter of Apache resistance took place when the Warm Springs Apache chieftain Victorio and his followers made a final desperate stand in the Tres Castillos Mountains of Chihuahua. Mexican troops under the command of Colonel Joaquin Terrazas ambushed and killed Victorio and most of the chief's followers. This brought an end to Indian raiding in West Texas. A second pivotal event took place in 1883 when the Southern Pacific Railroad completed track construction across the Big Bend. The arrival of the railroad opened the region to trade and settlement. The building of the railroad occurred because shortly after being admitted to the Union in 1845, the State of Texas set about making a number of improvements including the promotion of railroad construction and the establishment of public schools. The state encouraged railroad construction by granting railroad companies sixteen sections of land for every mile of track laid and put into operation. At the same time, Texas provided for public schools by granting three, and a few years later, four leagues of land in each organized county to fund the schools.[60]

When Presidio County was organized in 1875, most of the land within its boundaries belonged either to the schools or the railroad companies. In Presidio County, odd numbered sections contained railroad land and even numbered sections became school land. The state offered land for sale at two dollars an acre if the property contained no water and three dollars per acre for land with water.

Ranchers could lease land from the state for six cents per acre. The railroad companies offered land for sale or lease at similarly attractive prices. Since the railroads had been required to survey their lands in order to claim them, the railroad companies, as a rule, laid claim to watered land when possible. The availability of cheap land coupled with the removal of the Apache menace and the establishment of railroads made Presidio County very attractive to ranchers who came in droves during the 1880's.[61]

In 1885, trail boss Denton (Den) Gibbon Knight began a cattle drive of some eight thousand Durham and Longhorn cattle from Abilene, Texas, to the Chinati Mountains. Although only twenty-eight years of age at the time, Den Knight brought a considerable amount of cattle drive experience gained on the Chisom Trail and two drives on the Goodnight-Loving Trail. Two years previous, Den Knight drove a herd owned by O. D. Durant from Buffalo Gap in Taylor County to the open range land of Presidio County. An exceptional cattleman, Knight immediately recognized the Chinati Mountains to be some of the best cattle county he had ever seen. Following the 1883 drive, Den quit his job as Durant's ranch manager and went into the cattle business for himself. About that time, a terrible drought set in, forcing several Taylor County cowmen to seek the good water and open range of Presidio County. Knight and the other owners of a herd, including Otho Durant, Trav Childers, and Joe Humphris, left Taylor County following a terrible drought and resulting cattle "die up" of 1883 and 1884. The trail drive lasted two months before they reached the Chinati Mountains where Joe Humphris leased a ranch not far from Milton Faver. In later years, Humphris remarked that there were no fences in the Chinati Mountains when he arrived, and he thought there never would be because Humphris and his friends from Taylor County felt confident "they could keep the other fellow out." Joe Humphris was right, at least about the fences. W. F. Mitchell built the first barbed wire fence in Presidio County three years later in 1888 on his Antelope Springs Ranch when he enclosed a three section pasture. But few barbed wire fences existed in Presidio County until the mid 1890's when the price of barbed wire became more affordable.[62]

About the time Den Knight came to the Chinati Mountains, a Coleman County rancher by the name of James Pool brought a "good grade of cattle and turned them loose in Chinati Mountains on a part of the present Wood Ranch." That same year W. H. Cleveland drove 266 Longhorn cattle from Dimmit County into

Pinto Canyon on the north end of the Chinatis. Cleveland found the canyon rough and almost impassible since not even a trail existed at the time. He could hardly get through the canyon on a pack horse. But Pinto Canyon had plenty of water, and the hardy stockman established his new ranch by building a mud shack and a corral for his horses in the canyon.[63]

By the end of 1885, at least sixty thousand cattle roamed Presidio County, and all of the land with water had been claimed. According to Presidio County historian J. E. Gregg, "Fully ninety per cent of the cattlemen in Presidio County at the present time started their herds in the period from 1880 to 1890. The greatest rush was in the years of 1884 and 1885." While most of the larger ranches had been established in the eighties, there were untold numbers of small ranchers and settlers who tried and failed but nevertheless played a vital role in the development of the big spreads. These unfortunates who had their dreams shattered are remembered as "starve outs." Their names have mostly been long forgotten. Many of them came to Presidio County in the 1880's and others followed later well into the twentieth century, but they all shared a common experience in that they "starved out," lost their land and disappeared from the pages of history. In 1887, the State of Texas took action to prevent individuals from easily acquiring large tracks of state land by passing a new land law. The law stated that an individual could purchase only one section of land from the state if it contained surface water. Up to four sections could be purchased by an individual if the property contained no water. By the mid-1880's the range land in Presidio County became crowded as stockmen competed to purchase or lease the land. Those who controlled the water also controlled the range.[64]

Historian Gregg observed, "The squatters came in and took up the land, but could not make a living from it. They had to have water and could get none except when they secured it from the ranch men. Some of these people hauled water twelve miles for drinking purposes. They lived mostly in tents, but there were a few lumber houses and some of sheet iron. The number of these people was greater than can be imagined by one passing through the county today. They were from the North and East and thought that all the Texas lands were the same." One cowboy recalled that once on a Presidio County trail drive his herd became scattered during a stampede caused by a thunderstorm. For the next seven days he tried to round up his cattle and "during the whole time they were never out of sight of these squatter houses." When these squatters and small land owners began to starve out, they sold their land to the larger ranchers thereby enabling the formation of huge ranches in spite of state laws formulated to prevent such acquisitions. Gregg commented "There seemed to be no land law that the cowmen would not circumvent or break."[65]

By 1885, Don Milton had suffered heavy losses because so many of his calves, cows, and bulls remained unbranded making them easy prey to cattle thieves. He no longer had undisputed control over his Chinati ranch and since his land was unfenced, many of his cattle fell into the hands of rustlers and brand burners. The unwritten law of the range stated that any unbranded calf became the property of the first person to burn a brand on it. That same year, one state land agent found a brand burner on the outskirts of Marfa with 600 head of cattle. Don Milton lost large numbers of his branded cattle to brand burners who found his lazy F brand easy to alter with running irons. A running iron is a branding iron that, after being heated red hot in a fire can be used like a pen to alter an existing brand. Some brand burners became very inventive and skilled in their illegal trade using heated harness rings or wagon rods when they lacked a better running iron. Faver's fortune further declined when a severe drought set in that September. No rain fell in the Chinati Mountains until the following August. Don Milton's cattle, along with those of other ranchers, congregated along Cibolo, Cienega, and Oso creeks desperately trying to find places to drink. Cattlemen lost as much as forty per cent of their herds.[66]

About this time, Don Milton sent word to Den Knight that he wished to meet with him. The cattle baron had made an important decision. His health was beginning to fail, and the brand burners had made him decide to quit ranching. When the two met at the Cibolo headquarters a short time later, Faver made Knight a very attractive proposition. He offered to turn over his entire ranch including all the cattle, stock, and equipment to Knight for three years. In addition, Don Milton agreed to provide the money to operate the ranch during the first year. In return for running the ranch, the young cow man got every third Faver calf he branded and every eighth steer. Knight seized the opportunity and John Humphris drew up a contract covering the agreement. Evidently, Faver felt he would not live much longer since he made the contract with Knight in Francesca's name. Although Knight hoped to brand ten-thousand Faver calves, this proved impossible. He branded only twenty-eight-hundred cattle the following year. In 1888, Knight sold all the heifer calves and the three year old steers. His cowboys drove the cattle from Faver's ranch to Marfa where they loaded the cattle on a Texas and Pacific train bound for a buyer in Midland. Den Knight made little money on the transaction since he only got three dollars per head for the heifers and ten dollars each for the steers. In addition, because of the draught, the cattle were in poor condition and so wild they were almost impossible to handle.[67]

Knight's contract expired in 1889. Don Milton sold his remai n-ing cattle to Joe Humphris for eighteen thousand dollars. Humphris managed to round up only about seven thousand head. He then sold the cattle in New Orleans and in the Indian Territory. Falling beef prices made even this transaction unprofitable for Humphris. When the last cattle car rolled out of Marfa that year, Faver's remarkable era came to an end. Don Milton Faver died in the afternoon of December 23, 1889. He is buried atop a steep hill overlooking Cibolo Springs where his tombstone, written in Spanish reads, "If he had faults, let them be forgotten and only his good deeds be remembered."[68]

Faver bequeathed the Cibolo and Cienega ranches to his son Juan and widow Francesca. Since Francesca had lived most of her life at Cibolo Springs, Juan gave his mother the property, claiming Cienega for himself. Don Milton left La Morita to his good friend George Dawson and Dawson's wife Juliana. But several of Juan Faver's children including Avallino, a son by Juan's first wife, filed a lawsuit contesting the probate and succeeded in breaking Don Milton's will in a costly and bitter court battle. Francesca found herself in dire financial straits when lawyers and creditors filed claims against the estate. Unsure of the validity of many of the claims Francesca paid the demands, "until there was no money left."[69]

Juan Faver spent his final years traveling much of the time since he inherited enough from Don Milton to provide a comfortable income. He certainly was not the rancher that his father had been because, according to one source Juan, "had been brought up as a young aristocrat." Like his father, Juan Faver spoke several languages and had a considerable education but he did not share his father's good health. Juan smoked heavily, his wife rolling him "cigars and cigarettes herself from native tobacco." He suffered a stroke as a young man and died at an early age before his children were grown. He left the "considerable" property he owned in Mexico to Gavina and his Texas land and holdings to his second wife, Gomasinda. Several years after the death of his father, Avallino Faver, who had managed to gain title to a portion of the Cibolo Springs ranch, sold the property to J. D. Bunton for fifty cents an acre. Gomasinda Faver lived out her life supporting herself and her children by "renting rooms to drummers (salesmen) visiting the Shafter mill."[70]

For almost a decade after Don Milton's death, the Chinati Mountains remained open range land. Ever increasing herds of cattle roamed freely since few, if any, fences existed. Ranchers simply let it be known to each other the property they claimed. Sometimes and sometimes not, neighbors accepted each other's claims. More than one dispute broke out in gunfire. In the spring and fall, ranchers held round ups to brand new calves and drive those cattle they wished to sell to the shipping pens at Marfa. An important and highly skilled part of the round up took place when the cowboys had to separate or cut the calves from the cows, steers, and bulls. Since there were more than 60,000 cows in the Big Bend after 1886, this became quite a chore. Den Knight had standing bet that he "could cut one hundred calves and not make a mistake about their owners." Knight enjoyed an almost uncanny reputation for cow cutting. The first large general roundup in the Big Bend took place in 1886 after considerable numbers of cattle had drifted southward toward the Rio Grande to escape the cold winter storms. The herds became widely scattered, congregating around water holes with "a single owners brand being observed in a dozen different localities." Den Knight and about sixty men worked the range west of Alamito Creek while a smaller group led by Tom Ellison rounded up cattle east of the creek. The roundup took about two weeks with the cowboys covering fifteen miles each day. These large communal roundups took place until almost the turn of the century when barbed wire brought an end to unrestricted range land.[71]

While cattle round ups have been glamorized in the Hollywood tradition of motion pictures, most were simply filled with long days of drudgery. It was dangerous, difficult work that required highly skilled cowboys. More than one Chinati round up ended in disaster. F. A. Mitchell recalled such a round up in August 1896, when a group of thirty Big Bend cowboys from three different ranches rounded up some fifteen hundred steers driving them to a holding pen near a sheer cliff on the Mitchell ranch. That night, the cowboys didn't worry about keeping a watch over the herd since it was secured in the pen, and they spent the early part of the evening sitting around the campfire telling jokes and making bets about a horse race they planned the following day. Mitchell described what happened next in a way that only someone who saw it would know. "Suddenly a mighty roar, as of distant thunder, threw the camp into action. Every man recognized the reverberating din of a stampede. Snatching whatever was handy--a slicker, a saddle blanket or better still a flaming torch from the campfire, they were off like a flash. Heedless of danger, they leaped into the corral, brandishing their assorted weapons in the face of the maddened herd. Time sped by; excitement ran high. In the lull after the storm, the exhausted men could hear the groans of wounded cattle." That night the cowboys searched in the darkness for the source of the groans but it was not until the first light of morning that they discovered that hundreds of terrified cattle had plunged some eight-hundred feet to their deaths over a nearby cliff. Mitchell described the scene by saying, "It was an appalling sight--a gory mass of mutilated flesh, broken bones, and dismembered horns. By a miracle no human body had been added to this mound."[72]

Since the herd had not been counted before the stampede, it was impossible to know exactly how many cattle had been lost. The cause of the disaster could not be determined although Mitchell observed, "Perhaps the shade of some departed bandit startled a dozing steer; more likely a coyote or prowling panther disturbed his dreams. Be that as it may every man knew the cattle had not run headlong over the bluff. Their sight far surpasses that of human beings. The are cautious; they would have stopped or whirled. Evidently as the first cattle became frightened and ran, their fear was communicated though the herd. Cattle always run in the same direction. Just as people are swept with the crowd, the lead cattle were carried over by the terrific on rush of those behind."[73]

In 1887, Lucious D. Bunton brought his wife, Belle, and their family to the Chinatis. Lucious and Belle had five children, two boys and three girls. They settled not far from Shafter where Bunton found work in the Shafter mill earning three dollars a day. Bunton did not remain at the mill long before finding other employment, taking part in a cattle drive up the Chisolm Trail in 1889. About this same time, the Bunton family became acquainted with John Pool who lived nearby. Pool helped them build a house not far from Cienega Creek. The two families also erected a schoolhouse for their children, hiring a teacher whom they paid twenty-five dollars a month. In 1891, Bunton bought the Cieneguita Ranch from Don Milton's grandson, Avallino Faver. The Bunton family moved to the ranch, but tragedy struck the following year when Belle died, leaving her husband with five young children to rear. In 1893, Bunton married Amy Lewis, the teacher he and Poole had hired. During the years that followed, five more Bunton children were born of that union. Lucious Bunton was a successful rancher acquiring much of the property claimed by Don Milton previously including the Cibolo Springs Ranch.[74]

For ranchers, disease and drought have traditionally posed the greatest threat to their continuing existence. During the closing years of the nineteenth century, as West Texas ranchers began trying to upgrade their Longhorn herds by introducing Durham and Hereford Cattle, Texas fever decimated entire herds within a matter of weeks. Durham cattle proved to be most susceptible to the disease spread by the *Margaropus Annulatus* tick. Although a method of immunization against the disease had been introduced by the turn of the century, Texas fever seriously threatened Texas cattlemen as late as the 1940's. Vaccination and quarantine finally controlled the dreaded fever. While the advancements of technology have, in most cases, eventually overcome the rancher's struggle with disease, there is little the cattleman can do about drought. In West Texas, rain fall is dangerously unpredictable. While tree ring studies indicate that droughts in the western United States have occurred in twenty to twenty-two year intervals, serious droughts have struck the Chinati country during the last one-hundred-ten years in a much less foreseeable cycle. Severe droughts devastated West Texas ranchers in the mid-1880's, in 1918, in 1934, 1953-1955, 1963, 1980, and presently continue into the new century. These droughts impacted ranchers in various and sometimes not so obvious ways.[75]

The 1880's drought became significant in the history of the Chinati Mountains because it forced many West Texas ranchers to seek new land with water in order to save their herds as they began to starve when the grass disappeared. The eighties drought called the great cattle "die up" became widespread across West Texas and so extreme that it brought the attention of the Texas Legislature which voted into existence a relief fund of $100,000 to aid stricken ranchers and farmers who declared themselves to be in "destitute circumstances." The fund, however, provided only meager assistance and was used to purchase small cornmeal and flour allotments for those in need. Large numbers of Texas ranchers left their homes and moved their herds west of the Pecos in hopes of finding open range and good water. Many of these ranchers including James Pool, Den Knight, Joe Humpris, and W. H. Cleveland found that the spring water of the Chinati Mountains saved their herds.[76]

Like a lot of his fellow cattlemen, Den Knight, or as the Mexicans called him Don Daniel, looked for other ways outside the cow business to make a living. In addition to his considerable skills as a cowman, Knight possessed no small amount of political talents that served him well in the 1890's. Despite his future political antics, Den Knight enjoyed an apparently well-deserved reputation in Presidio County as being "honest and fair dealing." In 1892, Knight filed for election as sheriff of Presidio County against Sheriff Sam Miller. Sheriff Miller enjoyed the support of the Cibolo Mining Company in Shafter. Because of the large numbers of Mexican miners employed by the mine, the company controlled the votes of the miners and usually carried the county elections as a result. The Mexicans deeply resented the mining company and turned their support to Knight but only after "methods not exactly legal but not unusual in frontier days." About two weeks before the election, Den and a bunch of his political backers drove a cattle herd into Mexico along the Rio Conchos where they fed several hundred "starved Mexicans and on election day brought them over to Presidio and voted them." To show their gratitude for the beef, the Mexicans agreed to vote for Knight in the Presidio County election. In those days, polling places required no identification of the voters and Presido County consisted of present Brewster, Jeff Davis, and Presidio Counties. Both candidates simply marked and handed out ballots, and "to make it legal all the voter had to do was to place the ballot in the box." A big railroad crew working in the county also helped Knight carry the election when each man voted three times in the election as they rode two different work trains stopping to vote on the same day in Valentine, Marfa, and Murphysville (present Alpine). To counter Miller's accepted efforts to stuff the ballot box, Knight sent to Cuidad Chihuahua for two hundred "fancy Mexican straw hats." As opposed to most hats sold in Presidio County in those days, the hats Knight ordered had sweat bands running completely around the inside of the hat. Inside each sweatband a ballot marked for Knight awaited the recipient of the *sombrero.* On election day Knight and his friends gathered outside the courthouse and passed out the hats in exchange for marked ballot the voters had gotten from Sheriff Miller. Den Knight won the election by a landslide and served as Presidio County Sheriff for the next 18 years.[77]

Den Knight's lengthy career as sheriff of Presidio County was marked by a style as colorful as had been his first election. Knight married Zoe Edith Moore in 1888, but his new wife died in childbirth a year later. In July 1897, Den married Molly Pool and the couple moved into the Presidio County Jail in Marfa where they lived for the next nine years. "Miss Mollie," as the sheriff's wife was addressed around Marfa, bore Den four sons while the couple lived in an apartment above the jail. In later years, Miss Mollie recalled the night Den and a deputy got called out to deal with a drunken cowboy who was waving a gun. When Den tried to disarm the man, the two scuffled and the drunk pulled the trigger on the gun sending a bullet tearing through part of Knight's thumb and then wounding him a second time in the forearm. The wounds left scars and a "slight imparity which he bore the rest of his life." Many Texas sheriffs would have simply shot the drunk. But Den Knight did not pack a pistol on his hip although he was known to carry a handgun in a *moral* tied to his saddle. On another occasion, Sheriff Knight rode horse back to the St. George Hotel in Marfa to quiet down a big party that was going on inside the hotel barroom. The sheriff then rode inside the bar climbing a flight of stairs horse back to a landing where he gave a rebel yell which promptly broke up the party.[78]

Den Knight didn't make a lot of enemies in his years as a lawman but like any Texas sheriff, he had some. He became known for his generosity, reaching into his own pocket to bail out the some of very people he had just arrested. One notable enemy did not remain so permanently. Knight arrested a man known only as Humphries, who was brought to trial and sentenced to a term in the state penitentiary. While being led away to jail after his sentence had been passed, the man defiantly bellowed to the courtroom, "I hope I live to see the day Den Knight is stone blind!" It became a bitter prophecy for Den Knight lost his eyesight in last years of his life. Years later, after the man had been released from prison, the former sheriff and prisoner encountered each other at a "political barbecue" at a ranch outside Marfa in the 1920's. Humphries noticed the old sheriff from a distance but did not recognize him and asked one of his companions if he knew the old man. When the former prisoner discovered it was indeed the sheriff who years before had arrested him, Humphries approached

Knight and learned the old sheriff had lost his sight completely. It was the reason Den Knight eventually had to leave law enforcement. Humphries broke down, weeping. He apologized profusely to Knight for the remark he had foolishly made years before.[79]

Shortly after the turn of the century, Knight took up ranching again moving Mollie and his family to a ranch located west of the Sierra Vieja on Walker Creek. Mollie had homesteaded the property located only a few miles from the border north of Candelaria. The Knight family lived at the ranch until they were driven out by the growing violence of the Mexican revolution in 1910. The family returned to Marfa where they bought property and Den again took up law enforcement. In September 1912, Knight joined the Texas Rangers and became an acting sergeant under the command of Captain John R. Hughes. In 1918, following the massacre at Porvenir and the resulting resignation Captain Fox, Den Knight got an appointment as Captain of Texas Ranger Company N. The following year, Den Knight's eyesight began to fade and he became totally blind about 1927. In the last two years of his life, the old blind lawman kept children around Marfa fascinated with his stories about his days as a cattleman and sheriff. In March 1929, Den Knight fell dead of a heart attack.[80]

The cycle of droughts continued to dictate the lives of Presidio County residents as it always had in the past. In 1918, a severe drought again forced a generation of West Texas ranchers to pull up stakes and look for better-watered land or get out of the cattle business. Silas Tom Wood had ranched near Sterling City since his election as county sheriff in 1900. The drought caused Wood and his eighteen-year-old son, Tomas Doren, to look for a new ranch. Encouraged by J. M. Shannon, a prominent San Angelo rancher and banker, T. D. Wood bought a ranch from a Dr. Beakley located on the eastern slope of Chinati Peak adjoining the Bunton Ranch. A short time after purchasing the property, Tom D. married one of L. D. Bunton's daughters, Anna Belle. The couple raised a family and ranched in the Chinati Mountains for the next twenty-five years.[81]

While Chinati ranchers have weathered many droughts, without question, the most devastating dry spell of the twentieth century took place in 1934. It began in 1929 in Minnesota and North and South Dakota. During the next five years, the drought spread across the Great Plains to West Texas creating a national emergency. The chief of the U. S. Weather Bureau stated in 1934 that "never before in the weather history of the United States has so little rain fallen over so wide a territory throughout the entire growing season."[82]

John Schledbecker wrote of the drought, "Hell moved west. No bright spots appeared anywhere. Grasshoppers and rodents struck savagely, and devoured what little food they could find. Springs and streams dried up. Wheat dried up...the wild-hay crop never materialized, and by May, the alfalfa crop was lost. Almost everywhere, stockmen watered cattle only by pumping. When they could stockmen moved cattle off the Plains, and so swelled an already glutted market." In addition to the disastrous consequences of the drought, the Great Depression worsened an already grave situation. One out of four American workers lost his job, and ranchers flooded auction rings in a desperate attempt to sell their cattle. Cattle prices plummeted, and many stockmen found themselves unable to sell their herds at any price. By October 1934 circumstances became so bad that 241 Texas counties, including Presidio County, were designated disaster areas by the Texas Relief Commission.[83]

On April 7, 1934, Congress passed the Jones-Connally Act making beef a basic commodity and authorizing the use $63,400,000 of federal money for the Emergency Cattle Purchase Program. In addition the Federal Emergency Relief Administration made money available to stockman to drill water wells and encouraged railroads to reduce freight rates for shipping feed and moving cattle out of drought stricken areas. Cattle purchases in Texas commenced June 6, 1934. Brewster County led the state in participation in the program indicating the severity of the drought in the Big Bend. Ranchers in Presidio County sold 19,250 cattle to the government for $269,273. Texas led the nation in federal cattle purchases selling 2,015,570 head. Many of the cattle were in very poor condition, some almost dead when they were sold. In Texas 34 percent of the cattle were condemned. Most Presidio County ranchers participated in the program. One Texas newspaper commenting on the Emergency Cattle Purchase Program in August 1934 said: "the greatest movement of cattle since ranch men drove their thundering herds up the old Chisholm Trail to Abilene, Kansas, is now under way in Texas. From all directions come the herds to the government pens, preceded in clouds of dust that announce their approach."[84]

The federal government paid ranchers as little as $1 to $5 for a calf under one year old with one two-year-old cattle bringing $5 to $10. A "top cow" brought as much as $20. While the statistics give something of an indication of the enormity of the disaster, the impact of the drought and the loss of the herds can hardly be measured in human terms. For two long-time Big Bend ranchers, the drought of the 1930's left a vivid memory of those hard times. Tommy D. Wood was eight years old in 1934. Raised on his father's ranch at the foot of Chinati Peak, Tommy D. shared the fear and frustration brought about by the drought. He recalled the cattle purchase program and the fact that many of the Wood Ranch cattle were in such poor condition that they simply could not survive being driven to the government pens in Marfa. They received $12 a head for their condemned cattle. The cowboys shot the condemned cattle and skinned them to provide the government proof of their numbers before burning the remains. As many as a thousand head a day were killed in July 1934. Tommy D. saw it happen, as did nine-year-old Boyd Chambers who lived in Brewster County at the time. Chambers recalled that during the Great Depression, his father's "poor cattle" brought $4 a head and "thousands of cattle that were not suitable to eat" were shot and burned after the official tally had been completed.[85]

Federal cattle appraisers had the difficult task of determining the price ranchers received for their cattle, and they also condemned those animals that were too weak to make the drive to the government pens. The cattle appraisers were local ranchers themselves, and in some cases, they overstepped their authority to help a destitute friend. Kenneth Smith and George Benson were two appraisers who worked and lived in Presido County. Many times Smith and Benson "looked the other way" and allowed the ranchers to butcher the condemned cattle instead of destroying the cattle and meat as federal regulations required. Hungry ranch families made jerky from the condemned cattle since many Presidio County ranches had no other way to preserve beef. In some cases, federal appraisers allowed ranchers to transport condemned meat to town where it could be distributed to needy families. In taking such actions, the appraisers risked their jobs, and if they had been discovered, they might have been prosecuted. Long time Presidio County rancher Boyd Chambers summed up the effects of the Emergency Cattle Purchase Program of the 1930's simply by saying, "It kept the wolf away from the door."[86]

"Something like fifty years ago General William Shafter stood on the edge of the rim rock south of the Davis Mountains and looked with disappointment into what appeared to him to be the most desolate region that he had ever seen. A region of small mountains and miniature mountain ranges of dull reddish volcanic ash which rose barely high enough to reach the level of the rim rock which marked the end of the mile-high-table land known as the Marfa Plateau. And of all the desolate looking hills, the one in the elbow of Cibolo Creek seemed to be the most devoid of vegetation. Hardly a blade of grass sprouted from its rocky sides and, except for the cottonwoods, which grew at its foot; there was nothing of shade for the weary and sun-blistered jack rabbit, which sought the rocks as a sanctuary from hawks. But nature, in one of her ironic whims, had chosen to make this mean appearing and desolate hill the magnet, which was to draw civilization and capital to this desert region. Deep within those rocky sides she had hidden rich deposits of silver ore. And, not long after General Shafter had viewed the region with disgust, John W. Spencer drove his pick into the first silver ore that had ever been found by a white man in this part of Texas."

Robert Allen[87]

Spencer's Silver and Shafter

Chapter 3

The tiny mining village of Shafter lies in the heart of the Chinati Mountains along the banks of Cibolo Creek on U. S. Highway 67, forty miles south of Marfa. Today, it is a sleepy little community, almost abandoned except for a few hundred hardy Big Benders who presently comprise its citizenry. The nearby silver mines have been closed for over fifty years now, and no one in Shafter today makes a living from the empty limestone shafts located west of town. There is little indication that more than 100 miles of tunnels snake through the mountainside next to the village. The big white Sacred Heart Catholic Church built by Shafter miners in the nineteenth century and a tiny post office are the only remaining centers of activity in the community. Most of the mine buildings are now roofless crumbling adobe structures giving only a very faint glimpse of what Shafter must have been like when it was a booming silver town.[88]

Shafter had its beginnings more than a century ago. Legend has it that the Spanish found silver in the Chinatis although little documentation supporting the story can be found. According to one source, "If Spaniards operated mines in the region (West Texas) they were there no sooner than the early seventeenth century, following the colonization efforts of Don Juan de Onate, a wealthy mine owner of Zacatecas who brought up the Rio Grande in 1598 some hundred people." During this time, the Spanish had a keen interest in finding precious metals but their enthusiasm gradually diminished since no discoveries spurred them on and problems with hostile Indians became more pressing. Perhaps the most credible evidence of Spanish prospecting activities in the Chinatis was mentioned by Clyde P. Ross in a 1943 U. S. Department of the Interior study of the Shafter mining district. Ross noted the presence of some trenches about three miles west of Shafter that may have been dug by Spanish prospectors. Most accounts, however, credit John W. Spencer with the initial discovery of silver near Cibolo Creek in the mid 1860's. Old time Shafter residents were quick to point out that a Mexican goat herder by the name of Juan Chavarria actually made the discovery when he saw some interesting looking rocks not far from the creek and pointed them out to Spencer. Chavarria worked for Don Milton Faver. At any rate, even if Spencer was not the first person to take notice of the presence of silver bearing ore in the Chinatis, he certainly played a pivotal role in the history of the Shafter silver strike by initiating the first mining operations after years of prospecting.[89]

Like Don Milton, John Spencer was a Chinati pioneer who came to the region from an obscure past. Throughout his life he seemed reluctant to discuss details of his upbringing even with his immediate family. But according to a Mexican passport, John Spencer was born in Indiana in 1821. His descendents think he never attended school but learned to read from his mother and went to work as an apprentice mechanic at an early age. Then one day, the young Spencer caught a ride on a freight wagon bound for St. Louis and never returned to Indiana or his parents again. In 1846, Spencer set out from Saint Louis riding a good horse heading south to Mexico City. On the journey Spencer demonstrated his horse trading ability by acquiring "some ten or twelve fine horses and twenty or thirty scrubs" along the way. In Mexico City, he obtained a freight wagon and started hauling freight along the Chihuahua Trail. Begun in 1839 by a group of merchants who hoped to establish a shorter trade route than the Santa Fe Trail between Chihuahua and the United States, the Chihuahua Trail became an important route of commerce across the Big Bend until the coming of the railroads in the 1880's. Initially, the trail ran from Ciudad Chihuahua to Ojinaga where it crossed the Rio Grande and continued up Alamito Creek by passing the Chinati Mountains to the Pecos River. After the discovery of silver at Shafter, the Alamito Creek route fell into disuse as most commerce on the trail went from Presidio up Cibolo Creek and through the Chinati Mountains by way of Shafter.[90]

In Ciudad Chihuahua, John Spencer struck up acquaintances with several North American adventurers including Ben Leaton and John Burgess. Leaton, described as "a low character and deadly" had married into a Chihuahua family. Leaton's wife, Juana Pedraza "bought or somehow secured dubious title" to a large amount of land located directly across the Rio Grande from present Ojinaga. Ojinaga was then known as Presidio del Norte. John Burgess "a scheming rancher-entrepreneur, who dreamed of elusive fortunes," got the idea that the three men should establish a business in Presidio del Norte. Spencer, Burgess, and Leaton traveled to Presidio del Norte where Spencer married Jesusita Baisa in 1851. In November of that year, Spencer purchased land on the Texas side and founded the town of Presidio, Texas, although it was then called Spencer's Ranch. Ben Leaton settled not far away from Spencer's Ranch building El Fortin or Fort Leaton. At first, Spencer tried raising horses on the ranch, but Indian raiders made that venture less than successful so he continued hauling freight. Later, he got a beef contract with the U. S. Army at Fort Davis and started raising cattle he procured in Chihuahua. Spencer enjoyed better success in cattle ranching and, "made quite a lot of money." He and Milton Faver became good friends and business partners. A drought in 1855 forced the two to drive their herds to the Davis Mountains, and later they formed a business partnership in a flourmill.[91]

In the ensuing years, John Spencer became well acquainted with the Chinati Mountains, grazing his cattle, hauling freight, and prospecting. The Civil War brought a temporary halt to his beef contracts with the army when it withdrew troops from Fort Davis. Spencer sought other ways of making a living. He became a prospector. The exact date that Spencer first found silver ore in the Chinatis is not known although it probably took place near the end of the Civil War. At first, no one seemed interested in the discovery; so Spencer mined what ore he could and hauled it in burro carts to Cuidad Chihuahua to be smelted. Because of the low grade of this ore, his mining proved not to be "a paying proposition." But John Spencer continued his prospecting hoping to strike it rich. In 1876, Samuel B. Buckley, the State of Texas geologist, heard that Spencer had found silver and conducted a mineral survey in the Chinatis. When Buckley published the Annual Report of the Geological and Agricultural Survey of Texas he wrote that the Chinati Mountains, "were the most promising region in Texas for silver, lead, and copper." But even this startling announcement failed to produce any real interest in mining the Chinati Mountains except for John Spencer, who kept on searching.[92]

When the Civil War came to an end in 1865, the U. S. Army returned to the Big Bend and reoccupied Fort Davis in June 1867. Because of the war, the fort had been deserted for almost six years. The returning troops found the post had been destroyed by Indians in their absence. This prompted the army to begin rebuilding the fort and resume efforts to provide military protection from Indian raids in west Texas. Part of the strategy to increase military protection included the exploration and mapping of west Texas. To accomplish this task, the army placed Colonel William Rufus Shafter in command of the 10 th Cavalry, the 25 th Infantry, and a company of Seminole Indian scouts in the summer of 1875 to survey and map this vast territory.[93]

The hard drinking, heavyset Colonel performed his duties efficiently, finding and mapping the location of Indian villages and water holes from the Panhandle of Texas to the Big Bend. It was for his efforts during this time that the town of Shafter got its name along with Shafter Lake in present Andrews County and Shafter Canyon in Terrell County. The Colonel's military career began early in the Civil War when he enlisted as a lieutenant in the 7 th Michigan Infantry and lasted until after the Spanish American War when he received the Congressional Medal of Honor and a promotion to the rank of major general. Unlike many white army officers, Shafter readily accepted command of Negro troops after the Civil War. The buffalo soldiers, as the black cavalry men of the 10 th Cavalry were called, served Shafter with great distinction from the Indian campaigns of the 1870's through the invasion of Cuba two decades later. Shafter's troops nicknamed him "Pecos Bill." This was not an affectionate title born of great respect. Shafter's men knew their commander as a stern, aloof officer who seldom, if ever inspired, the admiration of his troops.[94]

The soldiers nicknamed their colonel because of an 1875 campaign when Shafter aggressively pushed the cavalrymen to the breaking point after they ran out of drinking water in the stifling heat of a West Texas summer. Some of the soldiers, their tongues so swollen that they could not eat, became convinced that they would not survive the ordeal and had to be tied on their saddles at gunpoint. However, after two more days, Shafter's exhausted troopers rode their horses into the Pecos River not far from present Carlsbad, New Mexico. All somehow survived. Shafter's biographer who found Shafter to be "an officer who got results" wrote, "William Rufus Shafter was no gallant hero. He drank heartly, gambled earnestly, ate plentifully, and cursed incessantly. He suffered from gout, varicose veins, and obesity. A victim of persistent and malicious gossip, he was constantly surrounded by controversy. Because he became associated in the public mind with American military blunders in Cuba during the Spanish American War, people often pictured him as a fat, incompetent buffoon of a field commander." In addition, Shafter's military career is marred by two court-martial proceedings brought against him.[95]

Shafter's association with John Spencer eventually led to the establishment of the town of Shafter. By the fall of 1880, most hostile Indians in West Texas had been subdued with the exception of the Apache chief, Victorio. Refusing to be forced back onto the San Carlos Indian reservation in Arizona, Victorio had sworn to "make war forever" on the United States. He led his warriors on a two-year rampage across New Mexico, Chihuahua, and West Texas that some sources say took the lives of some 400 whites. Others claim that as many as 2,000 whites died during this final uprising that became known as the Victorio War. Charged with the protection of the Trans-Pecos, Colonel Shafter's troops guarded water holes and after Shafter moved his command westward, watched for Victorio along important river crossings of the Rio Grande. The Colonel established a headquarters on Cibolo Creek, several miles north of Presidio. One day, a few miles away, as John Spencer rested against a low tree, the prospector noticed some rocks that looked "strikingly like the silver ore he had occasionally hauled to Mexico." Excitedly he collected samples and took them to Colonel Shafter's headquarters camp. When Shafter saw what Spencer had found, he too became enthusiastic about the discovery and offered to pay to have the samples assayed. The assay indicated that indeed Spencer had at last found silver, enough to make him and the Colonel rich.[96]

Since Spencer lacked the money to purchase any of the land or develop a mine, he entered into an agreement with Shafter and two other army officers. It proved to be an arrangement the prospector later regretted. Since they had been involved in the mapping and exploration of West Texas, most Fort Davis army officers came to recognize the potential of the region, and many of them invested in land. One of the largest land purchasers in the Trans-Pecos during this time was the post commander of Fort Davis, Colonel Benjamin Grierson. At one point, Grierson owned "at least 45,000 acres" in Presidio County including 126 lots in the small town of Valentine. Some of the property he purchased for as little as 12 1/2 cents an acre. Lieutenant John Bullis also acquired a considerable amount of land buying more than 53,000 acres in Pecos County. At least seven Fort Davis army officers bought land. Colonel Shafter certainly wanted to be involved in what became very lucrative ventures for his fellow officers, and John Spencer presented him with the opportunity. Shafter approached Lieutenant Bullis and Lieutenant Louis Wilhelmi at Fort Davis, and the three entered into a formal partnership with Spencer in the summer of 1882. The partners purchased nine sections of school land in the Chinati Mountains close to Spencer's discoveries.[97]

About the same time, Shafter and Wilhelmi became involved in an unfortunate incident that smacked of racism at Fort Davis and one that brought national attention. Shafter became post commander of Fort Davis on March 12, 1881. Almost immediately after taking command, Shafter became a bitter adversary of the Acting Post Quartermaster, Lieutenant Henry O. Flipper. The lieutenant had the distinction of being the first black graduate of West Point. During the Victorio War, Lieutenant Flipper served with the 10 th Cavalry. At Fort Davis, however, he apparently aroused the ire of several white officers by taking frequent horseback rides with a white lady, Miss Mollie Dwyer. Although Flipper denied ever having anything but a platonic relationship with the woman, his friendship with Miss Dwyer apparently enraged Shafter and the 1st Infantry Post Adjutant Lieutenant Louis Wilhelmi. One source wrote that Shafter and Wilhelmi "were determined to eliminate him (Flipper) from the officer corps." This, at least, was Flipper's view of the affair. Colonel Shafter had Flipper arrested in August 1881 on charges that he embezzled $3,791.77 of government funds that Colonel Shafter ordered him to assigned to his quarters. Curiously, Lieutenant Wilhelmi also had access to a key to Flipper's quarters where the money was kept. Flipper was brought before a Court Martial, tried and found guilty of "conduct not becoming an officer and a gentleman" even though the embezzlement charge was never proven. As a result, Flipper was dismissed from the army. The incident, according to one writer, "shocked and angered the black community" and served "as a painful reminder that justice for black soldiers was granted at the whim of white society." While the Flipper incident continues to be disputed, it certainly did not cast a very favorable light on the reputations of either Shafter or Wilhelmi.[98]

Colonel Shafter bought four sections of Chinati land, two in his name and two in the name of his wife to circumvent the state school land purchase regulations. Wilhelmi bought three sections and Bullis purchased two sections in the name of his wife. Since John Spencer apparently had no cash he wished to invest, his partners agreed that he would share equally in the venture, "on account of his being a known prospector of mines." Although the deeds to the property made no mention of this partnership, Spencer, Shafter, Bullis, and Wilhelmi were to each receive a one fourth interest in any profits made from the venture. Since the partners did not have the money or expertise to operate a mine, they leased the property in 1882 to Daniel Cook, a San Francisco mining speculator, for twelve months in order to "develop the mining potential of the leased property." It appears that the lease came about largely through the efforts of Colonel Shafter who had traveled to California, "to borrow money to organize a company to explore the minerals." On this trip, the Colonel convinced Daniel Cook to send some miners to the Chinati Mountains to dig test holes. Although the lease expired in June 1883, Cook remained interested in the property, and he and Shafter formed the Presidio Mining Company. Hoping to renew the lease, the company tried to contact the partners, who by this time, had become scattered across the country. The army transferred Colonel Shafter to New York City and Lieutenant Bullis to the Indian Territory. Wilhelmi went with the 1st Infantry to Arizona, and John Spencer returned to his ranch.[99]

In the summer of 1883, William Noyes, manager of the Presidio Mining Company, located silver deposits on Section 8, Block 8 that had a value of $45 per ton. Noyes found the ore on the surface beginning the exploration of the Mina Grande ore formation, which by 1940 had produced 30,972,286 ounces of silver then valued at $18,000,000. This was the property that had been purchased in Mrs. Bullis' name. Because of the discovery, the company offered each of the partners 5,000 shares of stock in the Presidio Mining Company and $1,600 for the property. Shafter, Spencer, and Wilhelmi sold their interests within a few months. Lieutenant Bullis, however, would not sell and obtained a court injunction ordering the suspension of mining operations claiming that the property belonged to his wife and not to the partners. The injunction expired in the spring of 1884, and the following year, the Presidio Mining Company began full-scale mining operations. The company filed a lawsuit against Mrs. Bullis claiming that the property belonged commonly to all the partners. Bullis countered by saying that the property was his wife's land and the company did not have permission to be mining on it. In a trial held in the 34th District Court in Marfa, the Presidio Mining Company lost the case when the court ruled in favor of Bullis. The company appealed to the Texas Supreme Court who overturned the decision in favor of the Presidio Mining Company in 1887.[100]

The town of Shafter grew quickly a little more than a mile east of the main Presidio mineshaft. A post office was established there in 1885. The Presidio Mining Company bought mining equipment and had it shipped to Paisano Pass by rail where teamsters loaded the cargo and hauled it cross country in mule drawn wagons to Shafter. The mining company's first foreman was a Californian by the name of S. A. Wright. E. M. Gleim became the first mining superintendent. Gleim oversaw the digging of the first Presidio Mining Company shaft and remained superintendent for many years. Gleim also tried a mining venture himself in the Chinatis by operating a mine in Section six, which is very near and just west of, present U. S. Highway 67.[101]

The smelting operation was a vital part of the mining venture from the start. Initially, wood for the smelter came from the higher elevations of the Chinati Mountains. Humphris and Company of Marfa contracted with the mining company to provide the wood. One four-year contract called for the delivery of 4,000 cords of wood at $5 per cord. Manuel Jiminez went to work hauling wood for Humphris in 1902. He hauled the wood in large wagons pulled by a team of six mules. Loads averaged a cord and one half, and the mine typically kept at least 500 cords of wood on hand. Later, when the Chinati timber began to play out, wood haulers brought wood to Shafter from the Sierra Madre of Chihuahua. Wood provided the fuel for the smelter until oil replaced it in 1910. The timber of the Chinati Mountains is just now recovering from the logging operations, which were used to supply the Shafter smelter.

Many of the stumps from the cut trees remain today in the mountains.[102]

The Presidio Mining Company employed experience hard-rock miners both Irish and Mexican. Apparently, many of the early miners were Irish although few records describing the Shafter miners before the twentieth century can be found. The 1890 Census of Shafter was lost long ago in a disastrous fire, and the business records of the Presidio Mining Company have not surfaced. However, later U. S. Census records and hard-rock mining research reveal a glimpse of the early mining operations at Shafter. Until the introduction of power drills early in the twentieth century, hard-rock miners drilled holes in the rock to place explosive charges using hand drills. The Presidio mine relied on hand drilling until 1910 when air powered percussion drills came into use. Hand drilling of the limestone shafts was a slow, laborious process requiring both a considerable amounts of physical strength and skill. Miners worked alone or in pairs depending upon their location in the tunnel. In tight narrow places, a miner used a technique called single jacking to drill into the rock. This meant the miner had to hold the drill with one hand and strike it with a sledge hammer at the same time. Many times a single jack miner had to swing the heavy hammer in an extremely awkward, upward motion in order to drill into the ceiling of the tunnel. Double jacking, when two miners had enough room to work together, was less exhausting since one man held the drill as the other swung the hammer, and the two miners could alternate taking turns at the hammer. Double jacking, however, could be much more dangerous since a missed swing could easily crush a hand or an arm.[103]

Once the miners finished drilling the blasting holes it was time to place the explosives, an extremely dangerous task requiring concentration and a fair amount of expertise. Miners placed the explosive, either powder or dynamite, in the hole and then very carefully tamped the charge snugly into place before a blasting cap or primer could be inserted. Miners used wooden sticks to tamp the charge to prevent the possibility of striking a spark with a metal tool. One miner wrote of the process, "Tamping is done very nicely--not too much--or the cap explodes and one is likely to go flying out of the shaft." The explosive charge was always set off at the end of a work shift to allow the powdery dust and gas time to settle before the next shift of miners cleared debris from the tunnel. The departing shift had the extremely important responsibility of counting the number of explosions to determine if all the charges had detonated so that the incoming shift would know an unexploded charge remained. Unexploded charges could easily be set off with disastrous results by a single blow from a pick, shovel, or drill as the new shift worked in the tunnel. One blasting accident in the Presidio Mine in 1908 killed one miner and badly injured another.[104]

The Presidio mine operated around the clock with the miners working morning, evening, and graveyard shifts. The Presidio Mining Company paid miners $1.25 per day and allowed them one day off per month. Since the shafts had no ventilation equipment, dust became a constant health problem and was probably the single most cause of death among the miners. Miner's consumption or silicosis claimed countless lives in the Shafter mines. "Miners con," as the illness was called, resulted from the prolonged inhalation of quartz dust. The poorly ventilated shafts and dry drilling techniques used at Shafter made consumption even more dangerous. Miners consumption struck without warning and produced symptoms similar to emphysema. The symptoms only appeared after the disease had reached an advanced state, and scar tissue had irreversibly damaged the miner's lungs. In addition, consumption frequently contributed to other fatal lung diseases such as pneumonia and tuberculosis. According to one source, consumption "killed several workers every year" at Shafter. Glenn Brooks, who worked in the mines, recalled seeing as many as five of his fellow miners buried in one day in the Shafter cemetery. Another Shafter miner Rufino Cortez, recalled consumption victims, "They just dried up and died. They'd get a cough and turn an ashen color. Sometimes strong Mexican liquor would help the cough a little. But nothing would stop it in the end." Miner's consumption usually claimed the older men, the men with families. While consumption appears to have been a considerable health threat to the miners, there were apparently few recorded accidents in the Presidio Mine because of the stability of the limestone rock through which the miners tunneled. Generally, the stable limestone made it unnecessary to shore up the tunnels with timbers. In the entire operation of the mines from the 1880's until the 1940's no cave-ins took place.[105]

By 1898, the Irish employed by the Presidio Mining Company had been mostly replaced by Mexican miners. One source claims the Irish miners had "transferred to Alaska," although this seems unlikely. Typically, hard-rock miners drifted from mine to mine, leaving employment at one place when the ore played out or when they learned of a new strike somewhere else where better wages had been offered. In other instances, hard-rock miners moved on after being locked out by mine management when they threatened to strike. Although no clearly documented evidence of labor disputes with the Irish miners at Shafter has been found, that possibility may better explain their rapid departure. The 1900 Census of Shafter shows only a handful of Irish miners still living at Shafter and most of them were in management positions with the Presidio Mining Company. When Charles Sheridan came to Shafter in June of 1900 to conduct the census, he found a thriving mining town with 1,037 residents. Most of the male residents were Hispanic and listed their occupations as day laborers in the mines. But there were other scattered occupations such as teamsters and wood haulers. The few women who gave their occupations to Sheridan listed their work as seamstress or laundress. The 1900 census reveals the existence of a few small business enterprises. Joseph Mosely operated a grocery store at Shafter and Ramon Gonzales had a blacksmith shop. His brother, Francisco Gonzales, made shoes.[106]

By 1910, Shafter had grown somewhat, at least in the number of business establishments. The Census of that year showed a population of 1,198 living in the community. The majority of the male residents worked as miners, mill hands, laborers, wood haulers, freighters, and teamsters. Practically all who listed these occupations were young Hispanic men with the exception of two Irish and two English miners. Mill foreman James A. Shannon came from Louisiana. The census reveals that by 1910, Shafter had a doctor, a minister, a deputy sheriff, and two saloon keepers. Carrie Driffil, the wife of a miner, listed her occupation as "post master." In 1910, the Presidio Mining Company ownership changed hands, but the company retained the original name. The new owners made a series of improvements at the mine by introducing a new cyanide process in the smelter and air-powered drills in the mine. Also, oil came into use in the smelter eliminating the need for wood as fuel. Three years later, the company replaced the old 50-ton pan-amalgamation mill with a new 200-ton cyanide mill to increase production. The new owners also built a cable tramway that carried ore from the east shaft of the Presidio Mine to the smelter in Shafter. Other improvements came when the company hired a doctor and built a hospital, a boarding house, a company store, a golf course, and a tennis court. The company also built several houses for executives and workers. A new company medical fund, however, required Mexican workers to contribute one day's pay a month while Anglo employees were charged one dollar per month.[107]

Although the Presidio Mining Company became the leading producer in the Chinati Mountains as well in the state of Texas, it was certainly not the only mine that sprang up near Shafter as a result of Spencer's discovery. There were at least nine other mines that, at some point, operated near but not in the lucrative Mina Grande ore formation. These included the Gleim Mine, the Stauber Mine, the Montezuma Mine, the Perry Mine, the Chinati Mine, the Cibolo Mine, the Last Chance Mine, the Ross Mine, and the Sullivan Mine. The Gleim Mine, located near U. S. 67, a little south of the Presidio mine, was operated about the turn of the century by the one time Presidio Mine Superintendent, E. M. Gleim. No significant production resulted from the several hundred feet of workings. Like the Gleim Mine, the Stauber Mine located about a mile west of Gleim's operation, did not produce significant amounts although some of the ore taken from the mine did contain small amounts of silver and lead. Durham Perry of Shafter operated the Perry Mine, located about a mile northwest of the Sauber Mine. The Perry Mine produced 5.4 ounces of silver per ton of ore during the early 1930's as well as small amounts of gold and lead. Perry also operated the nearby Chinati Mine. It first opened in 1890 but only one car of silver-lead ore was shipped from it. It opened again in 1902 and produced zinc ore during World War I. During the mid-1930's, 153 tons of lead-silver-gold ore came from Perry's Chinati Mine. The Chinati Mine had a small smelting plant at Shafter that produced ten cars of lead bars. Like the Chinati, the Montezuma Mine first operated in 1901 and 1902 and again during World War I. About a mile west of the Chinati is the old Ross Mine. Little is known about this mine except that it first opened about 1890 and was worked for about a year producing some silver-lead ore. The Last Chance Mine shipped small amounts of lead-sliver ore in 1910, 1915, and 1916. Harry Young reopened the mine in 1926 and worked it for about a year shipping three carloads of lead-silver ore before he closed the mine. Located between the Last Chance and the Ross Mine lies the Cibolo Mine. The Cibolo operation was short lived. The mine opened in June 1934, and when the shaft reached the sixty-foot level, water flooding forced its closure.[108]

Unlike the spotty production of the other mines in the Shafter area, the Presidio Mine produced over many years. From 1888 to

1955, it produced 93 per cent of the silver mined in Texas. Additionally, the Presidio Mine produced 99 per cent of the gold in the state between 1927 and 1952. The mine began to make a profit by 1888, and during the years from 1888 to 1913, the Presidio Mine averaged as much as thirty ounces of silver per ton for about half of those years. The mine suffered losses in 1906, 1907, 1909, and 1910 when the grade of ore dropped to about 20 ounces per ton. After the new cyanide mill went into operation in 1913, the amount of ore processed increased from about 20,000 tons per year to more than 84,000 tons. The grade of the ore, however, decreased to about 10 ounces of silver per ton. The tunnels of the Presidio Mine extend 900 feet beneath the surface in hundred foot levels below where the Mina Grande ore formation was first discovered on the surface. Interestingly, the stopes of the mine are named for the long forgotten miners or perhaps mining families who labored to excavate these caverns. A stope is the initial hole a miner digs to remove ore. Some stopes are identified only by numbers such as Stope 402 or 501. The largest stopes in the mine are the Auerlias Stopes located at the 200 and 400 foot levels. Pedro's Stope and the Salcidos Stope are not far away at the 400 foot level. The Librandos Stope is also at 400 feet and the Janitos Stope is at 200 feet. All the stopes bearing names are Hispanic names, none have Irish names.[109]

In the summer of 1916, Tracy Hammond Lewis, a New York newspaper correspondent who described himself as a "warless war correspondent" came to Shafter in search of some interesting material for the *New York Morning Telegraph.* Lewis spent two months traveling along the Rio Grande in search of newsworthy stories about the war in Mexico. Along the way the author wrote a number of articles about the people and places he encountered. Curiously, he wrote about the town of Shafter because of Bob Dent and, in the process, unwittingly preserved an intriguing glimpse into Shafter's past. Bob Dent was the Justice of the Peace in Shafter at the time. Lewis found his methods of dispensing justice strikingly similar to Judge Roy Bean, who years before had been Justice of the Peace in Langtry, Texas. Judge Bean had quite a reputation for his unusual methods of administering the law. According to Lewis, Bean once turned loose a railroad worker charged with killing a Chinese laborer because the judge said he could find no statute in his books against murdering a Chinese man. In another instance, when a man died after falling off the Pecos River High Bridge, and the judge investigated, Bean learned the unidentified body had been found with a pistol and $16. Judge Bean resolved the matter by fining the corpse $16 for carrying a concealed weapon.[110]

Lewis found that "Justice is manipulated a good deal the same way in Shafter." Owen White, a Shafter resident, gave Lewis more than one example telling the journalist, "Game laws are not strictly enforced in Shafter, but Jim Bailey had been violating them more frequently than we thought advisable. One day he came into town with three does he had shot and boasted to everybody in the place about it. It was decided that an example would have to be made of him. Bob Dent was a little nervous as to just how Bailey would take it. After figuring the problem out with Luke Russell, he planned to have the latter charged with killing forty-seven quail and then fine him to show Bailey others were receiving the same treatment. Russell agreed, and when his case was called before the court, he pleaded guilty. He was fined $30 and costs. He promptly paid with money that had been supplied him." Then Jim Bailey stood before Judge Dent who asked him if he was guilty of poaching. "Yes, I'm guilty responded Bailey, but all the men in Presidio County can help pull the rope that hangs me before I'll shell out any coin for it." The Judge thought for a minute and replied, "You're fined two barrels of beer." Lewis noted "Dent's judicial rulings frequently involved liquid refreshments."[111]

White provided Lewis with another instance of how the legal system worked in Shafter. "Frequently in Shafter, Mexicans working in the mines would get too much firewater in their systems and make the town uncomfortable, but Dent's methods proved effective in keeping them quiet during long stretches of time. We rounded up thirty of them one day. We didn't wish to keep them in jail because the jail wasn't big enough. It was an unnecessary expense anyway. Once more Dent's ingenious mind solved the difficulty. He hired an interpreter and a court stenographer in order that the expenses might be worth while. The he proceeded with the trial of the disturbers of the peace. They were all fined generously with the not insignificant items of costs attached. The mining company went bail for them and required them to work out their debt. It took a long time to do it. During that period, Shafter was not disturbed by these thirty Mexicans." The newspaperman thought for a moment and then asked White, "It's a rather picturesque form of legal procedure, but don't you think that justice would be doled out more effectively if the courts were conducted along accepted lines?" White answered, "No I don't. I've been a lawyer long enough to know that as a rule a legal man's chief ambition is to defeat the ends of justice. Take a man like Dent or Bean, for instance. They know the kind of people they are dealing with, and by using common instead of legal sense they get results which your courts in the larger cities can't touch."[112]

In 1926, the Presidio Mining Company sold to the American Metals Company. The new management included Richard Bosustow, general manager; C. E. Wheellock, mine superintendent; and Fred Gray, mill superintendent. By this point, the grade of ore had declined, and the price of silver fell made the operation less and less profitable. Finally, when the price of silver dropped to 25 cents per ounce, the company closed the mine in July 1930. Some 300 families whose livelihood depended on mining moved away from Shafter.[113] The mine reopened in the spring of 1934 when the price of silver recovered somewhat. Many of the miners who had worked at Shafter returned, and by 1937, the town had a population of 537 with 6 business establishments. That same year, construction of U. S. Highway 67 through Shafter was completed linking the community to the outside world. In 1940, the Shafter mill processed 144,558 tons of ore that produced 1,525,087 total ounces of silver. The main shaft descended to 900 feet by this time. But the end of an era had come. In September 1942 the Presidio Mine closed again, this time for many years. General Manager O. C. Rheinheimer summed up the reasons for the closing. "It's simply a matter of high cost of production. The mine is playing out, with the ore of such low grade that it is not profitable to produce... We hit water in what has been considered a dry mine. Since then we have been fighting water, pumping as we worked... There have been labor difficulties of various kinds...its no one's fault." The miners moved away and the community fell into ruins. All the mining and smelting equipment was sold and roofs, doors, and windows were removed from the company buildings and houses leaving only the bare walls. By 1950, only 20 residents remained in Shafter. In 1951, the Anaconda Lead and Silver Company tried to reopen the mine to produce lead, but the effort failed when no pumps could be found that were capable of coping with the water in the shafts.[114]

In the ensuing years, little changed in the community of Shafter. Several ventures tried and failed to restore lasting economic prosperity to the little town. A land promotion scheme called the Last Frontier Promulgated came about in the early 1960's. The promoters of the venture tried to develop and sell land on four sections located southeast of Shafter. They hoped to attract buyers by creating a lake on Cibolo Creek and providing a hunting reserve, but the enterprise failed rather quickly. About 1965, several Shafter residents tried to have some of the land surrounding Shafter declared a wildlife preserve, but this idea met with failure too. In February 1970 a Hollywood motion picture crew came to Shafter to film several scenes in Robert Wise's six million dollar production of The *Andromeda Strain*, starring Author Hill. While the filming of the movie produced some local excitement for a few days, it did little more. Then, in 1972, the price of silver began to rise at the most unprecedented rate in American history. Also, in the early 1970's, the American Metals Company, who still owned the Presidio Mine, permitted Teaton Exploration and Drilling Company to drill a number of test shafts near the Presidio Mine to determine the advisability of resuming mining.[115]

The Teaton testing produced very favorable results indicating that ore at 900 feet contained 75 per cent silver. The Gold Fields Mining Company purchased the property from American Metals in 1978 and 1979. In January 1980 the price of silver went to $36.50 per ounce, and Gold Fields made the decision to begin mining. The company planned to begin operating the mine in the spring of 1981 and hoped to process 1,500 tons of ore per day seven days a week by 1982. While Gold Field hoped to employ 160 people in the operation, the company made no plans to rebuild Shafter as a company town. The employees were to live in Marfa and Presidio with the company providing transportation to Shafter for their workers. Gold Fields invested five million dollars drilling some 200 test holes around the mine and building a new elevator in the main shaft of the Presidio Mine. They drilled a second emergency shaft about 40 feet from the main shaft. But, although the prospects looked very good at first, the entire operation had ceased entirely by August 1982. The reasons for the closure were almost the same as the 1942 shutdown. The price of silver had fallen almost as rapidly as it had increased and the lower levels of the mine had required the company to pump ground water at a rate of 300 gallons per minute. While Gold Fields claimed at the closing that it still had an interest in mining at Shafter and planned to invest another forty million dollars in the project, the Presidio Mine has not reopened.[116]

"I remember Mother remarked after about three days travel in Texas, 'This is the sorriest country in the world. Not a house or tree bigger than a Mesquite bush to be seen and the river water is muddy the year round...Poor Father and Mother.' It makes me feel sad yet when I think of the grief they suffered from losing all the cows, their only source of income and it looked so promising for them. They had just about exhausted all their cash. Now they were flat broke and had to start over."

Jesse A. Pruett

Coming to Texas: The Life and Times of Phillip Hawker Pruett

Chapter 4

When twenty-five year old Hawker Pruett came home from the Civil War, little did he foresee that his future lay in the Texas Big Bend. As a second lieutenant in Company C of the 10th Arkansas Infantry, Hawker Pruett served the Confederacy with distinction and courage. During the battle for Port Hudson, Mississippi in May 1861, Pruett fell wounded and found himself captured by Union forces. Because of his rank as an officer, Hawker spent the next four years as a Union prisoner of war. Before his release, Pruett somehow survived two terrible winters at the Union Depot of Prisoners of War located on Johnson's Island, in Lake Erie, near Sandusky, Ohio. After being freed in New Orleans, Louisiana in March 1865, Halker found himself far from his home in Romance, Arkansas with no money and only the remains of his ragged Confederate uniform on his back. He was certainly not alone. Many of his fellow southern prisoners faced similar circumstances.[117]

Pruett set out from New Orleans, on foot, slowly making his way home to Arkansas. Wounded and maimed Confederate veterans filled the roads. Somewhere along the way, a compassionate farmer gave the young man a "old wore out pony" with the agreement that if the horse got him back to Arkansas, Halker would pay for the animal. Pruett made a rope halter and rode the old horse bareback, frequently stopping to let the animal rest. Halker named the pony First Relief since the animal was his only relief from walking. Whenever he found a cornfield, he stopped and fed First Relief as much as the animal could eat. Frequently Halker and First Relief spent the night at the home of friendly southern farmers who opened their doors to the weary Confederate soldiers. Several months later, Halker arrived at his fathers' house in Romance "barefooted and almost with out any clothes on." Once he got back on his feet, Halker sent the kindly southern farmer ten dollars he owed for the horse. Halker found his father's farm devastated by the war. Union troops had stolen all of Ben Pruett's horses and live stock. The granaries had been emptied of corn and wheat.[118]

John H. Worshom, also a Confederate veteran, described those times, "When the Confederate soldiers returned from the army after the war the majority of them literally had nothing but the ragged clothing on their backs, not even a change. What a site met them on their on their arrival at home. Desolation every where. Many found their families scattered all over the state, different members having taken up their abode with relatives or friends in such sections as had not been over-run by the enemy."[119]

Worshom went on to say, "While some of the soldiers had their land, that was all they had, no stock, no farming utensils or provisions. If one had these, he was an exception. The world will never know the poverty these men were reduced to, and their conduct at this time shines with more brilliancy, if such could be the case, than did their services in the army! They literally turned the sword into the plowshare, and went to work with a determination to make a living, and, if possible, to recuperate their fortunes. Poverty is a great leveler, and all were on the same footing now. It was not uncommon to see a private and a colonel in their old uniforms, working side by side. All the money made by the men for several months was spent meeting actual needs, and generally it took all they made to feed the family. In consequence, the old soldiers were still wearing their old uniforms. This became a great annoyance to the Yankee army that was stationed in the South. The sight of the old Confederate soldier going about daily in his old uniform reminded them too forcibly of the hard times they had undergone in the last four years. In order to remove these uniforms from sight as much as possible, the military authorities issued an order that the brass buttons on the coats and jackets of the late Confederate soldier must come off by a certain date. They allowed them the choice of covering the buttons with some material that would hide the shining brass or cut them off, but the brass buttons must be off or hidden from sight by that date. If the brass buttons were found on their clothing after that date, the United States soldiers had orders to arrest the offender and cut the buttons off."[120]

Such was the life of Confederate veterans. But the Pruett family soon endured even greater hardships. Shortly before Halker came home from the war a band of bushwhackers raided Ben Pruett's farm. Bushwhackers were a product of the chaos produced in the south by the Civil War. These roving bands of Confederate guerillas and deserters who eluded capture because they knew the terrain well and knew how to live off the land hit Arkansas hard. Bushwhackers preyed on many isolated Arkansas communities, as well as in other states in the South, robbing and killing. The Union army considered them a substantial threat. Perhaps the best known bushwhackers were Jessie and Frank James and Cole Younger who rode with Quantrill's Raiders. In April 1864 Union General William T. Sherman expressed his frustration with dealing with bushwhackers when he wrote Judge-Advocate-General Col. Joseph Holt. "Sir: I wrote you from Memphis some time ago asking specific instructions as to the power of a commander of an army in the field to approve and execute the sentence of death. The question arises daily, and I expect to execute a good many spies and guerillas under law without bothering the president. Too many spies and villains escape us in the time consumed by a trial, review, and remission to Washington, and we all know that it is very important for the President to hang spies, even after conviction, when a troop of friends follow the sentence with earnest and *ex-parte* appeals. Spies and guerillas, murderers under the assumed title of Confederate soldiers, deserters on leave, should be hung quick, of course after a trial, for the number of escapes made easy by the changes on guard during the long time consumed by trial and reference have made that class of men bold and dangerous, and our own scouts and detachments have so little faith in the punishment of known desperados that a habit is growing of, 'losing prisoners in the swamp', the meaning of which you know. Forty or fifty executions now would in the next twelve months save a thousand lives."[121]

When the bushwhackers raided the Pruett farm, Halker was

still imprisoned at Johnson's Island. The armed bandits burst into the Pruett house demanding money from Ben. He told them he had none. Nancy and Aunt Annie tried in vain to convince the bushwhackers that there was no money. But the men dragged old Ben outside in the freezing night where they put a rope around his neck preparing to hang him from a nearby tree, when the two women intervened. Annie promised that if they would only release her father, she would give them money. Nancy put a blanket around Ben while two of the bushwhackers followed Annie into the house to get the money. She went to her work basket and got a pair of scissors before going into the bedroom where she cut open the corner of a quilt and pulled out a twenty dollar gold piece giving it to them. The men roughly pushed her aside and looked all through the quilt for more money but found none. Convinced that they had all they could steal, the men went out in the yard and released Ben before galloping off into the darkness. Little did the bushwhackers know that Ben Pruett had several hundred dollars in gold buried under the floor of his smokehouse.[122]

Once he came home from the war, Halker started farming along with his 17-year-old brother Elbert. It was not easy. The Pruetts and their neighbors had no work animals. Most of their horses and mules had been stolen during the war. As a result, a good plow horse or mule became priceless, since without them, crops could not be planted or fields worked. Some farmers were forced to use their milk cow to plow the fields. Fortunately, Halker somehow managed to obtain a plow horse to work his fields. Then, in 1866, another band of bushwhackers dealt the Pruetts the cruelest blow yet. One morning, as Elbert Pruett plowed a field, a shot rang out and the young man fell mortally wounded over the plow handles. No one knew why Elbert had been murdered, only that bushwhackers had been in the area. Grief stricken, Halker Pruett buried his brother and resolved to put the tragedy behind him. For a time he and Ben devoted all of their efforts to restoring the farm. Sometime later, after the crops had been harvested, Halker took a few days off and "dolled up in his new jeans suit, mounted First Relief and set out to see Mollie Brown." Halker and Mollie had been sweethearts before the war, and five years of separation had not diminished their feelings for each other. Mollie, or Martha Ann, was the daughter of John and Mary Brown who lived on the White River in nearby Woodruff County, Arkansas. Now that the war no longer stood in their way, the couple soon rekindled their relationship and married in

1866.[123]

In 1867, Mollie gave birth to the couple's first son. The child lived nine days. A second son was born in July 1868. They named him William Elbert after Halker's slain younger brother. Sometime before 1871, Mollie gave birth to a girl, but the baby died in infancy. In January 1871, Edmond Lee Pruett was born and lived. Jessie A. Pruett arrived in March 1872, and like his brothers survived. But tragedy stuck twice more following the birth of Jessie. Between 1872 and 1875 Mollie bore two more girl babies but neither lived.[124]In the first ten years of their marriage, Halker and Mollie lost four infant children to death. Sadly, in those days, this was not unusual. Disease claimed many infants. The list of the afflictions that took so many young lives in that time is long. Diarrhea, tuberculosis, small pox, mumps, mountain fever, and scurvy all took a dreadful toll. Probably the biggest single killer was cholera. Halker and Mollie decided that because they had lost so many children in the Kentucky Valley, the time had arrived to find a place that was, perhaps, more healthy. So they resolved to move west in search of "health and fortune." They had heard of opportunities in Colorado, New Mexico and Texas and set out, in pursuit of their dreams.[125]

In 1868 Halker bought an old, run-down sawmill in Des Arc, Arkansas and started selling lumber cut from the surrounding pine-covered woods. For the next seven years he operated the mill, doing fairly well but not content to continue the operation permanently. In the spring of 1876, he and Mollie made a decision that forever changed their lives and those of their descendents. They resolved to move west to the New Mexico Territory. It was not an easy decision, but one prompted out of concern for the health of their children.[126] In the first ten years of their marriage, four infant Pruett children died of various diseases. Most young couples living in Nineteenth Century America suffered similar losses. In 1800, only about half of the people living in the United States could reasonably expect to live to the "old" age of forty-five years. The death rate of women was higher than men due to the dangers of childbirth coupled with the fact that families tended to be large. Nineteenth century medical knowledge made few advances, and those living in remote sections of the country had virtually no access to even primitive medical care. Most people simply relied on home remedies or prayer. The children were the most vulnerable to diseases such as cholera, smallpox, and measles.[127] Hoping for better times, Halker and

Mollie loaded their surviving offspring, Willie, Eddie, Jesse, and Viola into a wagon and set out for the New Mexico Territory. The parting of the family became emotional. Jesse, only four years old at the time, remembered throughout his life "the kissing and crying that took place when it came time to say goodbye."[128]

Halker, Mollie, and the children rode in two wagons to Beebe, Arkansas about fifteen miles from Ben Pruett's place where they boarded a train to Saint Louis. In Saint Louis, a Union Pacific passenger train carried the family westward across the plains of Kansas before to Denver, Colorado. By 1876, railroads had dramatically changed the way Americans traveled. Rail transportation offered fast, dependable transport across the United States rapidly replacing turnpikes, canals, and steamboats. The Union Pacific was one of the first major railroads constructed after the Civil War when railroad construction, fueled by Federal land grants and subsidies, prospered. Following the Civil War, Congress, hoping to encourage railroad construction, offered the railroad companies grants of public land in the amount of 12,800 acres for each mile of track built. Once underway, the Union Pacific and other companies feverishly laid track sometimes at the rate of two miles per day. By May 1869, the Union Pacific completed more than 1,700 miles of track that stretched from Missouri River to the Pacific Ocean.[129] The building of the railroads encouraged large numbers of emigrants to move westward in hopes of obtaining railroad land offered for sale at cheap prices. New towns appeared almost overnight along the tracks as the railroad companies promoted land sales with glowing advertisements. Many emigrants, like Halker and Mollie, headed for the Rocky Mountains. In 1879, more than 100,000 newcomers arrived in Colorado. This set an immigration record in the state. Thousands traveled no further west than Kansas; a place described as "bewitchingly inviting to all of small means, whose only hope for a farm and home of their own is government land." [130]

Jesse Pruett wrote about his memories of the train ride across Kansas. "The first morning I woke up, I remember looking out and seeing trees and landscape all running the other way. So I asked Mother what made the trees move the other way. She tried to tell me that the trees were standing still and it was the train moving but I just knew Mother was wrong because I could see trees running the other way. I never did get it right until we ran out of the timber land country and to the grassy plains of western Kansas."[131] In those days, most passenger trains did not have dining cars. This compelled passengers to provide their own meals. Occasionally, when a train pulled into a station, passengers dashed hurriedly off the train to buy something to eat. The ever-practical Mollie brought along lunch baskets filled with fried chicken, boiled ham, cakes, and pies. At first, Halker became annoyed at having to carry along the baskets since he thought he could purchase food along the way. But the difficult traveling conditions and distance between dining stops caused the food baskets to be more than welcome. One of the few food items sold on the train by the "butcher boys" was bananas. Jesse had never previously seen or eaten a banana. Fascinated, he took great pleasure peeling and eating the mysterious new fruit. The conductor was amused by the Jesse's fascination with bananas, and he kept the boy well supplied. Jesse ate so many, "he felt like a monkey."[132]

Willie, Eddie, and Jesse sat wide-eyed as they listened to the stories told by their fellow passengers "with their long beards and heavy boots." The men talked of the New Mexico Territory and Texas where people "eat tortillas and chilies, and ride burrows, and wear big straw hats." These travelers came from every walk of life. The buffalo hunters, miners, loggers, cowboys, and soldiers greatly impressed Jesse. But along with these adventure seeking males came the capable, determined women like Mollie, upon whom the children depended so much. Fascinated by the optimistic talk about the New Mexico Territory and Texas, Halker pondered over the stories that he heard of wealth and fortune.[133] As the steam engine chugged across the almost endless prairies of Kansas and eastern Colorado, few houses came into view except those near railroad stations. Occasionally, groups of wagons drawn by horses, mules, and oxen belonging to buffalo hunters came within sight. When the Pruett children reached the Kansas-Colorado border, they stared in amazement when they passed near a huge herd of buffalo that stretched as far as the eye could see across the prairie. Little did they know that even more astounding sights awaited them.[134] When the train pulled into Denver, the Pruett children expressed wonderment at the size of the depot and the number of people milling around. About the time the Pruetts arrived, Congress granted Colorado statehood and made Denver the capitol. Nestled in the Front Range of the Southern Rocky Mountains, Denver, in little more than a decade, grew from a small mining camp into a bustling city. With the coming of the railroads and a silver boom, Denver became a thriving hub of transportation and commerce. The Union Pacific, the Santa Fe, and the Denver and Rio Grande Railroad all met in Denver.[135]

Halker left Mollie and the children in the waiting room of the depot while he went in search of a suitable boarding house. The family stayed in Denver for about two weeks while Halker looked the town over. Jesse marveled at the beauty of the snow-covered peaks surrounding Denver in the summertime. After several days, Halker concluded that his best course of action might be to try to get back into the lumber business in some way. After all, he knew the lumber business well and could not help thinking of the profit that the abundance of timber in the Rocky Mountains might bring him. Denver, however, proved to be too crowded so he resolved to head on to the New Mexico Territory as he had originally planned.[136] Pruett hired a freighter that had two wagons, and the family set out for Santa Fe. The trip took about six weeks. After the relative comfort of the train ride, the hardship of traveling in a covered wagon took some getting used to. The wagon's canvas top offered the children scanty protection from the heat of the sun and the drenching rains that poured from the sky almost every afternoon in the mountains. Weather permitting, Halker rolled up the sides of the canvas about a foot from the wagon box so the children could see outside. He sat up front in the seat with the driver. They loaded a second wagon full of baggage, tools, and farming implements. The journey to Santa Fe proved to be quite an experience for the children who greatly enjoyed watching all sorts of wildlife. At night they listened as wolves howled and owls hooted. Occasionally they spotted a wolf prowling near the camp before daybreak. Great numbers of deer and antelope grazed on the prairies.[137]

When the Pruett family reached Santa Fe, they camped near a creek lined with cottonwood trees on the edge of town. Halker and the freight man went into Santa Fe to try to find a house for rent. The dusty little town stood in stark contrast to the sprawling new city of Denver. Santa Fe, located in the valley of the Santa Fe River, is the second oldest town in the United States. When Pruett came there in 1876, Santa Fe had been in existence for more than 250 years. Originally established as the northern most outpost of the Spanish empire in 1609 some sixty Spanish governors once ruled the vast territory of New Mexico from the Governor's Palace north of the Plaza near the center of the town.[138] Halker arranged to rent a small house near the edge of town. An adobe structure, the house had dirt floors with whitewashed walls to make it more livable. One small window in each room proved a small amount of light. Although the house contained no furniture, the walls had recently been dusted and the floors swept. After they became acquainted with their Mexican neighbors, the Pruetts made friends quickly. The family of the landlord took a liking to the Pruett family and made every effort to make their lives as comfortable as possible. He sent two of his daughters to the house with dozen or more sheepskins, which Mollie put on the floor for use as a carpet. Each room had a fireplace, and Mollie cooked in one of them using utensils purchased to cook on campfires. Halker bought some lumber and built some beds and crude furniture.[139]

After the rigors of the wagon trip, everyone welcomed the opportunity to live under a roof again. The journey from Arkansas had been particularly difficult for the baby. Mollie fed Viola with a bottle and since fresh milk had been difficult to obtain on the trail, the infant developed a stomach ailment. One of the Mexican neighbors told Mollie to try giving Viola goat's milk, which she said, would be very good for the child. At first Mollie did not think much of the idea since she "had never heard of such a thing before." Finally, she consented and went to the back yard to milk a neighbor's goat. Within a few days, Viola recovered completely from her stomach ailment. Halker bought a milk goat and kept it to provide for milk for Viola.

The following year, Halker bought a one-half interest in a cow hide tanning operation selling processed hides and tanned leather to settlers along the Rio Grande and in Mexico. From his customers Halker learned of a great demand for purebred cattle in Texas where ranchers looked for ways to upgrade their Longhorn herds. Seizing the opportunity, Halker sold his tanning business and used the money to buy forty Durham cattle. He planned to drive the herd to Fort Concho in West Texas.[140] By the time Pruett made the decision to seek his fortune in Texas, the state had been firmly established as the leading cattle producer in the nation. Texas had a long history of cattle production dating from the time of the first Spanish colonial efforts. As the Spanish presence spread across Texas in the seventeen and eighteenth centuries so did the numbers of cattle and horses. Spanish cattle were of two types; the sharp-horned, generally black, fiercely behaving Castilian, and a more obscure, and equally unpredictable, unnamed breed of various colors and shades. Later Texans named the decedents of these Spanish cattle mustang cattle, and hunted them as they did deer, antelope, and buffalo.[141]

Halker was anxious to drive his Durhams to Fort Concho but waited until after Martha gave birth to her ninth child, a girl they named Ora Jane. As soon as the baby could travel, Halker hired a teamster named Wilson, who owned a large freight wagon, to move the family to Texas. By now Will Pruett was ten years old and accustomed to riding horseback, so his father made plans for the boy to help drive newly purchased the Durhams to Texas. Halker tied a mother cow to the wagon where the other children rode so that Ora Jane would have fresh milk for the journey. Wilson brought along his wife and children on the trip.[142] Pruett traveled from Santa Fe toward Las Vegas where they followed the meandering Pecos River in a southerly direction. The trail drive down the river proved to be a considerable challenge. Halker had no experience-herding cattle at night, and the cold pre-winter nights in the mountains turned out to be quite unpleasant. Snow covered many of the mountain trails. Occasionally, the children fished in the almost transparent headwaters of the Pecos where they could see perch swimming about clearly. Jesse used grasshoppers for bait with great success. Once, the boy became so excited when a large perch grabbed the bait that he jerked his pole over his head firmly hooking himself in the seat of his pants. When he couldn't extract it by himself, he walked to camp where Mollie plucked it out. Meanwhile, the other children caught more than enough fish for supper.[143]

Between Santa Fe and Las Vegas, the Pruetts encountered few settlements. At Las Vegas, Mexican and Indian farmers grew wheat in irrigated fields. Halker took an interest in learning the agricultural techniques of these people. When the farmers harvested their wheat, they piled it in round stacks, and drove goat's herds around the stacks to tromp the grain out. Then they shoveled up the wheat chaff, "dirt and all," and ran it through a wire sieve to remove the straw and chaff. Finally, they "winded" the wheat by tossing "shovelfulls" of the wheat into the air to further separate dirt and chaff from the grain.[144]

Halker spent a few days near Las Vegas observing the wheat farms. He considered going to St. Louis to purchase a thrashing machine for use around Las Vegas but decided against doing so because he thought the countryside lacked adequate wheat acreage to justify the cost of the machinery. Pressing on down river with the Durham herd, the Pruetts saw many other Mexican ranches and farms. Halker admired the practicality of the adobe construction methods he saw. Mollie commented that she couldn't imagine the possible uses for the long strings of red peppers hanging from the houses but soon discovered how essential the chili pepper was in the Southwestern diet.[145] The journey south along the Pecos River took longer than expected because the short-legged Durham cattle set the pace. Since the wagons traveled faster than the herd, frequent stops became necessary to allow Halker sufficient time to select camping spots located near good grass and water. After a few days of this routine, the cattle learned that usually the best grazing lay near the wagon where they congregated during the evening hours. Each day, the children passed the time by watching for good fishing places as they bounced along in the wagon.[146]

When Pruett reached Bosque Grande, not far from present day Roswell, he entered John Chisum's ranch. Chisum operated one of the biggest cattle ranches in New Mexico encompassing approximately 150 miles along the Pecos River. At one point, Chisum owned as many as 80,000 head of livestock and employed 100 cowboys. But as impressive as Chisum's operation seemed, he was almost put out of business by rustlers. Chisum estimated that he lost 10,000 head to theft in a couple of years. As a result, rustlers on Chisum's spread were often hung or shot by Chisum cowboys, and some of these cowboys developed a considerable reputation as outlaws themselves for their swift and sometimes merciless administration of frontier justice. Some of Chisum's men were not beyond a little rustling themselves.[147] Jesse remembered that on Chisum Ranch, the "prairies were literally alive with cattle and horse stock clear down the Pecos." As they crossed the ranch, Chisum hands frequently rode along with them to exchange news and look over the Pruett cattle. Halker's herd of Durams caused a great deal of interest among the Chisum cowboys and he got several offers to sell or trade them. Sometimes unsure of their motives, Halker would not set a price on his cattle and became afraid that his prize bull might be stolen, so much so that he roped the bull on several nights and tied to him to the wheel of one of the wagons.[148]

The Pruetts experienced a rather frightening experience not far from present Carlsbad, New Mexico. After finding a good camp near the Pecos River, they went fishing and had a fish fry. As they enjoyed their meal, a group of Mescalaro Apaches rode up and camped directly across the river. The Mescaleros burned fires throughout the night and danced and sang until dawn to the great discomfort of the Pruetts. Not knowing what to expect, Halker kept a nervous eye on the Apaches until the next morning when they ended their dancing and rode off. A little later, a Chisum cowboy came by and told Halker that he didn't think the Indians meant any harm since they occasionally came down from the reservation near Fort Stanton to fish and hunt. At daybreak, the Pruetts broke camp and crossed the state line into Texas.[149] Halker's uneasiness about the Mescaleros might have been justified because small raiding parties of Mescaleros were thought to have raided several stage stations along the San Antonio-El Paso road. Only a few months earlier, H Company of the 10 th Cavalry, operating from Fort Davis pursued a band of raiding Mescaleros into the near-by Guadualupe Mountains before losing their trail. But the Mescaleros were not the only Indian raiders operating in West Texas at the time; Comanche war parties also caused a considerable amount of trouble that year.[150]

In addition to Indian problems, the harsh terrain the Pruetts encountered in Texas made the journey more difficult. The further south they went, the more barren and inhospitable the land became. After three days of struggling to cross the rugged Trans-Pecos, Mollie remarked that West Texas is "the sorriest country in the world. Not a house or tree bigger than a mesquite bush to be seen and the river water is muddy the year round." Mexican accounts had long made similar observations for they called the Pecos, *Rio Puerco* or "Dirty River."[151] The harshness of the countryside stressed all that ventured there. Wilson, the wagon man, became extremely disagreeable, making his travelling companions very uncomfortable. According to Jesse, Wilson proved too lazy to hitch and unhitch the team without calling for help, and he abused and beat his wife. He wouldn't gather firewood or help with any of the work. To provide a more comfortable sitting place for Mollie and Ora Jane, each evening Halker removed the spring seat from the wagon placing it near the campfire at night so Mollie could sit comfortably and feed Ora Jane. To everyone's irritation, Wilson frequently took the wagon seat for himself and never helped place it back on the wagon.

One morning, about two days travel above Horsehead Crossing, Wilson slept late, and when he arose, he hurriedly filled his plate with breakfast before looking for a comfortable place to sit down. Seeing his wife sitting in the spring seat, he marched over, grabbed the woman roughly by the shoulder and ordered her to get up and move so that he could sit down. The woman meekly obeyed her husband's command. A little later he bellowed for his wife to fill his coffee cup. Having enough of Wilson's overbearing manner, Halker angrily told him to "get up and wait on himself." Infuriated, Wilson jumped to his feet and menacingly grabbed an axe. Sensing the trouble, Halker armed himself with another axe and stood glaring at Wilson from about eight feet away ready to meet any challenge. In the meantime, Mollie, who had been putting coals on the Dutch oven in the fire, quietly walked up behind Wilson, raising the shovel she had been using, and told him to "drop it." At first the man froze, but something in Mollie's voice when she told him to, "drop it," a second time convinced Wilson of the prudence of doing so. Then she turned to her husband and told him to put his weapon down which he did. Wilson emerged from the confrontation extremely embarrassed for having backed down from a woman and simmered about it as the others loaded the wagons. Just as they were about to get underway, he suddenly ordered the Pruetts to unload their possessions declaring that he did not intend to carry them any further. Upon hearing this, Halker rode up on his horse and, with his rifle handy in the scabbard, glared down at Wilson and told him that he had been hired to carry the family to Fort Concho. Halker further told the wagon man in no uncertain terms that he expected Wilson to fulfill his promise and if Wilson thought about leaving them in the middle of nowhere, "he had better have another think coming." Halker concluded by telling Wilson that if anyone would be left behind, it would not be any of the Pruetts or Mrs. Wilson but Wilson himself. As Wilson looked up at Halker, he became convinced that Halker clearly meant business and replied, "I finish my job." Following this second altercation, they all moved on to Horsehead Crossing. [152]

At Horsehead, they camped for the night. Halker struck up an acquaintance with a buffalo hunter who had set up a camp next to his large wagon not far away. Around the campfire that night, the two men talked. The hunter told Halker that he was headed for Fort Stockton and informed Pruett of the conditions they faced along the trail to Fort Concho. The following morning, Halker struck a deal with the hunter to carry the Pruetts to Fort Concho since he himself had a wagon and knew the trail. The Pruetts loaded their possessions in the buffalo hunter's wagon and gladly parted company with Wilson after Halker paid what he owed the man. Reflecting Mollie's concern for Mrs. Wilson when they left her with her husband, Jesse wrote, "Wilson didn't like it a bit but he didn't say or do anything. Poor Mrs. Wilson was the one to suffer because he whipped her and abused her whenever he wanted to. Mother was sorry for Mrs. Wilson and gave her lunch and bread enough to last her two days and that would get her to Fort Stockton, forty miles to the south."[153]

The Pruetts journeyed on in the opposite direction guided by the buffalo hunter who knew where to find the water holes and good camping places. Jesse noted the rapid change in the countryside as they approached the Concho River country. He recalled, "nothing but grass on the ground and the sky above and the land was literally covered with antelope." One evening, about three days travel from Horsehead Crossing, they camped near a pond to water the herd of Durhams. Suddenly a group of buffalo appeared over the horizon apparently wanting to water in the same place. Once they saw people, however, the buffalo stayed out of rifle range watching from a distance.[154] Halker found himself fascinated by the great shaggy beasts and "was anxious to kill a buffalo for the novelty of it as well as to get some fresh meat." The buffalo hunter told Halker that since he was riding a good horse he should try to rope one of the young creatures. Not realizing the futility of such an action, Halker tightened the cinch on his saddle, mounted his horse, grabbed his rifle, and galloped off in the direction of the wary animals. As he approached the herd, the buffalo scattered. Halker spotted a large bison calf about eight or nine months old and took out his rope. After several failed attempts to lasso the terrified animal, Halker managed to throw a loop over its head and drag the buffalo calf off its feet thinking it would fall like a cow. But as soon as he managed to get the calf down, it instantly bounced to its feet and took off running in another direction. Finally, the futility of the effort became plainly obvious. Unlike cattle, buffalo cannot be subdued by roping, no matter how skilled the person attempting such a feat. After repeated tries, Halker gave up and shot the beast. With the assistance of the buffalo hunter, the two men butchered the bison and carried the meat back to camp where quite a feast ensued. Since the Pruetts diet on the trail consisted mainly of deer meat, the availability of buffalo meat was a welcome change. After slicing the meat into strips, they stretched a rope around the wagon and hung it to dry in the sun making jerky.[155]

The buffalo Pruett encountered were part of the great Concho herds that migrated to the Concho River region because of the mild winter climate there. During the winter when bitter cold swept into the Texas Panhandle, huge herds of Bison moved southward to the Concho River country. In addition to the warmer climate, the North, South, and Middle Concho rivers provided plenty of water for the herds. The buffalo wintered in the Concho, returning northward in the late spring. It was an ancient cycle, one that the buffalo had followed since pre-historic times. The Comanche and Jumanos understood the migration and followed the Bison herds to the Concho to hunt them. Spanish explorers also hunted the animals. In 1684, the Mendoza-Lopez expedition killed more than 4,000 buffalo in one winter. But even a kill this large proved to be no threat to the survival of the huge herds. It was not until after the Civil War and the introduction of modern firearm technology that the herds began to disappear.[156]

In 1867, the United States Army established Fort Concho, and things changed rapidly for the buffalo. At first the shaggy beasts continued to graze not far from the new outpost, which caused numerous problems for the military. Their great numbers led to the contamination of the fort's water supply, and in more than one instance, thirsty buffalo charged into the Concho River and drowned. Their rotting remains fouled the river water resulting in epidemics of dysentery and diarrhea among the soldiers. Buffalo bulls also gained a considerable reputation for charging cavalry horses and causing them to stamped in fear. While the bison herd around Fort Concho caused considerable trouble for the army, they also provided the fort with a steady supply of fresh meat.[157] Although the soldiers killed some buffalo, large numbers still roamed near Fort Concho when Pruett arrived in 1877. One estimate placed the numbers of the Concho bison herd as large as 20,000 in 1876. Professional hunters systematically wiped out the entire herd in 1876 and 1877. Two reasons account for this incredibly rapid disappearance of the buffalo. First, although the United States Army had no official policy to destroy the bison, they realized that Native Americans depended almost entirely on the animals for survival, and the removal of the buffalo would, in turn, lead to the demise of the Indian. The army certainly understood that the buffalo hunters were "destroying the Indians commissary" and did nothing to prevent the killing of the animals. Professional hunters killed thirteen million buffalo on the Great Plains between 1866 and 1880.[158]

Another important reason for the demise of the Concho buffalo herds that the Pruetts saw was the strong market for buffalo products that made the killing a highly successful commercial venture. Leather made from buffalo hides provided the material for machinery belts, bodies for buggies, furniture covering, and even, in some instances, wall paper. Buffalo meat sold well in cities like San Antonio. At one point, when demand for buffalo hides peaked, prices reached $3.00 per hide. Because of the steady profitable demand for buffalo products, hunters developed very efficient methods of killing. Buffalo guns such as the extremely accurate Sharps .45 caliber rifle could kill even the largest buffalo from incredible distances. As soon as hunters felled the animals, hide crews moved in to skin the carcasses an butchers processed the meat. In 1876, one San Angelo meat seller sold five tons of smoked buffalo hams to the State of Texas. The buffalo hunters and their crews stayed very busy in the Concho country in 1876, 1877, and 1878. When the Pruetts came to the region as many as 5,000 men worked in hundreds of buffalo camps on the South Plains. One hunter, Joe S. McCombs, killed a reported 4,900 buffalo by himself in a single season. Several of his fellow hunters killed 11,000 more.[159]

In November 1877, the Pruetts drove their cattle to Ben Ficklin and made camp in a pecan grove just outside the little town. Ben Ficklin lay some four miles up the main Concho River from Fort Concho and San Angela. Originally established as a stage stop, Ben Ficklin served as the county seat of Tom Green County until a flood washed the town away in 1882. By the time Halker and his family arrived at Ben Ficklin, winter had set in forcing him to start an immediate search for a permanent shelter. He may have chosen to settle near Ben Ficklin because of the somewhat dubious reputation of San Angela. Colonel Benjamin H. Grierson wrote of San Angela in 1878, "... the so-called town [is] mainly made of gambling and drinking saloons and other still more disreputable places where murders and robberies are of frequent occurrence. Guards have been at time placed to prevent the soldiers from crossing the river into town in order to keep them from being robbed or murdered by desperate characters who infest the place...."[160]

After searching for several days, Halker became acquainted with a tall, redheaded Kentuckian by the name of Wash Delong, who farmed and ranched on the South Concho River. As one of the county's earliest permanent Anglo settlers, Delong and his wife, Sylvinia, first settled in the Concho county at Lipan Springs in 1865 where he started raising Durham cattle and farming to sell food to travelers on the Emigrant Trail.[161] Wash Delong knew from bitter experience how difficult life could be for settlers along the Concho. Five years after his arrival he almost lost his life during an Indian attack near his farm. During the fight, he fell victim to a wound in his arm that proved so serious that two Fort Concho physicians wanted to amputate the limb. Delong refused. He recovered after a long hospital stay. Undeterred by this misfortune, he continued farming until his business operation grew to be one of the largest in the area. At one point, he farmed eight sections of land on the South Concho River near present Christoval. Concentrating on livestock production rather than grain and vegetables, he raised cattle, swine, chickens, and sheep. A progressive operator, Delong introduced Egyptian Johnson Grass into the area to feed his livestock. [162]

Delong was a generous man. He allowed the Pruett family to move into a vacant one-room farmhouse in exchange for the promise of work. Halker immediately took him up on his offer. The next morning the Pruetts packed up their camp outside Ben Ficklin and moved their possessions and the herd of Durhams to the Delong farm. They arrived at the farm later in the day and drove the Durhams into a pen not far from the house. Delong, his family, and several neighbors welcomed the Pruetts to their new home. That evening Wash and Sylvinia treated their new neighbors to a fine meal.[163] That night the future looked very bright for the Pruetts. Their long, difficult journey from Arkansas appeared to have finally paid off. They had a new home, shelter from the approaching winter storms. Halker relaxed feeling confidant about the future. His herd of Durhams had made the trip in good condition. It was a fine herd. Word was spreading quickly in the Concho country about Pruett's Durhams. Halker hoped to "develop the finest herd of cattle in Texas."[164] The following day the Pruetts moved into their new home on the Delong farm. Wash Delong produced corn, potatoes, cabbage, and pumpkins and had a dairy herd that yielded enough for him to share with the Pruett family. Doing her part, Mollie took care of several cows and picked one to provide milk for Ora Jane. She named it "Old Redy." Mollie had learned from experience how to pick a cow to provide milk, "not too rich or too poor but about right for baby food."[165]

The winter proved to be a bitter one. Marvin Schultz wrote of that year at Fort Concho, "Severe blizzards marked the winter of 1877. Robert Parrack endured one of these storms while hunting on the South Concho, about five miles from the fort. One afternoon, this veteran of the buffalo prairies was following a herd when a norther blew up so quickly that he was unable to return to camp. Parrack wandered around lost, until well after dark. Realizing the hopelessness of his situation, he began firing his rifle in anticipation that someone would hear his distress signal. There was no reply. In desperation, he emptied his six-shooter. Fortunately, his companions responded in kind. So fierce was the blizzard, however, that in spite of being only two-hundred yards from the camp, Parrack could not hear the men's gunshots. He was saved only because he saw the muzzle flashes and was able to find his way back to safety." [166] With the winter winds came death and disaster. "Texas" fever struck Halker Pruett's herd of Durhams. The dreaded fever destroyed thousands of cattle during those years. Curiously, the disease affected only those cattle not bred in Texas. Unfortunately, Durham cattle proved to be particularly vulnerable to the fever. Most Durhams brought to Texas in the late 1870's became sick and died from the fever. In those days, no one knew the cause of the fever. It was only known that cattle coming in contact with Texas herds died mysteriously within a matter of days. In 1889, researchers discovered that the *Margaropus Annulatus* tick spread "Texas" fever. By the time of this discovery, the deadly tick had infected cattle in twelve states therefore making quarantine necessary from the Rio Grande River to the Atlantic Ocean. Although an immunization method had been developed by the dawn of the twentieth century, the fever constantly threatened the cattle industry in the United States until as late as 1945.[167] Like so many others, Halker's Durhams died very quickly. None survived. Within three weeks, the fever had wiped out the entire herd. Many years later, Jesse's memories of the disaster were particularly poignant, "Poor father and mother. It makes me feel sad yet, when I think of the grief they suffered from losing all the cows, their only source of income, and it looked so promising for them. They had just about exhausted all their cash. Now they were flat broke and had to start all over."[168]

In spite of his loss, the Pruett carried on. True to his word, Wash Delong employed Halker for twenty dollar a month to tend his cattle for the rest of the winter. Pruett oversaw the Delong herd of some one hundred head. Halker pastured the animals, driving them to pens during moonlit nights to keep Indians from "driving them off." Mollie borrowed an old spinning wheel and worked spinning and carding Delong wool into knitting hanks. Mollie made a profit from the spinning with Sylvinia Delong.[169]

The Pruett children occupied themselves with schoolwork. Even though the winter proved to be especially bitter, Pruett and his neighbors managed to construct a community school and hire a teacher. Although crudely built, the structure provided a functional environment for learning. The neighbors built long desks made of boards split from logs. They planed the desktops as smooth as possible to provide a level writing surface. The students sat on log benches supported by hand finished legs driven into auger holes in the logs.[170] The badly needed school opened its doors for classes in March of 1878. Some twenty students attended. They studied from Mc Guffie's Blue Book Speller and Reader. Since the school had no blackboards, they did their sums on slate tablets. They used turkey quills to write with red-colored ink made from pokeberries. Of the experience Jesse recollected, "When we got so we could make all the letters well, then we were advanced to words, and later sentences, after we would be required to compose and write sentences without aid, and the teacher would pass on the writing and correct mistakes."[171]

Three of the younger children, including six-year-old Jesse, were allowed to take long lunch hours, which they used to go fishing in a nearby pond. One spring day, as Jesse hurried through the brush to cut a fishing pole from the cane growing around the pond, he inadvertently stepped on a large coiled water moccasin. Before the frightened child realized the danger, the poisonous reptile wrapped itself around the child's leg and bit him on the ankle. Jesse's screams for help soon brought the teacher to his aid. The teacher immediately made Jesse lie down and pulled off his trousers to examine the bite. Taking out his knife, he carved a crude incision on the fang marks and sucked out some of the poison along with a considerable quantity of blood. Jesse later reflected that this action probably saved his live. After binding the wound, Jesse's teacher took him home in the back of a wagon. By the time they reached the Pruett house, the bite had swollen considerably and the child had become violently ill. The nearest doctor was hours away at Fort Concho, leaving Mollie to manage as best, she could. Jesse never forgot his mother's remedy saying she, "filled me full of whiskey and seared the wound with a hot iron." In spite of the treatments or perhaps because of them, Jesse remained "a mighty sick boy for several days."[172]

Meanwhile, Halker busied himself working for Wash Delong. Fortunately, he somehow managed to collect some back debts from his sawmill in Arkansas. Raising $500 in the summer of

1878 he purchased a sixty-acre homestead located some eight miles from the Delong farm. He also bought eighty head of cattle and some "wild hogs" on credit. The family moved into an old rock house on the homestead. It had a canvas roof with dirt floors. Several of the cows he bought were with calf so the herd grew to over one hundred head within a short time. In the fall, Halker butchered some of the hogs and found a good demand for pork at Fort Concho. By the spring, he managed to pay off his debt and bought more cattle. [173] In February 1878, Mollie gave birth to a baby boy in the rock house. They named him John Benjamin. The Pruetts worked hard to make the homestead more livable. They built a chicken house, a smokehouse, and an ash hopper to keep fireplace ashes, which they mixed with lye and grease rendered from hog skins to make lye soap. In the fall, the neighbors hired a lady teacher, and she moved into the Pruett house as a boarder. Miss Annie, the new teacher, and Mollie became close friends. The children gathered pecans in the near by Concho River bottom selling them to the merchants in Ben Ficklin.[174]

In the spring of 1880 Halker started to feel the effects of increased competition as the big cattle outfits "began monopolizing the whole country." By that time, Tom Green County had grown to a population of some 3600 residents with about 650 to 750 living in Ben Ficklin. Approximately 700 others lived on various ranches in the county. The 1880 census showed 548 people living at Fort Concho and about 1300 nearby in San Angela. Halker decided to move to the Davis Mountains in remote West Texas where it was still "all a wilderness", and land remained plentiful. He made plans to move to Fort Davis in June when early summer rains made more water available for his cattle. In May, Mollie gave birth to another child, a girl they named Lola.[175]

Pruett was not the only West Texas cattleman who wanted to move to Fort Davis. Halker's friend, Melancthon Glenn Jackson, who lived some 12 or 13 miles from Fort Concho also wanted to leave. Pruett and Jackson shared very similar backgrounds. Both men were about the same age, both were in the cattle business and they both were Confederate veterans. Jackson had been captured and confined in the Union prison camp at Vicksburg, Mississippi, within a few days of the time when Halker had been wounded at Port Hudson. Jackson did not stay long in Tom Green County. He arrived in 1879 and for a time sold milk to the army at Fort Concho. Jackson had about eighty cattle, a good wagon, and a team of mules.[176] By the time Hawker decided to move to

Fort Davis on the cattle drive with Jackson, he had managed to acquire 280 cattle. The Pruetts moved their belongings in a wagon. Halker purchased a two-wheel hack for Mollie to drive and carry the children. Jackson brought along his wife, Lucy, and their three children. Jackson's oldest son, ten-year-old Landa, rode horseback to help with the cattle. Will Pruett, 12, and his younger brother Ed also helped manage the herd since the boys were both good horsemen. Jesse had no saddle and had to ride bareback, so he rode most of the way in the hack with Mollie and the other children. In addition to the help supplied by the young cowboys, Pruett hired a wagon driver they called Butler and a Mexican cowboy named Faustian.[177]

In spite of their ages, the Pruett boys put in long hours alongside the men. Jesse recalled, "For the first two or three nights, we made two night guards of three each, father, Ed, and Landau took the first guard till midnight; Mr. Jackson, Fastino, and Willie on second guard until day light. It was understood that if the cattle were quiet and not trying to drift off that the little boys could, if they got sleepy, come in, stake their horses, and go to bed." [178] Mollie and Lucy also spent long days driving the hack, fixing meals, and caring for the children. Jesse recorded how they cared for babies on the trail, ".... two cows were milked whose calves had been tied to the wagon wheel the night before, and the milking had to be taken care of night and morning in order to have milk for Lola, the month-old baby. She had her regular cow; old Matt was her name. So Matt's calf wore a muzzle in the daytime and was tied to the wagon wheel at night and was only allowed to suck at milking time. Mother used to keep this milk in bottles wrapped in wet clothes suspended in the shade keeping it fresh from one milking to the next. We had no prepared baby foods in those days so we thought we were doing all right, and it was all right in as much as we didn't know any better."[179]

Following the stagecoach route to Grierson Springs, they drove the herd along the South Concho River before heading west. Heavy rains provided the cattle with sufficient water in the harsh, semi-arid environment. The early summer rains, at times, caused numerous travel problems. On the third evening intense rain started falling and continued most of the night. The cattle herd bedded down on one side of an arroyo with the wagons and camp on the opposite side. During the stormy night, the arroyo flooded leaving the herd cut off from the camp. The cowboys tending the cattle found themselves "marooned from the wagons till the water ran down." The intense downpour and resulting floodwaters prevented any movement until the following day and the party remained immobile until the afternoon sun dried out the trail somewhat.[180] Several days afterward, they reached Grierson Springs. Water, this time a lack of it, again presented problems. Located in present Reagan County six miles south of present Best, Grierson Springs was a water hole that has been used by travelers for centuries. The Comanche Indians knew of the springs. When the Pruetts and the Jacksons drove their cattle to the springs, they found it occupied by troopers of the 10 th U. S. Cavalry who the year before had established an outpost at that location. The reception the cattlemen received from the cavalry troops proved to be somewhat less than cordial. Because the output of the springs had been poor, the soldiers refused to let the any of the horses or cattle drink. "We tried to get water for the horses but the soldiers would only give us water for our own use..." Lack of water or an over abundance of it continued to plague the Pruetts as they drove the herd toward the Pecos River some 30 miles from Grierson Springs.[181]

The group drove the herd along a stagecoach route encountering stage stations every 20 or 30 miles. Each day a stagecoach passed by the herd as it slowly plodded westward. The passing stagecoaches and people at the stage stations kept the Pruett informed with the latest news as stage drivers relayed it up and down the trail. Jesse wrote, "The stage stand keeper would be a bureau of information for travelers as the stage drivers coming and going would tell the caretaker at each stage stand the news. So Father would always make it a point to visit with the stage stand caretaker and drivers to see what the happenings were on the road ahead. The only discouraging news each time was that the Pecos River was out of its banks, and all of our hopes were that it would run down before we got there."[182] Sometimes, when the stagecoaches ran behind schedule, the drivers could not take time to stop and talk. This greatly frustrated Halker, who depended on the daily exchange of news and information. One day, as a stagecoach approached, Halker's wagon driver waved his hat to the stagecoach hoping to get it to halt. Seeing the signal, the stage driver hollered, "Hell I can't stop!" The cowboy yelled back, "Bring me a plug of tobacco." Several days later when Halker rode into a stage stand he found a pouch of tobacco that had been sent to his teamster with a bill attached for seventy-five cents.[183]

When they reached the Pecos River in July, Halker found the

reports of the river flooding to be true. Deep, rapidly flowing floodwater ran bank to bank making the Pecos impossible to cross. Frustrated, the Pruetts set up camp on the eastern bank hoping the water might recede. A few days later, Halker left camp heading up-stream in the direction of Pontoon Crossing located on the Pecos about nine miles northwest of present Iraan. The Pecos River presented a great hindrance to travel well into the twentieth century. It snakes its way across West Texas making an incalculable number of turns and twists. The muddy Pecos has been described as the most winding river in the world for good reason. In addition to its many unpredictable turns and twists, the banks of the Pecos are extremely steep and muddy offering few suitable places to cross. The Spanish explorer Gaspar Castano de Sosa aptly named the river Rio Salado because of its high salt content. During the nineteenth century, west bound travelers primarily used two established crossing places of the Pecos in West Texas, Horsehead Crossing, and Pontoon Crossing.[184]

The site of the more famous Horsehead Crossing is located up-river from Pontoon Crossing some 20 miles northwest of present Girvin. It derived its name from the many horse and mule skulls that once littered the ground at the ford. Thirst crazed livestock frequently charged into the Pecos and died either from drinking the salty river water or became hopelessly mired in the quicksand of the treacherous river. Their bones marked the spot of their demise. Native Americans used Horsehead from prehistoric times. It lay on the Comanche Trail that Indian raiders used to attack Spanish settlements in northern Chihuahua. During the nineteenth century, Horsehead became a crossing point for the Butterfield Overland Mail Route that stretched from St. Louis to San Francisco. Horsehead Crossing was also well known to cattlemen. Charles Goodnight, Oliver Loving, and John Chisum drove many herds up the Pecos past Horsehead Crossing. Goodnight lost hundreds of cattle in the Pecos River causing him to declare, "The Pecos--the grave yard of the cowman's hopes. I hated it! It was as treacherous as the Indians themselves."[185] Down river at Pontoon Crossing, Butterfield Stagecoaches coming from Fort Lancaster crossed the Pecos on a pontoon bridge constructed by the U.S. Army about 1869. Previously a ferryboat crossed the river carrying mail and passengers. One account describes the ferry as being only a canoe that stranded both mail and passengers for weeks at a time when the river flooded. The army likely hauled lumber from Fort Davis to build the pontoon bridge. Although no detailed descriptions or photographs of the bridge at Pontoon Crossing have been located, the structure was probably constructed of a wooden bed supported by "boats" floating in the river and secured to the banks by "half inch chain". Pontoon bridges are typically used as temporary structures mainly by the military. Early pontoons may have been supported by inflated animal skins and later replaced by more modern floatation devices such as rubberized tubes or empty oil drums. Although most pontoon bridges are designed for temporary use, the bridge at Pontoon Crossing on the Pecos remained in use for as long as 16 years.[186]

Halker rode to Pontoon Crossing and "after getting acquainted with some of the older Mexicans, told them that he had a herd of cattle bound for Fort Davis and asked them if he would be safe in trying to swim his cattle across. They told him, 'you can cross your wagons on the pontoon bridge and we will help you swim your cattle.' So an old Mexican went with him down to the river and showed him how in small bunches of fifteen or twenty at a time [might cross] in a place where it looked like it was made for that purpose where a sand bars sloped into the water..." The Mexican also assured Halker that he could provide all the help needed in crossing the cattle.[187] The Mexican settlement at Pontoon Crossing where Halker found help crossing his herd was described in an 1870 Fort Davis Surgeon's Report: "The Pontoon Bridge was completed by1870 and a Mexican settlement was located there on June 2 (1870). They irrigate from the Pecos. They seem to be real poor--living in underground holes. They use an ancient plow consisting of a long beam, at one end of which a pointed stick is secured at an acute angle." By the time the Pruetts arrived in the summer of 1880, one farm operated by Cesario Torres had grown to as large as 600 acres with some fifty Mexican families working on the plot. Also, accounts in that year state that the pontoon bridge was in a very poor state of repair.[188]

Halker returned to his camp and told Jackson of his plan to cross the cattle and wagons at Pontoon. Jackson "declared that they would drown a lot of cattle, and that he wasn't willing to try it." So they waited, hoping the water would recede. After several days of waiting for the water to recede, Halker make up his mind attempt try to cross the river at Pontoon Crossing. He told Jackson that he was going to swim his cattle across near the bridge and if Jackson wanted to cut out his animals, he could wait as long as he wanted for the waters to drop. Jackson reluctantly relented and agreed to make the attempt although he "was just as ugly as he could be about the whole thing."[189] Jesse described the crossing: "After two weeks of waiting we broke camp early one morning and moved up to the Pontoon Crossing, and arrived there about noon time. Father went on ahead and secured the help of about a dozen young Mexicans by paying them a dollar an hour to help swim the cattle. When the cattle arrived, Fostino and the boys rounded up the cattle near the entrance to the river and held them there until we all had dinner. Then the orders were given to cut the cattle in small bunches and crowd them on to the sand bar and into the water. They swam across all right, easy enough. After some of them were across, they began to ball [sic] and it became easy to get the others to take the water. The river was only about 100 feet wide."[190]

After the herd made it safely across, Mollie and the children walked over the pontoon bridge, which constantly bobbed and swayed in the river. Halker unhitched the horses from Mollie's hack and led them to the other side and back to "get the bridge scare out of their minds" since the movement of the pontoons supporting the bridge in the river current spooked the horses. After another trip over and back, Halker hitched the team to the hack and drove it across. Using the same method, Halker and the teamsters unhitched the teams from the heavily loaded wagons and led them across the bridge and back to get them accustomed to the movement. Finally they rehitched the teams and one at a time drove the heavy wagons across. Disaster almost occurred when the Pruett wagon crossed and "the wagon and team weighted that old bridge down in the water until it almost went under."[191] Once the crossing had been safely accomplished, everyone was greatly relieved although the dangers they faced were far from over. In crossing the Pecos, they entered the Trans-Pecos that in the summer of 1880 buzzed with rumors of impending Indian raids as the crafty Apache Chief Victorio carried on his final struggle against the white man. Halker Pruett headed the herd and wagons in the direction of Fort Stockton. Although only a distance of approximately 10 miles, the trip from Pontoon Crossing on the Pecos River to Fort Stockton took the Pruett wagon train four grueling days because of constant rainfall and a muddy trail. Frequently, large mud holes forced the drivers to "double team" their horses and drag the heavy wagons across. When they reached the tiny settlement of Fort Stockton at Comanche Springs, the entire party was low on supplies and ready for a few days of rest.[192]

For centuries, Comanche Springs provided weary travelers a pleasant and unexpected break from the harsh Trans-Pecos desert. Jumano Indians used the springs in historic times to irrigate their corn crops. Since the springs lay on the Comanche Trail, the Comanche also frequented the place. Almost 200 years later, the U.S. Army established a cavalry outpost near the springs. Although many accounts speak of Comanche Springs in those days, most describe huge flow water pouring from the earth. Today Comanche Springs no longer flows due to heavy modern irrigation pumping.[193] Halker sought medical attention from a doctor at Fort Stockton for a painful "bone felon" on his hand that caused him a considerable amount of pain.[194] Fort Stockton bustled with activity as the buffalo soldiers of the 10 th Cavalry patrolled, ever watchful for Victorio and his band of Warm Springs Apache raiders. The buffalo soldiers were the Negro troops of the 9 th and 10 th Cavalry who served on the frontier fighting Indians following the Civil War. According to William H. Leckie, "The origin of the term 'buffalo soldier' is uncertain, although the common explanation is that the Indian saw a similarity between the hair of the Negro soldier and that of the buffalo. Since Native Americans considered the buffalo to be a sacred animal, the name demonstrated the respect the Indians held for the black horse soldiers. It is a fair guess that the Negro trooper understood this and willingly accepted the title."[195]

While the Apache and the buffalo soldiers held each other in great respect during those years, they remained deadly enemies. The accounts of both sides during 1879 and 1880 reveal mutual respect, great savagery, hatred, and an unspoken determination to fight each other to the death. Anglo and Hispanic settlers feared and hated the Apache. The Buffalo Soldiers found themselves caught up in the struggle and conducted their lives with great dignity and courage. The Apache fought against incredible odds to defend their homelands and continue their free-spirited, nomadic way of life as they had for centuries. Countless unrecorded struggles are lost in the past. The arrival of the Spanish in the sixteenth century brought a new onslaught and new methods of warfare. While the Spanish arrival threatened the Apache, it also provided them with two new weapons, the horse and the gun. Probably about 1660 various Native American groups, including the Apache, began acquiring Spanish horses placing them on a more equal footing with their enemies. After the establishment of San Antonio in 1713, the Apache remained in a constant state of conflict with Spanish and Anglo intrusions until the final battles with Victorio Nana, and Gernomo in the 1880's.[196]

Victorio emerged as a chief of the Mimbres Apache in 1863 after the death of Chief Mangus Colorado. Initially, Victorio had followed the path of peace leading his people to reservations at Ojo Caliente and Mescalaro, New Mexico and San Carlos, Arizona. But Victorio learned, as did so many Native American leaders, not to trust the white man. Reservation life, in many cases, threatened the very existence of his people. The conditions at the San Carlos reservation proved to be particularly distressing.[197] In August 1879, the Warm Springs Apaches led by Victorio, found themselves in an impossible situation. The United States government tried to force the Apaches to move to the San Carlos Reservation in San Carlos, Arizona. Twice before Victorio's people fled the San Carlos Reservation because of unbearable conditions. James Kaywaykla said of the reservation, "It is a place of death. Few people can endure the summer there. Before you were born I went to that terrible place. There was nothing but cactus, rattle snakes, heat, and insects. No game; no edible plants. Many, many of our people died of starvation. Victorio saw that if we stayed none would live so he took us and left. Even Loco, the Crazy One, joined us in that fight. Why is he called Loco? Because he trusts the White Eyes. Why do they want to put us there again? So that we may die. Their alibi is that they wish to civilize us. That means that they want to make thieves and liars of us like themselves."[198]

In frustration, Victorio swore in 1879 to, "make war forever" on the United States. Victorio proved to be a very formidable opponent. The Mimbres made Victorio chief because of his leadership abilities. Texas Ranger James B. Gillett wrote of Victorio, "This old chief was probably the best general ever produced by the Apache tribe. He was a far better captain than old Geronimo ever was, and capable of commanding a much larger force of men." For the last two years of his life, Victorio led his band of warriors on the war path in New Mexico, Chihuahua, and West Texas before being ambushed and killed in the Tres Castillos Mountains of Chihuahua in October, 1880. According to some estimates during this time some 400 whites lost their lives as a result of Victorio's rampage. Other estimates run much higher but the numbers are disputed.[199] Some historians contend the Apache were no more savage or bloodthirsty than other Indian tribes, but because they were one of the last groups of Native Americans to be subdued, their final days of hostility are better remembered and have become the subjects of countless books and motion pictures. The names Geronimo, Cochise, Mangus Colorado, Nana, and Victorio are forever preserved in southwestern folklore.[200]

About the time the members of the Pruett wagon train gathered provisions and rested for a few days in Fort Stockton, Victorio's warriors were not far away. During the spring of 1880, the Buffalo Soldiers of the 9 th Cavalry vigorously pursued Victorio across New Mexico and Arizona until he retreated into the mountains of northern Mexico. In May, Victorio's warriors crossed the U.S.-Mexican border once again and carried out a series of raids in West Texas. They attacked a wagon train in Bass Canyon near present Van Horn on May 12 killing a man and a woman and badly wounding two others. The survivors of the attack abandoned their wagons fleeing in terror to Van Horn Wells. The following day, a group of Apache killed yet another man and a woman and wounded two others not far from Eagle Springs. A short time later, the station keeper at the Barrel Springs stage station near Fort Davis was attacked by a war party but managed to survive.[201]

During that spring and summer, Victorio's raiders also fought several engagements with the buffalo soldiers of the 10 th Cavalry in West Texas. Victorio's band attacked a small detachment of troops of the 24 th Infantry in Vieja Pass west of present Valentine. First Lieutenant Frank H. Mills wrote of the attack, "Shortly after daylight, on the morning of June 11, 1880, while saddling to pursue the trail, my detachment was attacked by about twenty Indians, Apache. I ordered my detachment into the rocks and there made a stand, fighting about four hours. During the fight, I sent a detachment to occupy a height commanding the position of the attacking Indians, and when these men opened fire the hostile hastily retreated. I then came down the mountain to camp, took up the dead body of Sergeant Simon Olguin, who had been killed early in the fight, and proceeded to El Muerto, killing two horses that had been wounded in the fight, and were unable to travel. I also lost one other horse, killed; and abandoned one mule, wounded. I did not proceed further at Vieja, as my detachment was not armed sufficiently and my ammunition was running low."[202] This series of raids convinced 10 th Cavalry commander Colonel Benjamin H. Grierson that Victorio intended to bring his war to the Trans-Pecos instead of returning to New Mexico. Grierson's past experience with Victorio taught him that endless pursuits of the Apache merely exhausted his troops and their animals with few positive results. Grierson decided to try a new method, one that proved effective. Instead of continuing the seeming endless pursuit of Victorio, the Colonel stationed troops to guard the mountain passes and water holes that Victorio knew so well. The Colonel ordered Troops A, G, and I, 10 th Cavalry transferred from Fort Concho to move west.[203]

On July 10, Colonel Grierson left Fort Concho in route to Fort Davis to put his plan into operation. The Colonel and his troops likely passed the Pruett wagon train since they likely traveled the same route although Jesse made no mention of it in his writings. The Pruett's fears of Indian attack are plainly recorded however. After leaving Fort Stockton, the wagon train headed in the direction of Fort Davis, stopping to camp near Leon Springs, located eight miles west of Fort Stockton. From Leon Springs they pushed on to the Barilla Springs stage station near the entrance to Limpia Canyon, located approximately seventeen miles northeast of Fort Davis.[204] Along the way, one of the stage station caretakers warned Halker to be especially wary of Indian attack in Limpia because, the canyon was "a favorite place for Indians to make raids." However, once they reached the Barilla Springs station better news awaited. Twenty-three year old James Sherwood, the station keeper at the Barilla station, told Halker that he knew of no immediate threat in Limpia Canyon which the cavalry frequently patrolled because of past experience with Apache raiders. Also, the Pruetts would be able to get through the canyon before the full moon in September when the Apache traditionally attacked. For hundreds of years the Apache and Comanche raided to steal horses during a time whites called the "Indian moon" of September. According to Sherwood, Victorio's warriors would probably be some distance away in the Eagle Mountains located southwest of present Sierra Blanca. Halker learned what to expect once he entered Limpia Canyon. The stage keeper described the canyon to Pruett and advised him to attempt the trip through the canyon in a single day because it was not safe to camp in Limpia at night.[205]

The advice Sherwood provided proved sound because Limpia Canyon had always been a dangerous place for Anglo travelers. Even before the arrival of Anglo settlers or even Spanish explorers, the Davis Mountains and Limpia Canyon had been a dwelling place for ancient Americans. Although much of the ancient past in the Davis Mountains is obscure, the archaeological record indicates a long history of human occupation. The area abounds with pictographs revealing faint clues of age-old times. While it is impossible to construct a detailed history from such evidence, it is not hard to imagine why early Americans came to the Davis Mountains or Limpia Canyon. They came for the same reason man continues to occupy the place: an agreeable climate, good water, and abundant game. Although the buffalo did not venture into the Davis Mountains, the place abounded with deer, antelope, black bear, wolves, quail, turkey, and other wild game.[206] When Spanish explorers entered the Trans-Pecos in the sixteenth century they encountered the Apache who roamed the Davis Mountains periodically until the closing years of the nineteenth century. The Apache continued to inhabit the mountains near Fort Davis even after the establishment of the fort near Limpia Creek in October 1854.[207]

For the next 25 years the Apache used Limpia Canyon as a favorite place to ambush their enemies. The steep, vertical cliffs of the canyon walls offered countless hiding places for anyone waiting in ambush. In the canyon floor where Limpia Creek flows, unwary travelers had few places to take cover if fired upon. Albert O. Richardson wrote of an Apache raid in Limpia Canyon in 1859: "Sunrise overtook us in Limpia Canyon--The striking beautiful gorge soon widens into a secluded valley, where the Apaches often stole the stock of the San Antonio mails. Once they killed the driver and took mail bags and all. At their next camping ground they opened one sack and discovered several illustrated papers. They had never seen an engraving; and a new world opened up to them. Lying upon the ground with the pictures spread before them, these overgrown children were absorbed in wonder and delight. But suddenly the comedy was changed to tragedy. A squad of cavalry approaching unperceived dashed in among them, killing 14 and routing the rest. The Apaches believed the papers had revealed their whereabouts [sic]; and still supposing that pictures can talk they avoid them with superstitious dread."[208]

The Pruett wagons rumbled into Limpia Canyon. Halker thought it best to drive the cattle immediately in front of the closely spaced wagons. The Jackson wagon went first followed by Mollie driving her hack with the children. According to Halker's plan, the largest wagon brought up the rear. In the event of trouble, Jackson was to stop his wagon immediately allowing Mollie enough room to pull the hack alongside. Butler was to then pull the Pruett wagon next to the hack shielding Mollie and the children on two sides. Halker told the cowboys to turn the cattle loose in the event of an attack and take shelter in the wagons. If time permitted, Halker instructed Fostino to tie the saddle horses together shielding himself by standing among them. Halker and Jackson armed themselves with high-powered rifles. Butler loaded his muzzle-loading shotgun with buckshot. The old gun didn't have as much range as the rifles but could be devastating if the Indians got close.[209]

Fortunately none of these precautions proved necessary although Pruett had not seen the last of the Apache. Somewhere near Wild Rose Flat, the wagons met an army wagon train on the way to Toyah Creek hauling corn back to Fort Davis. The army also took precautions in Limpia Canyon. Six heavily armed buffalo soldiers guarded each wagon. Everyone was greatly relieved to hear that neither group had encountered any Apaches in the canyon. On the first day of August 1880 the Pruetts and the Jacksons arrived in Fort Davis and set up camp. Halker counted his cattle and found only one cow missing. However, the group soon parted company. Jesse recounted, "Our friend Jackson didn't find the Davis Mountains country to his liking at all. After about ten days rest, he started back to the Concho."[210]

Shortly before the Pruett's arrival in Fort Davis U.S. Census enumerator Sally Crosson completed a census of the village of Fort Davis and the military post. Her work on that 1880 census offers an interesting demographic view of the community. The total population of Fort Davis in 1880 was 1225. According to that census, the ethnic breakdown of Fort Davis listed 156 white, 360 black, and 709 mulatto residents. Racial stereotypes of the time are reflected in the Census that categorizes those of Hispanic origin as being "mulatto." Almost all of the black residents of Fort Davis consisted of the buffalo soldiers of Company C, 10 th Cavalry, and Companies B and H of the 24th. Infantry.[211] The Hispanic population of Fort Davis lived in a section known as Chihuahua located about one-half mile from the military post. Douglas C. McChristian wrote of Chihuahua in the 1880's saying, "Chihuahua was the original name given to the civilian settlement that grew up alongside Fort Davis. As with most such towns, Chihuahua was a rough place. It owed its livelihood to the soldiers supplying them with liquor, gambling, and women. By the '80s the name was applied to the southeast portion of the growing community, whereas the section east of the fort was known as

'New Town'. The sections are still known by these names among the residents." [212] According to the 1880 Census, the residents of Chihuahua worked in a variety of occupations, mostly related to the military post. They listed employment such as laundress, seamstress, shepherds, carpenters, adobe and stone masons, teamsters, butchers, and farmers. Some were quite candid about less respectable occupations such as dance hall keeper, or smuggler. The 1880's marked the beginning of a boom in cattle ranching in Fort Davis but surprisingly, in June 1880, only one Fort Davis resident listed his occupation as stockman. The white residents of Fort Davis living in New Town had equally diverse occupations and also depended on the military post for their livelihood. They included merchants, a bookkeeper, several U.S. Army officers, stage drivers and housekeepers. Two white residents listed their occupations as gamblers.[213]

Lawlessness in Fort Davis in the spring of 1880 reached an unprecedented peak prompting John M. Dean, County Attorney of Presidio County, to call upon Texas Governor O. M. Roberts for help. Dean wrote, "By today's mail you will receive a petition signed by the leading citizens of this county requesting your Excellency to send rangers to this place... during the last 12 months numerous murders and robberies have been committed by armed bands of desperados... The following are a few of the parties who have been robbed. E. P. Webster, Co. clerk John B. Shields, Merchant Moses E. Kelly, Rev. Joseph Hoban, the Catholic priest; C. T. Wilcox, August Diamond, F. W. Rouff, E. G. Gleim, A. Underwood, George Crossen, Charles Mahle, Diedrick Dutchover, and on the 19th of this month Joseph Sender and Charles Siebenborn were robbed in their store."[214]

The Pruetts spent ten days in Fort Davis camped on the edge of town. Since the bone felon continued to cause him considerable discomfort, Halker went to a doctor at the fort for treatment. A few days later, Pruett moved his family to a new camp on the opposite side of Limpia Creek near the home of Miam McKinney and his family who had moved to Fort Davis from Fort Concho the previous year. A few days later, Halker rented an adobe dwelling located on Limpia Creek some two miles northwest of Fort Davis near the "Picnic Rocks" and started ranching. Although only one Fort Davis resident listed his occupation as "stockman," several others kept cattle including E. C. Webster, Charlie Mahle, and Dedrich Dutchover, who raised dairy cattle. They all warned Halker that "he was making a mistake to turn cattle loose," and the Indians would drive them out. [215]

The Fort Davis military post fueled the local economy. The army purchased a great deal of milk and butter and the Pruetts took advantage of the opportunity. Halker and Fostino build a pen for the dairy cattle using "the bluff on one side and poles and brush on three sides" not far from the rented adobe house. Before long the Pruetts owned some 50 milk cows requiring Mollie and the children to milk them twice a day. Using a "dasher" churn, Mollie churned butter two or three times a day. At one point, the quartermaster at the fort bought 100 pounds of butter a week from the Pruetts paying 50 to 75 cents per pound. As long as the grass stayed green before the onset of winter, the milk and butter production remained strong. Many years later, Ora recalled, "Officers and their ladies came to our place on horseback and in hacks to drink buttermilk at a dime a glass. Mother kept the milk cool in wet cloths. In a little more than a year she took in $1500 on milk and butter sales, which was more than pin money in those years."[216]

Although the quartermaster at Fort Davis purchased large amounts of butter and milk in 1880, the majority of the troops of the 10th Cavalry and 24th Infantry had few opportunities to enjoy meals at Fort Davis because most remained in the field guarding the mountain passes and water holes and patrolling the Rio Grande in search of Victorio. In late July, Mexican army reinforcements increased the pressure on Victorio. Colonel Aldolfo Valle and 420 soldiers headed for the border area opposite Colonel Grierson's command. An additional 120 Mexican cavalry troops trailed Victorio in the direction of Eagle Springs. Grierson ordered increased forces at Vieja Pass, Eagle Springs, Fort Quitman and the Guadalupe Mountains and ordered, "the concentration of troops at any threatened point." [217] A few days later, Grierson left Fort Davis in hopes of intercepting Victorio in case he again crossed the Rio Grande into Texas. Meanwhile, Colonel Valle reported that the Mexican troops engaged Victorio in a fight in the Borracho Mountains, killing four Apaches. Grierson proceeded on to Fort Quitman and on July 28th was surprised to find Colonel Valle's Mexican troops at the border exhausted and out of food. Victorio once again had eluded them. Grierson reported: "On account of their destitute condition, having been without food for three days, I furnished Colonel Valle, subject to the approval of higher authority, one thousand pounds of flour, and one hundred thirty pounds of grain." Believing Victorio planned to cross the border a short distance upriver, Grierson moved in the direction of Eagle Springs the following day.[218]

A short time later, couriers brought Grierson word that Apaches had crossed the river a short distance away. Grierson wrote, "Deeming it my duty, I camped directly in their line of March, and at the only water for a long distance north. I then had only with me First Lieutenant William H. Beck, 10 th Cavalry, one non-commissioned officer, and five privates--two of whom were team-sters--and my son, Robert G. Grierson, who, just through school, was out in search of adventure and suddenly found it." [219] Grierson and his small party sent for help and dug in as best they could on a ridge overlooking the surrounding countryside not far from the Tinaja de las Palmas water hole in Quitman Canyon. Early in the morning of July 30, Grierson received word that Victorio's main force had camped a few miles away and engaged several patrols resulting in the death of one army scout. Grierson held his position on the ridge and refused to be escorted to a place of safety. About 9 a.m. Grierson's command saw a large party of Indians approaching and the fight was on. After a four hour battle, the Colonel's son, Robert, recorded in his journal, "We then let fly from our fortifications at the Indians about 300 yards off and golly you ought o have seen 'em turn tail and strike for the hills....As it was the sons of guns nearly jumped out of their skins getting away." [220]

The younger Grierson continued, "From all accounts and evidence it was the effective force of Victorio's command (about 100 men) that we were engaged with. It is remarkable how quick the Indians jump from their ponies, lie flat on the ground and blaze away. The Indians were wonderfully surprised to see the troops come from both directions, and they concluded it was bad medicine." [221] Colonel Grierson noted his reasons for standing his ground in a letter to his wife, "It may seem to have been a very rash and dangerous undertaking to get ready to fight Victorio and his hundred Indians with only (at first seven men), but I had looked over the ground well before going into camp, and saw clearly what a strong position I had, and with what ease it could be fortified. I decided immediately what to do, and it turned out to be the best thing that could have been done under the circumstances. If I had attempted to run away, I would have never forgiven myself, and myself and the whole party would very likely have been killed.... If I had not made my stand as I did, Victorio and his whole outfit would have got through without a fight, and we would have only the uncertain chance of pursuit." [222] Victorio retreated but clashed again with the buffalo soldiers on August 6 in a fight at Rattlesnake Springs. That same day, the Apaches raided an army supply train heading for Fort Davis. The soldiers guarding the supply train fought off the attack. Companies B, C, and G of the 10th Cavalry commanded by Captain L. H. Carpenter pursued the Apaches into the mountains. Victorio retreated back across the Rio Grande into Mexico.[223]

A few weeks later, Milam McKinney galloped up to the Pruett house calling out loudly for Halker. Earlier that morning Halker, Will, Ed, and Fostino hitched the horses to the wagon and headed up Limpia Creek to cut wood and haul it to the ranch. Mollie and the girls stayed behind to attend to the butter making chores. Mollie told McKinney that Halker was not home. McKinney asked her if Halker was on horseback and had his gun. She replied that he had his gun but had left most of his cartridges behind hanging in a belt on the head of their bed in the house. McKinney hurriedly told her to fetch it since a group of Apaches had raided the stage stand in Limpia Canyon not far away and stole several horses. During the attack, a Mexican horse-herder fled in terror barely managing to escape with his life. [224] McKinney said he thought the Indians were presently on their way to Cook Flat. He wanted to find Halker and try to trap the Apaches at the entrance to Frazier Canyon. Mollie gave McKinney the cartridge belt and he galloped off. Although he was alone, McKinney had been, "raised on the frontier," and was "no stranger to Indian troubles." A short time later, Fostino and the boys returned and reported that Halker and McKinney found each other and were trailing the Indians. Before he left, Halker told Fostino to gather the horses, hobble them near the house, and keep a close watch. In the meantime, Halker and McKinney rode to Cook Flat. Since it was late in the day, the two men decided that it was best to return and form a posse before following the trail any farther that day.[225]

That evening, a posse including Halker, McKinney, Charlie Mahle, Frank Dutchover, two Mexican neighbors and several Texas Rangers assembled supplies and made plans to leave before daybreak the following morning. Near a lake on Grierson Mountain they discovered where the Apaches had camped for the night and found the remains of a butchered Pruett cow. For the next five days, the posse stayed on the trail until it grew cold near present Kent.[226] On October 15th Mexican troops under the command of Colonel Joaquin Terranzas ambushed Victorio's band in the Tres Castillos Mountains of Chihuahua. During the resulting battle some sixty warriors and eighteen women and children died. Victorio met his death also although accounts of how the chief died are conflicting. According to the Mexicans, Victorio died when hit by a long distance shot fired by a Tarahumara Indian soldier named Mauricio. As a reward for the deed, the governor of Chihuahua presented Mauricio "a fine nickel-plated rifle." Apache accounts differ, however, saying Chief Victorio chose to take his own life rather than face imprisonment. [227]

News of Victorio's death brought a great feeling of relief to Fort Davis residents who lived in constant fear of Apache attack. Colonel Grierson and the buffalo soldiers who, had pursued Apaches for the previous three years marching an incredible 135,710 miles, expressed similar feelings. Grierson wrote "a settled feeling of security" was present at Fort Davis and he looked for a rapid increase in the population and wealth of the area. Halker Pruett grazed his cattle in Limpia Canyon and although he didn't always pen them at night, kept a watchful eye over his herd. [228] In November, milk production slowed allowing the children the opportunity to attend school in Fort Davis. Jesse wrote: "Will, Ed, and myself had to go to school. We would take our lunch, climb the mountain in back of the house, cross Hospital Canyon and over a second mountain then across the flat to the school. The Pruett boys attended classes with Billie and George McKinney, Annie and Bill Keesie, Rob and Lizzie Robinson, and Joe, Louis, Mary and Dora Dutchover along with Eddie Webster. Jesse remembered the Fort Davis school as being much better than their previous school. "Our desks and seats were quite an improvement over the ones we used on the Concho. We had carpenter made desks of lumber and long plank benches with back rests."[229]

While the older children went to school in Fort Davis, Halker and Mollie stayed busy at the ranch. Mollie cared for Viola, Ora, John Ben, and Lovina. Most days Halker spent on horseback tending the herd and looking for Indian sign. Some days Halker loaded a packhorse and took it with him to stay out overnight. Frequently he stopped before sundown, unloaded the horses, and made camp. He then lit a fire and ate supper but after dark moved his camp a short distance where he could watch for any Indians that might have followed him or spotted the campfire. When spring arrived and the grass greened again, Halker rounded up the milk cows driving them near the house to begin butter and milk production.[230]

Halker's overnight trips allowed him to become more familiar with the country around Fort Davis. He ventured into Musquiz Canyon south of Fort Davis and liked what he saw. The canyon had an abundance of water, rich soil, and excellent grass in scenic meadows. The canyon was named for Manuel Musquiz, a settler who established his home in the canyon about 1854. Musquiz built, "a substantial ranch home" in the canyon, and a tiny settlement remained there for a time. But in the summer of 1861, while Senior Musquiz was away on a trip to Presidio Del Norte, a band of Apache warriors attacked the ranch killing three members of Musquiz family before stealing the livestock. Following the raid, Senior Musquiz abandoned his home and moved to San Carlos, Mexico, where he felt safer than in the canyon that bears his name.[231] Halker discovered that in spite of the problems Victorio had caused settlers, a number of Anglo families lived in Musquiz Canyon. Cal Nations lived near the mouth of Musquiz with his family. Other nearby settlers included James Dawson and Joe Dorsey. Halker purchased 160 acres of land located twelve miles southeast of Fort Davis in 1881 and hired some Mexican workers to build one-room adobe house while Mollie and the children remained at the Limpia Canyon ranch. Halker hurried completion of the adobe in Musquiz, hoping to have it completed before winter arrived. [232]

The building of the adobe went smoothly although Halker remained absent from the Limpia Canyon much of the time. Mollie and the children tended the dairy herd, sold milk, and made butter. The children helped as best they could. Occasionally Mollie and the children visited Musquez Canyon but the trips were not frequent for she was pregnant with her twelfth child. Halker and Mollie planted some trees near the new adobe. Six-year-old Viola and her little four-year-old sister Ora hauled buckets of water for the newly planted trees. Then came September and the Indian moon returned. Although he was only ten, Eddie did his best to chip in with the chores at the Limpia Canyon ranch. Every evening, shortly before sunset, Eddie mounted his horse and rounded up the milk cows to pen them for the night. One evening, as he rounded up the herd, Eddie rode into the mouth of Keesey Canyon near a spring in the mountainside where he made a terrifying discovery. As he looked for Old Babe a, "strawberry roan milk cow," he found the freshly butchered carcass of the animal. Sensing trouble, the boy wheeled his horse and started to ride away when he noticed two other Pruett cows not far away on the mountainside. He rode toward the cows, when suddenly a shot rang out and he heard the bullet whiz closely by. Undaunted, Eddie drove the cattle back to the house where he told his mother what had happened. Mollie immediately feared an Indian attack and sent Eddie to William McKinney's house for help. That night, a group of Indians murdered a sheep-herder not far from Leon Springs.[233]

As they waited for help to arrive Mollie prepared to defend the ranch house. She sent Willie and Jesse to milk the cows and tie the horses in the front yard before darkness set in. Willie loaded an old shotgun with buckshot and took up a position in a darkened room with a window overlooking the tied horses. Mollie told the boy not to fire unless the Indians tried to steal the horses. She gathered up a number of axes, picks, and shovels and brought them into the house. Mollie hid several knives out of sight in the house where they could be quickly recovered if the Indians managed to get inside the house and she needed weapons to protect the children. She barred the door and shut the curtains on the windows so no light escaped. After building a fire in the fireplace, Mollie spent most of the evening molding bullets and loading cartridges for Halker's Sharps buffalo rifle. Jesse wrote, "I don't know whether Viola, Ora, Ben, and Lola went to sleep that night or not. I do know that Mother, Will, Ed, and I didn't sleep a wink. Ed and I kept peeking out through different cracks to see if we could see any Indians sneaking around."[234]

Sometime after midnight, Halker and Texas Ranger Captain C. L. Nevill, accompanied by seven or eight Rangers and several other men arrived at the ranch house. Mollie and the children were very glad to see them. Although Nevill and Pruett both came to Fort Davis about the same time, they came for different reasons. Halker moved his family to Fort Davis for a fresh start in the cattle business. Nevill came to help local authorities quell a wave of lawlessness that had gotten out of hand. The captain had a considerable reputation as an Indian fighter. Walter Prescott Webb said of Neville "He was primarily an Indian hunter and really continued to hunt Indians after they were all gone from Texas. Even in his last report, written in November 1882, he talked more of Indians than of white men." Outlaws and Indians alike avoided Nevill and his fellow Rangers because of their fearsome reputations. [235] Since his best horse needed shoes, Halker shod the animal using only candlelight to avoid attracting attention. Once this task had been accomplished the posse set out on the trail reaching Pruett's butchered milk cow about daybreak. The trail led them up Limpia Canyon and into the Apache Mountains near present Kent. There the posse sighted the Apache approaching the tracks of the newly constructed Texas and Pacific Railway. As the Indians neared the rail grade, which was only a few months old, they hesitated, "puzzled by that ridge of earth extending to right and left as far as they could see. They began to gallop back and forth, flourishing their weapons and war whooping. It was as if they believed the fresh earth embankment was a fortification with soldiers concealed on the other side. A red warrior chanced to glance back and see the posse. He let out a shriek and pointed; all the Indians stared momentarily. Then one of them, shouting and motioning with his rifle, sent his pony scrambling up the bank. The others followed and all vanished in a fog of dust." By the time the posse reached the Texas and Pacific rail grade, the Apache band of some eleven warriors had vanished. Captain Nevill and Halker found several fresh sheepskins left behind when the Apache beat their hasty retreat.[236]

For the next nine days, the posse stayed on the trail of the raiders as it snaked through the Guadalupe Mountains into the New Mexico Territory. At one point, a troop of buffalo soldiers joined in the pursuit, but they returned to Fort Davis after a short time. The posse continued on without the soldiers. In the meantime, another Apache band was driving a large herd of stolen horses southward. The two Apache groups met and combined their forces that by then greatly outnumbered the posse. In an effort to scatter the trail and confuse the posse, the Apache spread out "over a space of a quarter mile wide," leaving several trails to follow. The Apache assembled a mile or so further on and waited hoping to ambush the posse at the end of a flat patch of ground. Sensing trouble, Captain Nevill called the posse together and explained the danger. The posse was greatly outnumbered, the men and horses exhausted, and it appeared that the Apache were ready to make a stand now that the soldiers had returned to Fort Davis. The men voted to turn back and did so. Halker returned to the Limpia Canyon ranch after being gone about ten days.[237]

While this may or may not have been the "last Indian affray" in the Trans-Pecos, as it has been called, it can be safely said that by the fall of 1881, the Apache ceased to be a significant threat to ranchers and settlers in the Davis Mountains. Other raids probably took place, but the elimination of Victorio effectively quashed the last significant Indian uprising in the Trans-Pecos. The year

1881 is also an important transitional year because of railroad construction that linked the Trans-Pecos to the outside world for the first time. That year also brought an end to Apache raiding and signaled the beginning of the end for the buffalo soldier in the region. The great cattle ranches suddenly had access to markets by rail. Halker finished building the adobe house in Musquiz Canyon in October and hired Lonjino Silvas to move the family possessions to their new home in a big ox drawn freight wagon. Once the move had been completed, Halker and his several of his new neighbors, including Cal Nations, James Dawson, and Joe Dorsey, built an adobe brick schoolhouse near the Pruett house. The neighbors shared in the building expense and hired a teacher by the name of Jacobs. Classes began in the school in November 1881. A Texas Historical Commission marker proclaiming the school as being the first rural school west of the Pecos River presently stands on State Highway 118, twelve miles south of Fort Davis.[238]

Jesse wrote of the school: "Our principle [sic] amusement at recess and noon was marbles and town ball. The three month session was soon completed, then we had another three month session in April, May, and June. This time we had a new teacher, a Mr. Crawford, an old man with a long white beard that was a very interesting old man and a good teacher for us little folks as none of us were very far advanced. Our books and line of study was about the same as our former schools on the Concho and Fort Davis."[239] On November 5, 1881, Mollie gave birth to another boy whom they named Charles Elmer. The birth of the new baby made life in the small adobe house even more uncomfortable for Halker and Mollie and their remaining eight children. Once the adobe had been finished Halker promised Mollie as soon as the new railroad reached Murphysville he would, "ship in some lumber and build her a good house." There was much talk of the new rail road. The tracks of the Southern Pacific Railroad were then being built from El Paso although it would be another year before they reached Marfa and Murphysville. Seven years later, in 1888, Murphysville became known as Alpine. Halker planned to haul lumber from the new section house in Murphysville once it was finished.[240]

In July 1882, Halker hired a carpenter and an adobe brick mason to build the house he promised Mollie. He ordered the lumber for the house and had it shipped from California. Since no road existed between Musquiz Canyon and Murphysville, Halker hauled the lumber in a wagon across the grassy prairie establishing a trail that later became State Highway 118. The workmen completed the house in the fall. Jesse remembered, "That was the best ranch house in Presidio County with a (Redwood) shingle roof and lumber floors. Now mother was some happy woman to move into a real house with plank floors out of the dirt that she lived in for several years."[241] The availability of rail transportation brought other conveniences as well. Mollie got a cook stove and a sewing machine. Jesse wrote about his mother, "Just think she made all her own clothes and for the children too as there was no ready wear to be had in the stores of those days except overalls for men and all her sewing was by hand. When I think of the past, I still wonder how mother kept clothes on our backs when there was so many of us." That fall, school continued for the children with a new teacher, Miss Lena Vanhorn from Indiana. The new teacher was "well educated for that day and time and brought new and more modern ideas of teaching" to the school. Miss Lena boarded with the Pruetts and became a close friend to Mollie.[242]

Ora and Viola began their first school session with Miss Lena. She introduced the children to "discipline and modern manners." Miss Lena also knew how to operate the new sewing machine that Mollie "was having considerable trouble with" since she had little experience with such a modern contraption. Under Miss Lena's tutorage, "All the children in the school did better than they ever done before." But Miss Lena only remained at the school for a single session. She met a book keeper in Fort Davis, and "didn't remain single long enough to teach another session."[243] Although the Pruetts took great pride in their new home, they did not remain in Musquiz Canyon long. In November 1882, Colonel Benjamin Grierson passed by the Pruett place on his way to Fort Davis. Grierson and a troop of buffalo soldiers camped for the night near the Pruett house and, according to Jesse, "made father's acquaintance". The Colonel complemented Halker on his fine new home and the beautiful location. Halker told Grierson of his plans to build a dam in the creek to irrigate the valley below. The Colonel left the following morning, "very much impressed with the location and possibilities," he saw at the Pruett place.[244] Grierson had just assumed command of Fort Davis, transferring from Fort Concho, where he had been post commander. Although he had only been commander of Fort Davis for a short time, the colonel was well acquainted with Fort Davis due to the time he had spent in the region campaigning against Victorio and his

Warm Springs Apaches.

The Colonel had a distinguished military career beginning in the Civil War. During the war, Halker Pruett and Benjamin Grierson had been mortal enemies since Pruett wore the gray uniform of the Confederacy and Grierson fought for the Union. Almost 20 years earlier, the two men faced each other in the struggle to control the Mississippi River at Port Hudson. Halker fought for the south in the 10th Arkansas Infantry while Grierson commanded the 6 th and 7th Illinois Cavalry. In the spring of that year, as Halker fought from the trenches of Port Hudson, Grierson led some one-thousand Union cavalrymen across the state of Mississippi successfully destroying the tracks of the Southern Mississippi Railroad east of Jackson, cutting off supplies to the besieged Confederate garrison at Vicksburg. The action became known across the United States as "Grierson's Raid" and gained Grierson considerable notoriety. Union General William T. Sherman called the raid "the most brilliant expedition of the war." Even General Ulysses S. Grant could not overlook Grierson's accomplishment following the raid when he wrote, "It was Grierson who first set the example of what might be done in the interior of the enemy's country with any base from which to draw supplies." *Harper's Weekly* and *Leslie's Illustrated* carried Grierson's picture on their front covers. The *New York Herald* and the *Memphis Bulletin* carried a number of articles about Grierson's raid.[245] Grierson and Pruett apparently held no animosity toward each other following the war although Halker must have known of Grierson's reputation. At the same time, there is no evidence that the Pruett and Grierson were particularly friendly. Both men recognized the economic potential the Davis Mountains offered once the Apache had been removed and the railroad came. Also land prices in the early 1880s were quite cheap when compared to today's market. Some land could be purchased for as little as 12 1/2 to 15 cents per acre.[246]

Halker Pruett's 160 acres in Musquiz Canyon was a fine piece of property with abundant grass and good water. In February 1883 Colonel Grierson returned to the Pruett Ranch and according to Jesse, "offered him (Hawker) a handsome price for the place and left it a standing offer that would make father a nice profit above his investment up to that time."[247] Pruett considered the offer and found two sections of land for sale at the Lone Cottonwood Ranch located some seven miles to the north. The Lone Cottonwood property had good water and a beautiful valley with good grass.

Halker wrote the owners of the property who agreed to sell it to him for $1.50 per acre. He contacted Grierson and sold him the Musquiz Canyon place for $1800 in April 1883. Jesse wrote, "So now it was up to the Pruett family to move again. It almost broke mother's heart to give up her new house. Father told her that it would be the last move because he had at last found the place he had been looking for and that it would be their life long home."[248]

Hawker Pruett moved his family and some 450 cattle to the Lone Cottonwood Ranch where he built a new home. Pruett built a dam on the creek to provide water for the cattle and a 150-acre irrigated farm. He fenced the farm with a new invention, barbed wire. According to Jessie Pruett, this was the first use of barbed wire in Presidio County. Because of its uniqueness, the fence attracted considerable attention from the local cattlemen who came to see it and "all declared they wouldn't have it on a ranch because it would cut the cattle and horses all to pieces." Pruett broke the ground for the new farm with oxen and produced his first crop in 1884 raising corn, Irish potatoes, sweet potatoes, watermelons, and cantaloupe. The farm produced abundantly. Some weeks Hawker hauled two wagonloads of produce to Fort Davis. The foodstuffs sold for about $50 a load. In the Davis Mountains, the years between 1880 and 1885 brought good rains. Jessie wrote, "The whole country looked like green wheat field, every canyon was a running creek." Because of the considerable rainfall, many of the newcomers arriving in those years thought they had found "cow heaven." These new ranchers prospered and assumed the situation to be permanent and saw no need to build windmills or stock tanks. The life-giving rains stopped in August 1885, however, and no rain fell again in the Davis Mountains until September 1886. According to Jessie, "...the whole country suffered a fifty percent loss." In addition, Pruett noted that nearly all of the surface water quickly disappeared in the Davis Mountains with the exception of Limpia Creek north of Fort Davis, Keesey Creek, and in the Musquiz Canyon drainage. Since fences in those days were nonexistent in the Davis Mountains, large numbers of thirsty cattle converged in these areas and quickly wiped out the grass near the water. Jessie observed, "they died until it looked like they were all going to die." He wrote that he saw as many as 3,000 dying cattle along Keesey Creek.[249]

In addition, the new ranchers soon began to realize the danger posed to livestock by an innocent looking plant growing along the banks of the creeks and streams of the Davis Mountains. The plant produced abundant purple flowers and while beautiful, it could be deadly to cattle, horses, and mules. The plant, *astragaulas mollissimus*, is better known by its common name of locoweed. During the drought of 1886, Jessie observed that "the locoweed was the only green thing on the land." The hungry cattle consumed the plant and soon began to exhibit strange symptoms as a result of the toxin. Locoweed got its name from the Spanish word *loco* or crazy because of the abnormal behavior exhibited by animals that have been poisoned by it. Symptoms begin to appear after 2 or 3 weeks of continuous grazing. The animals become lethargic and depressed and become confused when approached by humans or other animals. They suffer neurological damage, lose weight, have abortions and congestive heart failure in higher altitudes. It is said a "locoed" animal will not go downhill, might attack his own shadow, and cannot be roped. Some die of starvation when they lose their ability to find food or meet their end as a result of some demented misadventure. Jessie Pruett felt that locoweed claimed as many cattle during the 1886 drought as the lack of water. [250]

The Pruetts endured the drought and the locoweed at the Lone Cottonwood Ranch. During the 1890's, the children started reaching adulthood and left the ranch to marry, see the world, or get an education. In the spring of 1892, Jesse wrote that, "the wonder lust bee got in my bonnet" and he joined a trail drive delivering 2,500 cattle from the E. F. Ranch in the Davis Mountains to Pueblo, Colorado. The following year, Jesse took part in another cattle drive to the Belle Fourche River in South Dakota. When he returned, Jesse sadly learned that his brother Ed had been killed when a horse fell on him. Jessie wrote, "Surely was a hard blow for the Pruett family to lose Ed, just 22 years old, tall, handsome, a lovely character and one of the most popular cowboys in the whole country." In 1894, Will Pruett married and left the ranch. Jessie stayed on helping his father as range foreman.[251]

Hawker Pruett continued buying, leasing, and fencing land in the Davis Mountains in spite of the fact that, "Everybody said he was a damned old fool to buy and lease land when he could run the open range for free." It became a considerable burden to keep his leases and taxes paid. He pastured many head of cattle and bought more when he could get them for a good price. Before long Hawker Pruett faced a considerable debt. By the last part of the

1890's, the Pruett Ranch comprised some 80,000 acres of deeded and leased land. In 1897, Ora Jane married Andrew G. Prude "a resident of Limpia Canyon". Mollie died in 1898, and Hawker buried her in the family graveyard at the old ranch. A year later, Viola married S. W. Ward. Lola married J. W. Espy in 1900. After the turn of the century, Hawker Pruett found his ranch a very lonely place with his wife gone. In 1910, he married Laura Brown, and the couple lived in Alpine for a time. In 1912, Pruett sold his ranch and cattle to H. L. Kokernot for cash and divided the money with his children. For a time he lived in California but returned to El Paso, Texas, where he lived out the last four years of his life. He died February 24, 1924, at El Paso, and the family buried him next to Mollie in the family graveyard of the old ranch that "he loved so well" at the end of his "long and useful life."[252]

"...the Villistas captured about forty-five women from the Carrancistas at El Coyote. Most of these women were put in a corral. The soldiers sat on a corral fence and at a signal from an officer they would run for the woman who was stood up in the middle of the corral. The first soldier to get his hands on the woman would rape her on the spot in front of the people. Before the fight we came onto a wagon that was loaded with pigs. A dead man was laying [sic] near the wagon. The man had about six wounds from bullets in his body and about three knife or bayonet wounds close to the region of his heart.... We investigated the killing of the man laying near the wagon and learned he was killed by the Carrancistas who accused him of being a Villista. From all the information we could gather, the man was a peaceful citizen on his way to Ojinaga to sell the pigs."

John Farjas

Revolution on the Rio Grande

Chapter 5

Beginning in 1910, during a decade of terrible destruction, as many as a million Mexicans perished or disappeared in a bloody civil war known as the Mexican revolution. It was the first great revolution of the twentieth century. The uprising brought to an end the long-standing regime of Porfirio Diaz, who had become president of Mexico in 1876. Under Diaz, Mexico experienced a period of unprecedented economic prosperity, at least for a privileged few. American, British, and German investors poured enormous amounts of money into the country, creating a boom in mining, railroad building, manufacturing, and after the turn of the century, petroleum exploration and production. During Diaz's rule, Mexicans fought no major civil wars, and the peace and stability under the dictator assured foreign investors that their property was safe and their ventures profitable.[253] Peace and stability came at a high price, however, because Diaz secured his regime by ironfisted repression of the peons. The landless poor suffered the most, while the wealthy of Mexico lived comfortable, even lavish lifestyles. Affluent *hacendados* exploited the peons, who found themselves trapped in an endless cycle of poverty. For the *peon*, the system offered no escape as the debts of their fathers were passed on to the next generation. The revolution offered the *peons* hope and a chance to realize their dreams of land owning land. In 1910, as Diaz celebrated his eightieth birthday, frustrated political opponents who had tried unsuccessfully to unseat the dictator by legal means took up arms. From exile in San Antonio, Texas, Francisco I. Madero, a *hacendado* turned revolutionary, issued his Plan de San Luis Potosi, calling for an end to the tyranny of Diaz. Joining the revolution were, of course, the *peons,* but the rebels came from many different circumstances. They came from the *sierras*, the *haciendas*, the villages, and the towns. They came from every segment of Mexican society.[254]

In Chihuahua, Pancho Villa, a bandit turned revolutionary, joined the rebel cause. Villa's comrades in arms in Chihuahua included Pascual Orozco, a muleteer who had fallen on hard times. Villa and Orozco would not remain allies for long, but in the first days of the revolution, they provided the catalyst for the revolutionary movement in the north. It was only after their early victories that Madero returned from the United States to assume a military and political leadership role in the uprising. Villa and Orozco provided Madero with the rebellion's first major military victory at Ciudad Juarez in May 1911.[255]

In the south, Emiliano Zapata, a horse trainer who had never been a peon, took up arms in Morelos. After the capture of Ciudad Juarez, which provided the rebels with a vital supply of arms and supplies from the United States, the revolt grew in intensity. The fall of Juarez marked the end of the Diaz regime. Within days, the defeated dictator went into exile, opening the way for Madero to become the new president of Mexico. After being elected in 1911, Madero found the role of revolutionary president filled with unforeseen challenges and dangers. He hoped, idealistically, to bring democracy to Mexico; however, he proved unable to achieve his goal and lost his life in the attempt. After Madero's murder in February 1913, General Victoriano Huerta assumed the presidency. A military man, Huerta had been loyal to Diaz and was probably responsible for ordering the murder of Madero. Huerta's seizure of power plunged the nation back into revolution when the general's opponents again took up arms. Venustiano Carranza, himself a Madero supporter and military governor of Coahuila, found political support in the north and was joined by Villa and other rebels in overthrowing Huerta. For Carranza, the revolt against Huerta led him to the presidency, following Huerta's ouster in July 1914. Carranza managed to remain in the presidency until 1920, when he fell victim to an assassin's bullets.[256]

The Mexican revolution was not a unified single movement but rather a complex series of regional uprisings. Chihuahua, Morelos, Coahuila, and Sonora experienced distinct, separate revolts. In Chihuahua, for example, the beginnings of the revolution can be traced to the displacement of small landowners from their land by the powerful Terrazas family.[257] Before the revolution, the Terrazas family became the largest single landowners not only in Mexico but also in Latin America. In Chihuahua alone, the Terrazas acquired 3.5 million acres by 1884, using their political and economic power to obtain expropriated church properties. They were the state's biggest employers with some 13,000 Chihuahuans on their payroll. The Terrazas maintained a political stranglehold on the state government, controlling it entirely. They owned the majority of the businesses in Chihuahua, dominating banking, mining, railroads, and meatpacking. Terrazas also land holdings in the Durango and Coahuila states. [258]

The Chihuahuan revolution was a rebellion of landless *peons*, small landowners, merchants, artisans, and tradesmen. These unlikely revolutionaries suffered great losses in an economic depression beginning in 1907. Mineral market prices plummeted on world markets and there were massive crop failures; interest rates rose and taxes increased considerably, making Chihuahua ripe for revolution. Near Ojinaga, small landowners took up arms in 1910 when their lands were stolen from them by the Terrazas clan particularly by Enrique Creel, a son in law to Luis Terrazas, who made huge profits selling land to American investors as the construction into Chihuahua of the American-owned Kansas City, Mexico, and Orient railroad progressed.[259]

By December 1913, open warfare had broken out across Chihuahua. The Terazas financed Federal army retreated to Ojinaga in the face of Pancho Villa's Division of the North. Many considered Ojinaga impregnable because the Mexican border town lay on a hill surrounded by a flat plain and was heavily defended with artillery. Across the Rio Grande in Presidio, Texas, American military and law enforcement authorities closely watched the Federal defense of Ojinaga.[260]

The Federals, some three thousand strong, fortified Ojinaga with rifle pits, slit trenches, and machine-gun nests. They placed ten artillery pieces on the hill and strung as much barbed wire as could be procured. On December 28th the Constitutionalists ambushed about a thousand Federals at La Mula Pass, 28 miles northwest of Ojinaga. The defeated Federals routed and panic stricken, retreated to Ojinaga. Ordered to fight to the death, several Federal deserters were shot as they tried to cross the river.[261]

Orozco's orders had little effect. Food and ammunition ran low in the besieged Mexican town as desertions grew by the day. U.S. authorities warned the competing Mexican commanders to aim their guns so that no shells or bullets fell on the Texas side. The Mexicans promptly complied with the American request. A battle at Ojinaga began on December 29th as the Villistas shelled the town with mountain howitzers and began to move in heavier pieces. Federal desertions grew into the hundreds as the artillery fire took its toll in their shallow trenches. Numerous fires could be seen up and down the river each night for a week. Each night, after the artillery barrage, grenade-hurling rebel cavalry attacked the town, but the Federals fought them off.[262]

On January 10 th 1914, Pancho Villa personally led the final assault on Ojinaga. With a battlefront ten miles wide, some nine thousand cavalry, headed by Villa, approached Ojinaga, sending up an ominous dust cloud of considerable size. The spectacle of the approach of the then undefeated Pancho Villa was sufficient to convince the Federal army that it was time for a hasty departure to the safety of Texas. Ojinaga fell in about two hours.[263]

A flood of refugees crossed the Rio Grande to Presidio, Texas. Some 4,500 of them, including many Federal soldiers and countless civilians, were interned in a hastily constructed compound near the Catholic Church in Presidio. The freezing January night drove the refugees to burn saddles and parts of wagons and other military gear brought from Mexico. The Americans built a Red Cross hospital as rumor spread of a smallpox epidemic in Ojinaga. The road from Presidio to Marfa became jammed with a constant flow of refugees fleeing Villa's wrath.[264]

The refugees came from every segment of Mexican society. Mixed among the Federal soldiers and the peasants were the elite of Chihuahua, including Luis Terrazas, the millionaire cattle baron and head of the wealthy family. The proud old *haciendado* crossed the Rio Grande, bringing with him a herd of thoroughbred horses, some of which he gave as gifts to the waiting American soldiers. The departure of Terrazas from Chihuahua signaled a new wave of violence as Pancho Villa regained control of the city.[265]

While the plight of the refugees in Presidio was unfortunate, their misery paled when compared to the orgy of bloodshed that took place when Villa occupied Ojinaga. The dead and dying lay everywhere. For two days firing squads disposed of Federal prisoners. The Villistas stacked bodies like cordwood and burned them in the main *plaza*, the unbearable stench drifting across the river to Presidio.[266]

Villa remained in the rubble of Ojinaga only forty-eight hours. The Lion of Chihuahua responded by allowing some wounded Federal prisoners to cross for treatment at the American Red Cross hospital in Presidio. Then he departed, leaving Ojinaga guarded by a few young boys and old men, those that could be spared as he prepared to march on to Mexico City. Villa accomplished his objective at Ojinaga. The vital Chihuahuan border ports of entry at Ciudad Juarez and Ojinaga lay in his power, for the moment. For Pancho Villa and the other contending revolutionary leaders, control of these two vital border ports was a military necessity and continued to be so until the end of the revolution. Domination of the border assured Villa of the constant flow of arms and supplies from the United States that kept his army in operation.[267]

Pancho Villa financed much of his revolution by trading stolen Terrazas cattle for American arms, ammunition, and supplies. A considerable amount of this trade took place in the Big Bend, where Villa frequently smuggled cattle across the border to a ready market. Texas ranchers bought cattle from Villa's agents and changed the brands before they sold them. Border merchants and businessmen who were already established gun dealers enjoyed a lucrative arms trade across the border throughout the revolution. Dishonest U.S. soldiers stole machine guns from U.S. armories and sold them in Mexico. Some Texas Rangers traded arms for cattle across the border.[268]

Sometimes the arms deals took strange twists. Howard Perry, the millionaire owner of the Chisos Mining Company in Terlingua, faced a serious business difficulty that Pancho Villa was able to solve. Before a coal mine was developed to provide fuel, the mine's wood supply was imported from Mexico, where the Villistas exchanged firewood and silver bullion for guns and ammunition. Hipolito Villa, Pancho's half-brother, regularly smuggled arms at Santa Elena, Chihuahua, in the lower Big Bend, trading with Perry's agent and a number of ranchers, and merchants, as well as one physician.[269]

As the revolution in Chihuahua escalated, so did the price for smuggled arms and ammunition. Rifle cartridges delivered on the Mexican side of the river brought fifty cents each in exchange for cattle at five dollars a head. This arms-for-cattle trade proved to be quite profitable, especially when the traders neglected to pay U.S. Customs duties imposed on imported cattle.[270]

The violence of Mexico's social and political struggle was not confined by its borders. Disorder spilled across the Rio Grande into the Texas borderlands in many forms. Thousands of refugees crossed into Texas to escape the chaos in Mexico. At first, Americans responded to these events as spectators. In Texas border towns, curious onlookers braved stray bullets and shells to stand on their rooftops and watch pitched battles on the Mexican side as various revolutionary armies struggled to the death. Wholesale cattle and horse thefts and border raids plagued ranchers living in remote areas who found they lived dangerously close to the war across the border. Because of its location far from population centers and its rugged geography that made law enforcement nearly impossible, the upper Big Bend of West Texas and eastern Chihuahua experienced a particularly violent era between 1910 and 1920.[271]

By October 1915, Pancho Villa's fortune as a revolutionary leader reached a turning point when Woodrow Wilson granted *de facto* American recognition to the government of Villa's sworn enemy and arch political opponent, Venustiano Carranza. Wilson's decision caused Villa to lose stature as a revolutionary leader. With the chance of his winning the struggle for national political power having virtually disappeared, the Lion of Chihuahua resumed his guerrilla tactics and border raids on the United States.[272] United States recognition of the Carranza government forced Villa to operate outside the law. Along with the recognition came a trade embargo against Villa, barring arms and ammunition and even medicine and food from making their way to his forces. Arms smugglers increased the price of their weapons since trade was now illegal and their risks increased. Thus, while the embargo did not stop the flow of weapons to Villa, his costs went up, and he found credit more difficult to obtain. Villa believed the American president intended to intervene in Mexico and that Carranza had become a tool of the Americans.[273]

Villa also felt betrayed by the American president because Wilson permitted Carrancista troops to reinforce the besieged garrison at Agua Prieta, Sonora. When Villa attacked Agua Prieta on

November 29 th, he used a favorite tactic, the night assault, but the Carrancistas surprised Villa's army, wiping out most of the Villistas in a short but decisive battle. Because of this U.S. support, Villa's losses were heavy, and his army was almost destroyed.[274]

Wilson's arms embargo and military assistance to Carranza made Pancho Villa furious. Four months later, on March 9, 1916, the lion of Chihuahua raided Columbus, New Mexico. During the famous raid, eighteen Americans were killed, with many more wounded. Villa burned Columbus, destroying much of the downtown section of the tiny border town. Americans were outraged. On the floor of the United States Senate, New Mexico Sen. Albert B. Fall called for an American occupation of Mexico. Responding to public pressure, Pres. Woodrow Wilson ordered some 5,000 (this number was later increased to 10,000) American troops under the command of Gen. John J. Pershing to enter Mexico and kill or capture Villa. Within a week of the raid, the American cavalry charged into Chihuahua and remained there chasing Villa for the next eleven months.[275]

According to one account, Villa originally planned to attack Presidio, Texas, rather than Columbus but changed his mind when part of his forces deserted. Had Villa chosen Presidio, Pershing's pursuit probably would have been slower in coming because Presidio, unlike Columbus, lacked a railroad and is surrounded by mountainous terrain offering Villa's forces a better chance of escape. But while Columbus was his second choice, the raid worked well enough, for Pancho Villa received an unexpected benefit from his bold raid and the resulting American intervention. In Mexico, and particularly in Chihuahua, the wily guerrilla became a symbol of national resistance to the Yankee invasion, augmenting his waning popularity.[276]

On May 5, 1916, while Pershing's army chased the elusive Villa across Chihuahua, Mexican bandits raided the remote Big Bend villages of Glenn Springs and Boquillas, Texas. At Glenn Springs, the raiders shot to death three American soldiers of the Fourteenth Calvary and a four-year-old boy and put the village to the torch. Several hours later, the bandits struck at Boquillas, Texas, where they ransacked a general merchandise store and took captive an American store keeper and his clerk. Across the Rio Grande at the International Mining Company in Boquillas, Mexico, the bandits seized seven American employees including the mine's physician and superintendent, and robbed the company store.[277]

Three days after the raid, troops of the 8th Cavalry, 14th Cavalry and various Texas lawmen assembled from across the state began pursuit of the raiders into Mexico. Also accompanying the expedition was a group of American newsman, including reporters, photographers, and even a motion picture crew. The American expedition remained in Mexico for two weeks before returning to the United States after capturing five of the bandits and killing and wounding several others.[278]

In the days following the raids, all of the American captives managed to escape unharmed, but the attacks and the killings terrified border residents. Rumors circulated that some of the raiders were Mexicans who lived on the Texas side of the Rio Grande. As a result, there was a considerable amount of mistrust of Mexican-Americans by Anglo-Americans living along the border. Many Anglo residents left the area and sought safety in the towns of Marathon, Alpine, and Marfa.[279]

In addition to heightening tensions along the border, the raids caused President Woodrow Wilson to order the National Guards of Texas, New Mexico and Arizona to the border on May 9, 1916. Mexican officials, outraged at Pershing's presence in Chihuahua and the crossing of American troops after the Glenn Springs raid, demanded that all American troops be withdrawn. The prospect of war loomed between the two countries. On June 18th, to bolster American troop strengths along the border, President Wilson ordered the National Guards of all the states into active duty to defend the border. By the end of July there were more than 110,957 officers and enlisted men of the Guard stationed on the border.[280]

After the Pershing expedition withdrew from Chihuahua in February 1917, Villa frequented the Mexican side of the Big Bend, where he launched a new military offensive to regain control of the state and its border ports of Ciudad Juarez and Ojinaga. In October 1917, a group of Villistas attacked a small Carrancista garrison at Barrancas, Chihuahua, across the Rio Grande from Ruidosa, Texas. During the fight, the Villistas drove the Carrancista command across the border, where they were detained by waiting U.S. Army troopers. In November Villa recaptured Ojinaga. Shortly after the battle, the guerrilla chieftain established his headquarters in the Mexican border town. The port of entry at Presidio, guarded by the U.S. Army, remained closed to Villa. His agents attempted to buy arms in Presidio but were not permitted to do so. Villa's 1,000 to 1,500 men were low on ammunition;

each soldier had five or fewer cartridges remaining.[281]

In Ojinaga Villa announced himself head of a new faction, *El Partido de la Convencion.* He denounced the Carranza government and called for Carrancista soldiers to desert and join his army. Villa hoped to be recognized as the head of a major political and military force and regain his legitimacy. Before Wilson recognized Carranza, Villa enjoyed a certain amount of support in the United States, particularly in border communities where he purchased arms and supplies.[282]

By late November, Villa and his personal command withdrew to the upper Big Bend amid reports that he was still suffering from a bullet wound in his leg and had withdrawn into the mountains to recuperate. Villa had been shot in late March 1916, and the wound was slow in healing. According to newspaper sources, Villa turned command of his troops over to his trusted general and fellow Columbus raider, Martin Lopez. One month later, on Christmas Day, 1917, a group of Mexican raiders attacked the Brite Ranch, west of Marfa, setting in motion a series of punitive retaliations by American authorities that continued well into 1919.[283]

In Texas, public reaction to the raids called for American authorities to protect the border. The United States Army responded by building up its forces along the Rio Grande. After raids at Bouqillas and Glenn Springs, Texas, increased border tensions in May 1916, the army constructed a number of new border outposts in the upper Big Bend to prevent raiding and stop the smuggling of arms to Villa. In the Big Bend Military District, the Rio Grande was guarded by eleven cavalry outposts located at Boquillas, Glenn Springs, Terlingua, Lajitas, Redford (also known as Polvo), Presidio, Indio, Ruidosa, Candelaria, Holland's Camp, and Evetts' Ranch. Each of the camps was garrisoned with at least a troop of cavalry, about 75 to 100 men. Some of the larger camps, such as the Holland Camp, housed as many as 400 cavalry troopers, infantrymen, scouts, guides, and pack train personnel.[284]

Each of the upper Big Bend outposts was caught up in the savagery as the revolution in Chihuahua wore on. The camp at Presidio, also called Camp Fulton, was located on the road to Marfa, near Pineda's Store. Occupied initially by the 3rd Cavalry in March 1911, Camp Fulton's troopers guarded Presidio as Villa's armies repeatedly struggled for control of Ojinaga during the next nine years.[285]

Located between Presidio and Ruidosa, across from the Mexican village of Buena Vista, Chihuahua, the Indio camp was home to L Troop of the 8 th Cavalry. On December 1, 1917, an unidentified group of Mexicans across the river in Buena Vista, Chihuahua, fired on a Troop L patrol near Indio. In an action that lasted only five hours, Troops I, K, and L of the 8 th Cavalry, accompanied by a machine-gun troop, crossed into Mexico and killed some twelve Mexicans before burning Buena Vista to the ground. One American trooper, Pvt. Albert A. Riggs, died of wounds received in the fight.[286]

Located five miles upriver from the Indio camp, the Ruidosa Camp sat atop a hill overlooking Ruidosa and Barrancas, Chihuahua. It was typical of the border posts. The camp consisted of a barracks, mess hall and kitchen, officers' quarters, corrals, and hay sheds. A power plant generated electricity at the remote post to provide lighting and charge batteries for the telephone and radio system.[287] Another outpost, located upriver at Candelaria, became an important addition to the army's line of defense. The beginnings of the Candelaria camp can be traced to July 1916, when a small group of cavalrymen were assigned to guard the small Texas community, located across from San Antonio, Chihuahua. At first the troopers set up camp in a flat in old man Ingles cotton patch near the road to Presidio in the south part of the village. Later, a permanent facility was constructed on a hill that overlooked both Candelaria and San Antonio. Troop K, some 100 strong, remained stationed at Candelaria until late 1919.[288]

A large outpost sat on the Candelaria rimrock near Viejo Pass at Holland's ranch. This camp, located several miles from the Rio Grande, was used as a stopover point between Marfa and the river for mule trains supplying the border outposts. In July 1919, Troop B of the Fifth Cavalry, Company H of the 37th Infantry, and three army pack trains occupied the Camp Holland.[289] Camp Evetts, a smaller outpost a few miles away near Van Horn Creek, was constructed of timbers taken from the abandoned San Carlos Mine railroad which ran nearby. Troop G of the 8th Cavalry remained stationed at Camp Evetts for two years.[290]

Camp Marfa, established in 1914, became the headquarters of the Big Bend Military District because it was located on the Southern Pacific Railroad. The camp, later known as Fort D. A. Russell, served as headquarters of the 8 th Cavalry, the 37 th Infantry, and various supply troops, veterinary detachments, pack trains, and wagon and motor transport companies operating in the district.[291]

In many respects, Camp Marfa was a nineteenth century cavalry camp; however, it was equipped with much twentieth century technology that allowed the horse soldier briefly to continue as an effective military force on the Texas border. Communication was important to the U. S. Army because of the ruggedness of the Chihuahuan desert in the Big Bend and because Marfa was a two-day cavalry march from some of the border outposts. Camp Marfa was linked to the border cavalry outposts by a communications network that included aircraft, radio, telephone, and telegraph. While a ten-kilowatt radio station at Marfa received transmissions from as far away as Fort Bliss in El Paso and Fort Sam Houston in San Antonio under optimal conditions, the mountains generally blocked radio communications with the border outposts. Telephone and telegraph lines made communication with all the Big Bend border outposts possible but with uncertain reliability.[292]

One of the duties of military intelligence personnel stationed in the Big Bend military district was the gathering of intelligence information on both Villista activities and arms smuggling. The Marfa intelligence officer got information by using paid spies and informants who had legitimate reasons for frequent trips to Mexico, such as employment in mining, agriculture, or cattle buying. Army intelligence wanted only qualified informants and not "ordinary Mexicans of mediocre intelligence who can only give facts of a general nature." These informants, some of whom had confidential identities with code names, proved to be very useful for the army in exposing smugglers. Army Intelligence cooperated with the Department of Justice and U.S. Customs officials in the exchange of intelligence information.[293]

Some of the intelligence activity was intended to facilitate an effective intervention in Mexico. Anticipating the possibility of an American military takeover of Chihuahua following World War I, when the American Expeditionary Forces returned from Europe, the U.S. Army engaged in secret contingency planning detailing an invasion of Mexico. Pershing's pursuit of Pancho Villa in 1916 had proven how ill prepared the American army was for operations in Mexico. The army plan called for the 8 th Cavalry to reinforce border garrisons against Mexican retaliation while American Expeditionary Forces crossed the border at various strategic points from Brownsville, Texas, to Yuma, Arizona. American military intelligence did extensive mapping of the border, noting possible river crossings throughout the Big Bend. After the occupation of Mexico, the American forces were to "establish military government through out the occupied enemy territory." The contingency plans included extensive lists noting physical descriptions and other information about Mexicans on both sides of the border who were to be arrested upon the invasion. The plan certainly would have had the enthusiastic support of American investors, who had lost their business interests in Mexico as a result of the Mexican revolution.[294]

"The first incident that came to my attention which disclosed the vindictive and cruel nature of J.J. Kilpatrick Sr. was the finding of Ventura Garcia in the camp with a fractured scull. Garcia was taken to the camp and given medical treatment by military doctors. J.J. Kilpatrick Sr. represented himself to be a Justice of the Peace and had arrested Ventura Garcia, tried him and fined him ten dollars. The day following the fine he told Garcia that he must work out the fine for Kilpatrick for fifty cents a day. The poor ignorant old Mexican went to work in good faith and worked for about three months when he fell ill and went to the home of Naverto Jaso who took him in through sympathy for his condition. The following morning J. J. Kilpatrick Sr. went to the home of Jaso and in the presence of the Jaso family struck Garcia over the head with a pistol, knocked him out of the house and fired two shots at him. Garcia reported this case to the civil authorities and Kilpatrick was arrested and tried and I understand pled guilty to the aggravated assault and paid a large fine."

Captain Leonard F. Matlack
8th Cavalry, U. S. Army

The Captain and The King of Candelaria

Chapter 6

The Reverend James Hinds Kilpatrick and his wife, Cornelia Hall, enjoyed comfortable lives on their fine cotton plantation just outside White Plains, Georgia. J. H. Kilpatrick, "one of the most prominent Baptist ministers in the South" lived well on the plantation tending to his ministry and his slaves. His father, James Hall Tanner Kilpatrick, also a well-known Baptist preacher, made a name for himself by performing innovative agricultural experiments. J.H.T. Kilpatrick developed the seedless Kilpatrick watermelon that bears his name. He invented a peach grafting technique that allowed peach trees to produce naturally ripe fruit year round. Large and successful, the elder Reverend Kilpatrick's plantation flourished until one night near the end of the Civil War as General William Tecumseh Sherman pressed his searing march across Georgia to the sea. A distant cousin in a Union uniform came to dinner at the Kilpatrick plantation at Hephzibah in present Greene County Georgia. Cousin Brigadier General

Hugh Judson Kilpatrick arrived at the Kilpatrick plantation at the head of a large force of the dreaded Union cavalry. Described by his commanding officer General Sherman as, "a hell of a damn fool", Brigadier General Hugh Judson Kilpatrick earned a reputation for having a, "tendency to lose his head when beset with self invited perils".[295]

In what must have been a confrontational meeting, the Reverend Kilpatrick invited his Yankee cousin into the reverend's elegant southern mansion for dinner. It is said at the dinner table, Reverend J.H.T. Kilpatrick offered the following prayer to his astonished dinner guests, "God have mercy on the barbarians from the north." Apparently following the blessing, the meal somehow continued without violence. After the dinner, the Kilpatrick cousins coolly said goodnight. As General Kilpatrick walked from the front porch to his horse he was overheard ordering his soldiers to "torch the place." The soldiers burned the house to the ground according to one source. Another account states that someone extinguished the fire and "they were able to save everything except for an out building used for the storage of food." Reverend J. H. Kilpatrick, "who had more slaves than most," later accepted the outcome of the war, freed his slaves, and got on with his "ministry, water melons and peach farm".[296]

James Hinds Kilpatrick fathered ten children with Cornelia. A relative described Reverend J. H. Kilpatrick, "He was of strong character and a strong mind. He served as pastor of the White Plains, Georgia, Baptist Church from1854 to his death in 1908, nearly fifty-four years." The eldest son, James Hall Kilpatrick, born in 1857, proved to be a little rebellious. So did his younger brother Hugh Hall born in March 1860. Their father was a strict disciplinarian, and the boys on numerous occasions found themselves in trouble. According to family lore, James and Hugh grew up in a very strict religious environment rebelling against it until they were old enough to escape the world of their controlling father. One family story suggests that James Hall changed his name to James Judson in an effort to "upset his father." He used the name James Judson or J.J. for the rest of his life. A Kilpatrick ancestor observed that J.J.'s choosing to name one of his son's Darwin, and two daughters Huxley and Livingstone can be explained as another attempt by J.J. to spite his father's fundamentalist religious teaching.[297]

Although J.J. and Hugh apparently could not free themselves from their controlling father during their youth, they learned skills and received a good education that served them well during their lives. J.J., Hugh, and their sister, Mary, grew up in their father's cotton fields and peach orchards. During those formative years, they learned a great deal about farming and agriculture. J.J. studied at Mercer University in Macon, Georgia, before graduating from Carson and Newman College in 1880. He married Lula M. Dawkins on May 13, 1881, in White Plains Georgia. The couple's first child, a girl they named Mary Macon, born February 12, 1882, was followed by the birth of a boy who died in infancy. Following his graduation from college, J.J. took up teaching. He taught school in Georgia for a time but "got in trouble for falling in love with one of his students." Kilpatrick and his family left Georgia, and he became principle of the Masonic Institute of Alabama. In 1882 he accepted a professorship at Columbia College. Professor Sandford, author of *Sanford's Arithmetic and Algebra*, described J.J. Kilpatrick as, "the best mathematician he had ever seen during his thirty-two years of professorship at the university."[298]

In 1888, Kilpatrick became a school superintendent in Eufala, Alabama. According to a newspaper account, J.J. Kilpatrick "built up those schools to a high pitch of excellence and raised, through hard work, $10,000 to construct a handsome school building." In 1895, Professor Kilpatrick journeyed to Europe studying the educational systems in several countries. He spent a year in Germany when his heath gave way and he sought the high county of Marfa, Texas to recover. Kilpatrick then became principle of a school in Seguin, Texas. J.J. and Lula had a third child, Darwin Dawkins, born on the first day of August 1887. James Judson Kilpatrick Jr., or Jim, was born January 11, 1894. [299]

Hugh Kilpatrick came to Marfa, Texas in the late 1880's and established a law practice. It is said Hugh also left Georgia and came to Texas in an attempt to escape his domineering father. Also, at about this time, J. J. purchased land on the Rio Grande at Candelaria, Texas. For a time, Hugh edited the Marfa *New Era* newspaper and served as Presidio County Judge and, later, tax collector. Apparently, the two brothers did not get along well for a time, "having strained their brotherly relationship in a dispute over a side of bacon." About 1900, J.J.'s daughter, Mary Kilpatrick, accepted a teaching job in Valentine. The following year she began instructing some fifteen Hispanic students in the Candelaria schoolhouse. Mary taught in Candelaria on and off for the next 40 years. In 1903, she wrote of being "offered the purchase of a store building with a very meager stock of groceries" which she bought at Candelaria. Her brother, Dawkins Kilpatrick, came to Candelaria about this time to operate the store. Their father, fifty-two year old J.J. Kilpatrick Sr., arrived in Candelaria in 1909.[300]

Candelaria, Texas, is a tiny, secluded village located on the banks of the Rio Grande River in remote western Presidio County. Isolated from the outside world by the Sierra Vieja Mountains, Candelaria lies in a Chihuahuan Desert valley watered by the Rio Grande River. The valley separates the Southern Rocky Mountains of North America from the vast Sierra Madre of Mexico. Candelaria lies directly across the Rio Grande from the Mexican hamlet of San Antonio del Bravo, Chihuahua. Candelaria was originally called La Gallina, meaning, in Spanish, "the chicken." Sometime in the late nineteenth century, an unknown party of engineers came to La Gallina and renamed the village Candelaria. Their inspiration is said to have come from a beautiful Mexican [301]girl they found living there. Henry Shane and Company manufactured the bell at the adobe Catholic Church in 1881 giving an indication its age. Candelaria got a post office in 1901. William B. Preuit served as the first postmaster. Dawkins Kilpatrick became postmaster in June 1908 and remained in that office until 1918. D.D.'s sister, Mary, became postmaster of Candelaria in July 1928. [302]

The Mexican Revolution broke out in 1910, dragging those living in Candelaria into a bloody and very near at hand civil war. Because of its close proximity to Mexico, the tiny Texas village soon became caught up in the conflict. The uprising had its beginnings not far from Candelaria, some 40 miles down river at Ojinaga, Chihuahua, when small landowners and *peons* took up arms to prevent their property from being seized by a group of powerful *hacendados.* These rich elite few hoped to profit from the sale of land along the roadbed of the Kansas City, Mexico, and Orient railroad that was being built across Chihuahua. At this time, Candelaria was home to some 540 residents who suddenly found themselves thrust into the war raging just across the river, only a mile away, where pitched battles took place in Candelaria's sister village called San Antonio del Bravo. In early 1914, Pancho Villa's dreaded Division of the North captured the vital border port of Ojinaga across from Presidio, Texas, and, for a time, Villa dominated the Mexican side of the Big Bend border. More than half of the inhabitants of Candelaria fled their homes on the river seeking the safety of Marfa or Alpine or El Paso. Most never returned. In 1925, Candelaria contained only 250 residents.[303]

Born and raised in Georgia, J.J. and Dawkins Kilpatrick came to Texas, "well acquainted with cotton and its culture." One of the Kilpatrick's earliest undertakings at Candelaria was to construct a cotton gin and begin farming cotton. In 1910, they raised 7 bales on 12 acres of land producing what J.J. bragged was the first cotton ginned west of the Pecos River. The Rio Grande provided the vital irrigation water for the desert valley farm. The Kilpatricks utilized large mule-drawn wagons to haul bales of cotton and loads of cottonseed over the steep, mountainous Candelaria rimrock trail to the railroad station at Marfa. In the spring of 1912, the Kilpatricks hauled 30 bales over the rim rock, and the following spring they transported 40 bales. They completed a new cotton gin in Candelaria in 1914 and built a second gin in 1917. In addition to ginning cotton, J. J. and Dawkins farmed and milled wheat and corn. By 1919, J.J. owned 1,000 acres of tillable land with approximately 800 acres in cultivation. In that year about 45 Mexican families worked for the Kilpatricks in Candelaria producing more than 300 bales of cotton. Dawkins Kilpatrick paid his workers with scrip issued in the domination of 5 cents, 10 cents, 50 cents and one dollar. D.D. Kilpatrick script could only be redeemed in their Candelaria general merchandise store. Kilpatrick paid his Mexicans 50 cents a day for their labor.[304]

An unknown San Angelo Standard Times newspaper reporter journeyed to Candelaria and penned an article titled, "King of Candelaria Reigns Over Thousand Acre Farm in Presidio Valley." The account presents a snapshot of James Judson Kilpatrick and his farming operation at Candelaria. "Candelaria is a few adobe shacks, a mud plastered post office and adobe thatched palace of the ruler of the village. There is a general store and a few houses in which his Mexican tenants live, long strings of *chilis* swinging in the breeze. The King of Candelaria rules on in Candelaria, pioneering in America's last frontier, directing agricultural development in the area, destined to become one of the state's richest farming sections."[305]

Kilpatrick's store served as the center of the Candelaria community for most of the twentieth century. Initially, the emporium only sold a few groceries and supplies but by 1910 offered the largest variety of merchandise available on the river in those days.

In that year, Candelaria had the Kilpatrick store along with a post office, a school, the Catholic church, a pool hall and bar, and a two-story hotel with a barbershop. Kilpatrick's store offered the village a wide variety of merchandise. The Kilpatricks owned the town and controlled the people. During those years, Dawkins greatly expanded the inventory and the original structure of the building that housed the store. He sold groceries, beer, hardware, clothing, guns, ammunition, and gasoline. The store housed Candelaria's post office and J.J. Kilpatrick's living quarters. When J.J. became justice of the peace, he held court in the store. It should be remembered that the remote location of Candelaria made the Kilpatrick store essential to those living near Candelaria on the river. Modern roads did not reach Candelaria until 1985 with the paving of FM 170. As a result, for most of the twentieth century, Candelaria remained isolated from the outside world. The village lies in a great natural flood plain, and even as late as the 1970's floodwaters cut the community off from the outside world.[306]

J. J. Kilpatrick's business interests were wide spread, and his location on the Mexican border brought him a more than a fair degree of prosperity. Sometimes this came at the expense of being in trouble with the law. For in addition to the flourishing farming operation and the store, Kilpatrick's border town proved to be a place where fast money could be made. Pancho Villa fought a desperate war in Chihuahua and found his revolutionary armies land locked from their constant need for arms, ammunition, and supplies. The United States became Villa's chief supplier of weapons and ammunition. Like more than one Big Bend border merchant, cattleman, and lawman in those days, Kilpatrick sold guns and ammunition to Pancho Villa and others in exchange for stolen cattle and mules.[307]

The arms for cattle trade along the border fueled the war in Mexico. The vast *haciendas* (landed estates) of Chihuahua were ripe for the picking when the revolution broke out in 1910. More than one million cattle roamed northern Mexico with many being located in Chihuahua. The wealthy *hacendados* planned to market these cattle in the United States and had, from the turn of the century, imported Hereford bulls from the U. S. in an effort to improve the quality of their cattle. When the revolution broke out, the Luis Terrazas interests produced a "meatier, more valuable animal on the Mexican ranges." The war in Mexico eventually stripped the ranches of these cattle and completely wiped out the entire Mexican cattle industry as roving bands of hungry revolutionaries rustled almost every cow in Chihuahua and sold or traded the herds for gold, guns, or ammunition. In 1914, Pancho Villa seized the Juarez slaughterhouse and rebuilt the place so that it would comply with U.S. slaughtered beef import regulations. In addition to the cattle theft problems, the huge influx of cattle brought fever tick and foot-and-mouth disease into Texas. During the revolution Mexico lost 67 % of its cattle bringing about meat shortages and high prices to those who could ill afford it. It took another thirty years for the Mexican cattle industry to rebuild to pre-revolution levels.[308]

In March 1916, the violence spilling into the borderlands escalated with Pancho Villa's famous raid on Columbus, New Mexico. Two months later, raiders said to be Villistas struck Glenn Springs, Texas, in Brewster County, killing three U. S. soldiers and a child before burning the village. In nearby Boquillas, Coahuila, the Glenn Springs raiders robbed a store and kidnapped seven American mining employees. On Christmas Day 1917 Mexican raiders attacked the Brite Ranch not far from Candelaria killing mail coach driver Mickey Welch and two of his passengers. J.J. Kilpatrick wrote a letter to the *El Paso Herald* stating that only a dozen U. S. troops had been stationed at Candelaria, and he considered this an inadequate force for the protection of his town and store. [309]

In late 1916, the U. S. Army responded to the growing border crisis and Kilpatrick's pleas for help to protect his town by constructing a new cavalry outpost garrisoned by Troop K of the 8th Cavalry atop Ananias Hill, overlooking Candelaria. Captain Leonard F. Matlack commanded some 125 mounted troopers at the outpost. The captain was a tough, hard-nosed five-foot-seven career horse soldier who rose through the ranks from private to captain in his twenty-plus-year military career. Born June 6, 1880, at Beard Station, Kentucky, Matlack began his military service during the Spanish American War enlisting June 6, 1898, as a private in Company A, 1st Regiment, Kentucky Infantry. During the hostilities, Matlack served in Puerto Rico before returning to the United States. Following the end of the war, Matlack received an honorable discharge in February 1899 at Louisville, Kentucky. Matlack again enlisted in the army at Jefferson Barracks, Missouri, with Troop H, 8 th Cavalry in December 1904. In June 1908, Matlack attained the rank of corporal while stationed on Jolo Island in the Philippine Islands at Fort William

McKinley. By 1912, Matlack had advanced to the rank of sergeant. In September 1915, Matlack and the 8 th Cavalry departed Fort William H. McKinley for the United States arriving at Fort Bliss, near El Paso, in October. By this point Matlack had risen to the rank of first sergeant and he saw service in the Big Bend Military District at the border outposts at Indio and Ruidosa. On July 11, 1917, Leonard Matlack received his commission as a second lieutenant and in August 1918, while stationed at Candelaria Matlack was commissioned captain.[310]

Matlack demonstrated his knowledge of military tactics in Candelaria by moving the old army camp to a more easily defended location on Ananias Hill. Previously the camp lay on the indefensible low ground near the Rio Grande in "old man Ingle's cotton patch." The captain chose to move the cavalry outpost to the foot of Ananias Hill. Ananias Hill is the steep, rock-covered elevation overlooking Candelaria, the Rio Grande, and San Antonio, Mexico. J.J. Kilpatrick named the hill referring to the biblical story of Ananias and Sapphira. According to the Bible, Ananias lied to God in the book of Acts making him the biblical liar. The King of Candelaria gave Ananias Hill its name because the rocky incline was home to Captain Matlack, who Kilpatrick considered to be a prevaricator, the stature of Ananias.[311]

From the top of the hill, soldiers in the observation post could scrutinize every house in Candelaria and clearly look into San Antonio. Because its steep rock covered slopes are nearly impossible to climb even under the best conditions, the fortification of the new camp proved a less daunting task. This meant the construction of a trail above the camp to the top of Ananias Hill and a large rock corral for the horse and mules. The narrow steep trail snaked its way to the observation post. During Matlack's time at the Candelaria outpost, Troop K consisted of two officers and at least 100 troopers. For a time the camp became known as Camp Kenney, in honor of Private Joseph D. Kenney, formerly a member of Troop K, 8th Cavalry who was "accidentiently shot on April 29, 1918. " In the event of an attack on Camp Kenney, all 100 K troopers could mount their horses in the camp's rock corral and take cover with their mounts behind boulders lining the trail to the observation post. From such a position each trooper could defend both sides of the hill with rifle fire. Troop K riflemen armed with 1903 Springfield rifles and machine guns could literally fend off an attack from the largest force Pancho Villa could likely muster at the time.[312]

Matlack and J.J. Kilpatrick butted heads almost immediately, and the strife continued between the pair until well after the army left Kilpatrick's town. Describing the feud, Candelaria schoolteacher Pat Greene recalled, "it was like having two roosters in the same barnyard." Matlack was a man with a mission, that being his dogged determination to see any or all of the Kilpatrick family behind bars. The hatred ran deep. Even before construction of the Candelaria cavalry outpost took place, Matlack busied himself by conducting an extensive investigation of the Kilpatricks. The investigation came at the order of his commanding officer, George T. Langhorne who played a very active roll in the Kilpatrick investigation. Langhorne's zeal for jailing Kilpatrick equaled or exceeded Matlack's determination. In a letter to his commanding officer Colonel Langhorne described from his viewpoint what Matlack faced in Candelaria, "Ever since I have been here, I have heard of the evil doings of the Kilpatrick family. At one time this J.J. Kilpatrick, Sr. was a Justice of the Peace in Candelaria, his brother H. H. Kilpatrick was the county judge in Marfa, and it was impossible to have any of the Kilpatrick family brought to trial, and it is difficult to get convictions here at any time. Like in many places local politics play an important part in the life of the community, and local politics are very bitter. Kilpatrick had quite a following among the Mexicans. They control the situation in Candelaria. Things were so bad there that I sent an officer (Captain Matlack) with a great deal of energy to Candelaria, and placed a sufficient number of men there to keep order, and to attempt to suppress the smuggling and other evil doings. They had not been there six weeks before there were a number of charges against the Kilpatrick family and their henchmen for illegally selling liquor to soldiers, illegally selling out of hours, smuggling, etc." As a part of the investigation J.C. White wrote, "Colonel Langhorne is very anxious to find something that will convince Washington what a big liar and a jail bird old Kilpatrick is. Dig up all the information you can in regard to this." Captain Matlack summed up the situation he faced: "When I assumed command of the district, Mr. Kilpatrick ruled Candelaria and it's vicinity somewhat in the manner of a feudal baron, recognizing no law but his own, and treating those of the United States and Mexico with equal contempt."[313]

A General Order issued on March 25, 1917, at the Headquarters of the Big Bend Military District in Marfa outlined the mission of Big Bend border outpost commanders. The first priority of the U.S. Army troops guarding the border was to "preserve the peace by preventing raids". It also dictated border outpost commanders to "use all possible efforts to prevent the exportation of ammunition" to Mexico. The method chosen by the military accomplish this goal was by "constant patrol of the border and following up on any information received." Officers and soldiers were forbidden to cross the border except in cases when they were following a "hot trail." In addition "certain officers can be authorized to visit Mexican authorities across the river." Recognizing the arms for cattle trade problems, the order cautioned unit commanders that any livestock crossing the border from Mexico should be done under the supervision of U. S. Customs inspectors. Army captains also had the responsibility to report to Customs any information received about the importation of livestock and to assist Customs inspectors in their duties.[314]

In early March 1915 twenty-two year old Pat Greene made his first trip to Candelaria. Greene stayed in Candelaria for some three months before returning to the border village following his graduation from the University of Texas at Austin. The young teacher took pride in his marksmanship skills since he had competed and done well on the National Rifle Association sponsored University of Texas shooting team. Greene's shooting ability and education impressed J.J. Kilpatrick so much so that he hired him to teach at one of Kilpatrick's ranch schools. When Greene accepted the job, the King of Candelaria presented him with a 7mm Mauser rifle and 1,500 rounds of ammunition. Greene came to fully appreciate his need for the Mauser after spending his first year at a tiny, primitive rock schoolhouse situated about five miles north of Candelaria on Capote Creek. The school lay only a short distance from the Rio Grande and was located closer to Mexico than to Candelaria. The new schoolmaster taught the children of the Duke, Tarrango, and Corales families who lived nearby farming a five-acre corn patch. Utilizing ancient Native American farming techniques, they also raised goats and cattle on the little farm called a *temporal*. In wet years, Patricio Tarrango planted his corn with a steel bar jamming each corn kernel deep into the rocky desert soil hoping it would germinate and draw life from the subsoil moisture.[315]

During Greene's time at the rock school house on Capote Creek rumors frequently circulated along the river that Pancho Villa was in the Sierra Madre not far away. It should be remembered that Pat Greene taught at the Capote school during the time of the border raids at Glenn Springs, Brite's Ranch, and Columbus, New Mexico, forced many people to leave the border. Greene recalled that one night the "river grapevine" reported that Pancho Villa and a small party of his men were on the Texas side of the river coming in the direction of Candelaria. Illustrating the terror felt in Candelaria with the news of Villa's reported approach, Greene recounted the incident. J.J., Jim and Dawkins were out of town, leaving Pat Greene as, "the only grown white man" in the community. At the time, Greene's sister, Frances Marian Greene, lived in Candelaria and taught school with her brother. Greene recalled his sister, "She was a pretty fair shot with a .45 automatic and I had a 30-40 Winchester and one .45."

Upon hearing the rumor about Villa Pat Greene went to a group of about a dozen U. S. soldiers camped in Candelaria, "in old man Ingle's cotton patch" seeking help protecting the town. According to Greene, the soldiers refused to help by saying, "they had to look out for themselves." Amazed at the soldier's response, the two schoolteachers grabbed their guns and climbed up a ladder to the roof of their adobe house to await Villa's rumored arrival. About three o'clock in the morning, Greene heard the sound of a large number of horse hooves loudly striking rocks in the road not far away in the darkness. Dogs in the village started barking and a group of horsemen approached within a hundred yards of Greene's house. Suddenly someone in the darkness fired a shot and the barking stopped completely. After the gunshot, the riders turned into a sandy *arroyo* that led to the river and disappeared into the night. Although Greene personally did not see Villa among the riders, he stated "that plenty of the Mexicans saw him." When the teacher later related the story to the Presidio County judge, the judge said, "you ought to have shot him (Villa). Greene replied, "I told the judge that I thought I was born with enough sense not to tackle Pancho Villa and his bodyguards by myself."[316]

During his time in Candelaria, Pat Greene developed a close friendship with J.J. Kilpatrick Jr. or Jim as everyone called him. Jim was Dawkins Kilpatrick's younger brother. Jim and Pat Greene roomed together in Candelaria for a time. Jim grew up in the border village and spoke better Spanish than a lot of Mexicans. He had been the constable of Candelaria since he turned eighteen years of age. An excellent horseman and pistol shot, Jim Kilpatrick knew the Candelaria river country as well as any man. Other lawmen including Texas Rangers and even the U.S. Army on several occasions sought his help as a scout in the wild country around Candelaria. Fifth Cavalry 1st Lieutenant James M. Adamson, Jr. wrote a letter of recommendation for Jim Kilpatrick saying, "He possesses an exceptional knowledge of the Spanish language, is a good horseman, and is familiar with this sector on both sides of the river. During the time, which I have known him, I have never had occasion to question his veracity or his trustworthiness. This recommendation would have been made sometime ago but for the fact that I have been desirous of observing Mr. Kilpatrick's actions, in lieu of the questionable reputation which his family bears. He has however proven to my entire satisfaction that he is undeserving of this reputation."[317]

Although Jim wore a badge, he was also a Kilpatrick and like his father he drank heavily. Also like his father, Jim had more than a few encounters on the wrong side the law. Jim's criminal record started when he was charged at age sixteen for unlawful carrying a pistol. Jim Kilpatrick killed his first man at age eighteen. Apparently Jim Kilpatrick became constable of Candelaria sometime in 1912. A few months later, the young Kilpatrick got arrested for the murder of a man named P. S. Boyd. At an examining trial held in Marfa, Judge Hugh Kilpatrick testified in Jim's defense stating, "The facts show that my nephew acted in self defense and it was either shoot or be shot." Few details about the shooting survive; a resulting murder case against Jim Kilpatrick "was dismissed".[318]

In April 1914 U.S. Customs Inspectors arrested Jim Kilpatrick for "receiving and having in his possession cattle smuggled and illegally imported into the United States." The case lingered in court for the next three years before being dismissed because the court could not "secure the presence of important witnesses." [319] In August 1914, Jim found himself again charged with "theft of cattle and receiving stolen property." The charges came about when Jim tried to sell cattle bearing the brands of the Terrazas *hacienda* and the TO Ranch. The case was dismissed because of "an illegally drawn grand jury." The court finally dismissed the case for lack of evidence on April 2, 1917. An assistant U. S. Attorney commented he "thought very little of the merits of the case and it was not worth while to re-indict".[320]

Greene described how Jim Kilpatrick altered the brands of the Terrazas and T.O. cattle after Jim bought a big herd of Mexican cattle from Jesus Baisa. Following some experimentation, Jim devised a method to distort cattle brands so that brand inspectors and customs officers had difficulty reading the original brand. First he heated a branding iron in a forge getting it red-hot. He then put 3 or 4 folds of a wet gunnysack against the cow and re-branded it. This procedure caused steaming, blistering, and distorted the brand. Brand burners also used running irons to alter the brands. One enterprising brand burner figured out how to change the TO brand to a J8 brand using a running iron.[321]

Pat Greene did his best to keep Jim Kilpatrick out of trouble. According to Greene, "His (Jim Kilpatrick's) folks created jobs for me because they thought I could keep him from getting drunk and getting in trouble." The best thing Greene could do for Jim was to keep him at the ranch, out of Candelaria, and away from the beer. During the time the two roomed together, Greene got to know Jim Kilpatrick well. Greene recounted the five stages Jim usually went though when he got drunk. At first, Jim "got witty and told stories." Then he got generous buying drinks and giving little kids and pretty women his money. At this point Jim, "got to be a hero, ready to fight a circle saw." Jim's next step was to find a woman before he had to sleep off the drunk. According to Greene, "Both J.J. and Jim were alcoholics."[322]

On December 10, 1915, Jim had been at the ranch for a month and sober most of the time. He spent the days breaking horses and working his cattle with the Calache *vaqueros* (cowboys) and others who worked for him. Jim and Pat decided to go to town to get supplies and "play a little *dolares* (dollar) pool." In the game players bet a dollar and drew a numbered ball from a leather jug and placed it in their pocket. When a player made the ball with his drawn number, he won the game and all the dollars bet. On the way to town Jim started telling stories. The two men got to Candelaria just about sundown and Jim went to the bar. Jim Kilpatrick looked very much as if he had been on the ranch for a month. His beard had grown long and when he entered the bar, he conversed with all the Mexicans in Spanish. It was Saturday night and the pool hall was filled with soldiers and Mexicans. Only the Mexicans knew Jim to be a *gringo*. Late in the evening, an intoxicated 6th Cavalry sergeant went to the bar and ordered a sack of beer to take with him. As he made his way out of the bar with his beer, he drunkenly began cussing Mexicans as he walked past them. Greene recounted, "after he had cussed the first one, it felt so good, he just kept cussing them all down the line." When he came to Jim Kilpatrick, who the soldier thought to be just another Mexican, he cussed him too. He cussed the wrong man because Jim Kilpatrick pulled his pistol and told the astonished soldier he was under arrest. Then the unexpected happened when the soldier dived under the pool table, drew his pistol and fired a shot. When Jim returned fire, he missed his target and his errant round killed O. M. Keyser, a German-American horse soldier who had the misfortune of standing behind the pool table when gunfire shattered the night. Presidio County authorities arrested Jim Kilpatrick and charged him with murder. A Fort Stockton jury later found Jim guilty of a lessor charge of manslaughter on June 22, 1916, and sentenced him to ten years in the penitentiary. Five months later, the Texas Court of Criminal Appeals overturned the case again making Jim Kilpatrick a free man.[323]

The violence on the border continued. In the fall of 1917, Pat Greene awoke early one morning in Candelaria to the sound of gunfire in San Antonio del Bravo. He hurriedly climbed to the flat roof of his adobe house located next to Kilpatrick's store to discover the cause of the gunshots. The teacher looked across the river in time to observe "200 or more" Carrancista cavalrymen gallop into the Mexican community. The Carrancistas under the command of General Salvador Mercado surprised Chico Cano and the some 25 Villistas in the border village. Greene watched from his rooftop as the Villistas fled San Antonio riding their horses into the mountains, faster according to Greene, than "horses could be ridden." After Cano's retreat, rumors circulated around Candelaria that Cano and his men would return. Greene remembered Chico Cano as "a pretty fine gentleman, except for taking a cow or two when he was hungry." The teacher summed up Cano's leadership in the Candelaria area by saying "he was a leader and nearly as popular as Pancho Villa." Early the following morning Chico Cano returned with more men, and a second battle broke out this time with a different result. The Villistas drove Mercado's soldiers out of San Antonio in the direction of the Rio Grande. Then, "a lieutenant colonel with the Carrancistas made a break with as many men as he could get away with" to the river and the comparative safety of Candelaria on the other side. Some of the fleeing Carrancistas rode two men on a horse and many of them "looked awfully bad when they crossed over." Indicative of the popularity of Pancho Villa at the time, Greene noted that the Candelaria Mexicans jeered the defeated soldiers and that, "it was shameful the way the native Mexicans made fun of them." To his credit, a Carrancista Lieutenant Colonel rode his horse back into the river more than once to save one of his wounded men who nearly drowned in the river. A short time later, individual gunshots rang out. Dawkins Kilpatrick said the Villistas were killing the Carrancista wounded who had been left behind. U. S. soldiers rounded up the defeated Carrancistas in Candelaria and the army transported them to El Paso. [324]

In addition to his arms dealings, the King of Candelaria managed to run afoul the law with a frequency that strains his credibility. Assistant U. S. Attorney R. E. Crawford considered a federal charge of peonage against Kilpatrick in 1917. Peonage is the holding of a person to service or labor to pay a debt when the employee desires to quit or leave. As a result, Kilpatrick was arrested and "pled guilty to aggravated assault and paid a large fine." Although the United States Attorney considered that both J.J. and Dawkins might both be guilty of peonage, he did not to come to an opinion on the case or file formal charges. Matlack reported that none of the Mexicans in Candelaria wanted to talk about the incident. The captain wrote, "People here very much afraid of Kilpatrick and will not talk much."[325]

Unfortunately the incident may have not been the only time J.J. Kilpatrick mistreated the Mexicans who worked for him. According to Captain Matlack, Kilpatrick, "struck Bartolo Torcero with a scale weight in his store simply because the poor old man did not know where Kilpatrick's son was."[326] While the King of Candelaria's writings clearly document his personal hatred for Captain Matlack and Colonel Langhorne, the two army officers bore an equal amount of resentment for the Kilpatricks. In a report Matlack wrote, "My station is at the home of J. J. Kilpatrick, Sr., and his actions at times are most outrageous and dangerous. I have been greatly worried by him coming to my camp drunk and disorderly. He has caused much trouble in and around Candelaria. He has interfered with my military duties but I considered him an unresponsible person at times; therefore made no report previous to this one. His two sons came to my camp and asked me not to take action of any kind, as their father was demented. They stated that if he caused any more trouble they would tie him up until he was in a normal condition."[327]

Colonel Langhorne was equally critical reporting, "Kilpatrick's mania seems to run to writing newspaper articles and abusing certain people. At one time he may have had a bright mind, and he probably had a good education, and may have been respected at one time in Georgia. He is said to have drunk sotol, a vicious drink, which is a distilled product of a plant of that name, for so many years it has ruined his mind." The King of Candelaria, on the other hand, summed up his feelings about Matlack and Langhorne to U. S. Senator Morris Shepard, "Langhorne is persecuting us, and it should be stopped."[328]

Dawkins Kilpatrick had his own problems with the Captain; the most serious relating his arms dealings. In October 1914 U.S. authorities charged Dawkins with attempting to smuggle a machine gun across the border to the revolutionary forces of Constitutionalist General Toribio Ortega. The government seized the machine gun along with a number of other guns and a quantity of ammunition holding the cache as evidence. Charged with a violation of the U. S. neutrality law, a court later acquitted Kilpatrick in the case. In January 1918, Captain Matlack sent a telegram to Colonel Langhorne describing an ammunition sale the captain believed Dawkins Kilpatrick made to a Villista agent near Candelaria. "About two weeks before the Christmas holidays, D.D. Kilpatrick left Valentine with one-thousand rounds of 30 caliber and a like amount of Mauser which he delivered by a round-about way though Foley's, Pooles, and Perry's ranches to Mickey Welch at the intersection of Perry's road and Brite's road. This ammunition was taken over the rimrock and turned over to an agent of Alfonso Sanchez who paid six-hundred dollars for it." The man packed the ammunition on a mule and went across the river. According to Matlack, this ammunition was later used in a fight against the Carrancistas.[329]

The captain kept a close eye on Dawkins. When Dawkins left Candelaria hauling cotton, Matlack telegraphed ahead to Marfa of Kilpatrick's movements. On at least one occasion, "prohibition officers" acting on Matlack's tips found the powerful and illegal liquor *sotol* hidden beneath loads of cottonseed in Kilpatrick wagons. When the cotton wagons returned to Candelaria Dawkins utilized the large hauling capacity of the wagons to transport heavy crates of guns and ammunition. According to Captain Matlack, "Dawkins Kilpatrick and Ramon Villalva gave two boxes of ammunition and a pistol to Chico Cano. He (Matlack's informant) did not know how much ammunition was in the boxes but that they were very heavy." Matlack also accused Dawkins of providing Mauser rifle ammunition to Jesus Renteria, who claimed to have been a Villista at the time. The Captain also learned that two other Villistas, a General Salazar and Colonel Jose Godoy, "passed mules across the line to the Kilpatricks" in exchange for cash.[330]

Matlack's scrutiny of Dawkins Kilpatrick extended beyond the smuggling of guns and ammunition and into Kilpatrick's personal life. The Captain observed, "Sometime ago the wife of Francisco Tarin left him and lived illegally with Dawkins Kilpatrick having one baby girl with Dawkins as the father. They were never married. This woman now lives in Valentine, Texas. After the Tarin woman went to Valentine, Dawkins took Baria Hinojos as his second choice and lives with her at present almost under the nose of his mother and father. Some few months ago Dawkins imported into Candelaria an immoral woman who was deported the following day." Matlack continued, "To my personal knowledge Dawkins Kilpatrick is familiar and even friendly with some of the most notorious bandits of Mexico who operate in this vicinity." Indicating the depth of the personal hatred the captain felt for the Kilpatricks, Matlack wrote, "This family of Kilpatricks who I have found after two years of living within a stones throw of their home to be the most vindictive, dishonest, immoral and filthy family in the town of Candelaria."[331]

Shortly after the United States declared war on Germany in April 1917, thousands of young American men got draft notices and J.J. Kilpatrick's two sons were no exception. In early October 1918, Dawkins received his draft notice ordering him to report for a physical examination at Camp Travis, Texas. Prior to leaving Marfa for the exam, Dawkins produced a letter from a Dr. Dysart of El Paso stating that Kilpatrick was under his care for an unspecified medical condition and he was unfit for military service. Captain Matlack looked into the draft status of the Kilpatrick boys, telegraphing Colonel Langhorne that he suspected them to be draft dodgers writing, "There is no record of J.J. Kilpatrick, Sr. performing any kind of labor or aiding his country in any manner during the recent war. Both his sons, Dawkins and Jim, were of the draft age and apparently sound and health but nevertheless did not serve their country in any manner whatever." Marfa 8th Cavalry District Intelligence Officer Captain J. S. Tate found Dawkins medical exemption suspicious. Tate interviewed Dr. J. C. Daracott, the Presidio County Exemption Board physician who had examined Dawkins previously and found him fit for service. Captain Tate found, "It is of our opinion that it is possible for Dr. Dysart, of El Paso Texas, who has a cloudy record to give subject something which would make him unfit for military service. It is suggested that Dr. Dysart be investigated."[332]

Jim Kilpatrick's criminal record complicated his draft status. J.J. Kilpatrick, Sr. wrote of his son's dilemma in a 1918 letter to the Attorney General of the United States. "The facts are these: after his (Jim Kilpatrick) case was reversed and remanded the draft call was issued, he promptly responded and registered, claiming no exemption. The local board however, rejected him because he was under indictment. He appealed to the District Board and won his appeal; and was ordered sent to the Army, yet the military would not allow him to enlist. My son is anxious to go to the front. He is a fine shot and horseman. My wife and I want him to go. In fact, we feel rather chagrined because none of our immediate people are represented in this Great War for freedom and democracy. Our ancestors fought in the Revolutionary War and some of our people in the Civil War; and it seems too bad our son should be denied the privilege of fighting for his country simply because while in the discharge of his duty, he accidentally shot and killed a soldier against whom he had nothing in the world." Kilpatrick proposed the following solution. "It is our earnest request that you, the Attorney General, hold up the case until the war is over and he is mustered out, so that he may enter the army and go to the front. If he is killed, he will surely pay an ample price for any criminal debt he may owe the State of Texas. If he lives through the great conflict when he returns home, the machinery of the court can again be set in motion and the mandate of the law carried out." The war ended in a few months making the draft status of the Kilpatrick boys a dead issue.[333]

In January 1918, Matlack telegraphed Colonel Langhorne, "Please have Mr. Ryman Meet Lt. White and party on road at Kilpatrick ranch Jan 24 at 8 a.m. or come to Candelaria tonight. Want to look over mules and seize horse. Please answer at once." The following day, U. S. Customs Inspector Ryman seized 26 horses and mules from Kilpatrick and Sons near Candelaria. Ryan found in Dawkins' possession one of the horses in the herd that had been stolen from Carrancista General Murguia. Matlack telegraphed Langhorne, "Kilpatricks have a horse and claim that they bought him across the river. They also claim they have an order from Dowe (U. S. Customs Inspector O. C. Dowe) to cross animals anytime and pay duty at any time. Told (Customs Inspector) Holden they would not give horse up." While it is not clear what happened to the General's horse, the Customs men did manage to seize 1,400 rounds of rifle ammunition and an unknown number of guns from the Kilpatricks that day. J.J. Kilpatrick demanded the return of what he considered to be his legal property and was not alone in his condemnation of the seizure. W. E. Love, chairman of the Presidio County Democratic Executive Committee, wrote Democratic congressman W. R. Smith in Washington D.C., "We understand the Kilpatricks have had some arms and ammunition seized from them by the U.S., such arms and ammunition being now held for investigation in the matter of neutrality with Mexico. Their reputation in the county as law-abiding people is such that we bespeak for them all favorable consideration and trust they may be given an early showing to the end that the property may be released."[334]

J.J. Kilpatrick's difficulties with the government did not abate because he unceasingly antagonized his opponents with rambling letters and articles defaming the military, Captain Matlack, and Colonel Langhorne on the pages of number of newspapers such as the *El Paso Times*, and the *San Antonio Express*. The King of Candelaria possessed a keen ability to embarrass Colonel Langhorne with his stinging criticisms. Langhorne wrote, "His dementia seems to run to vilifying certain individuals, and the last object of hatred of his dementia seems to be myself." Kilpatrick's war started as a war of words that, depending on the former professor's mood and condition, could turn violent unexpectedly. Following Jim's stolen cattle trial in El Paso, J.J. Kilpatrick had to be removed from the court room after a raving outburst in which he insulted Sam Neill, foreman of the Brite Ranch, who had testified in the case. That evening J.J. got thrown in jail for, "shooting out the lights of a bawdy house in the tenderloin district" of El Paso. Following his arrest, the El Paso and San Antonio newspapers stopped publishing any writings penned by the King of Candelaria. This, however, failed to silence J.J. Kilpatrick for after this time he simply printed his articles in the Marfa *New Era*, a newspaper edited by his brother Hugh. Kilpatrick also paid other newspapers such as the *Fort Stockton Herald* to print his writings. Colonel Langhorne observed, "Mr. Kilpatrick in his normal condition is said to be a brilliant and educated gentleman but, even as members of his own family admit that, under the influence of intoxicants, he becomes erratic, spiteful and revengeful, and it is at such times that he writes his venomous letters."[335]

Early in 1918, J.J. Kilpatrick's reelection as Justice of the Peace attracted Matlack's scrutiny. The captain telegraphed Colonel Langhorne, "Just received wire stating that Kilpatrick is no longer a Justice of the Peace. If so he has no authority to arrest or try persons. He united in marriage Guillermo Nunez with Cristina Tarrango and Miguel Banches." While the source of Matlack's information is unclear, Lucas Charles Brite certified that Kilpatrick had been elected Justice of the Peace by running unopposed in the 1917 election. Brite added, "Would a disloyal citizen or a man of unsound mind (at times) be given such a position by his neighbors?"[336]

Pat Greene found himself caught in the middle of the feud. While Greene and Jim Kilpatrick continued to be close friends, Greene also developed camaraderie with Captain Matlack, for whom the young teacher held a great deal of respect. Greene observed, "Captain Matlack was a good friend of mine." He also described the captain as a, "loyal friend" and "a man that knew what he was doing." Shortly after his arrival in Candelaria in 1917, the captain declared the community to be "under military law." The Mexicans called it *ley secreta* or secret law. Matlack ordered all Mexicans living in the village disarmed. An army search of the Mexican houses in Candelaria turned up little, only a few old guns. The captain then issued identification cards bearing a thumbprint to persons living legally in Candelaria. When Pat Greene learned of Matlack's decree, he went to see the captain and told him he had several guns and wanted to know if Matlack wanted him to turn in his guns. Matlack replied, "hell no, you can have your guns" and issued Greene an identification card. The captain and the teacher got along well. Pat Greene took his meals in the Camp Kenney officer's mess on Ananias Hill each day with Captain Matlack and Lieutenant Tompkins for two years. Greene remembered, "It was good eating, good for my health and I got to hear all the gossip in the officers mess."[337]

In 1918, Pat Greene agreed to become the new postmaster of Candelaria taking over the office from Dawkins Kilpatrick. At this time Greene lived with his wife Inez and the couple's newborn son, Pat K. Greene, in their home located next to Kilpatrick's store. The couple chose the middle initial of the baby's name to be the letter K in honor of the K Troop physician who delivered the child in that house. This was 1918 and anti-German sentiment across the United States ran high as World War I raged on. J.J. and Mary Kilpatrick made no secret of their distrust of anyone of German heritage. When a German-American woman accepted an appointment as head the American Red Cross chapter in Marfa, school trustee Mary wrote, "There are many pure blooded Anglo-Saxon American ladies in Marfa, and there has been some speculation as to why a German-American woman should have in the first place appointed the head of the Red Cross."[338]

Inez Greene, Pat Greene's wife, was the daughter of first generation German-American parents. J.J. Kilpatrick wrote a spiteful letter to Washington about Inez Greene's racial heritage. When a copy of the letter filtered down to Colonel Langhorne in Marfa, he showed Pat Greene a copy of what the King of Candelaria had written about his wife. Captain Matlack recounted what happened next. "J.J. Kilpatrick entered the home of the Postmaster of Candelaria, Mr. Greene, and insulted his wife for which Mr. Kilpatrick was knocked down several times and thrown through the front door. Mr. Kilpatrick stood in the streets of Candelaria and defamed his own wife by making utterances against her character that would discredit the lowest contemptible white slaver who ever walked. The Postmaster, Mr. Greene and his wife heard Kilpatrick accuse his wife of everything that could be attributed to decency and they state that Mrs. Kilpatrick came into in to their home weeping bitterly."[339]

During a 1984 interview, the former Candelaria postmaster described the incident by simply saying, "I guess I should be ashamed of it but I gave the old man a thrashing." Ninety-three year old Pat Greene then said "I never have let anybody insult my wife and get away with it." He added that Kilpatrick's tantrum had taken place because the King of Candelaria, "hated me being a friend of Matlack" Greene left Kilpatrick's border town in 1918 and he did not return for almost sixty years. "I didn't want to be on either side of it and I not could stay there with taking sides." The couple settled in Rockport, Texas, where Greene continued his career as a teacher. Although Greene did not return to Candelaria until shortly before his death in the 1980's, he recalled the last time he saw J.J. Kilpatrick sometime in the early 1930's. " I saw him on the street in Austin walking in the direction of the capitol, he was on the west side of Congress Avenue, I was driving north on the east side." The traffic moved on and that was the last time Pat Greene saw the King of Candelaria alive.[340]

Following Pat Green's departure from Candelaria, J.J. Kilpatrick's problems with the government continued. In a 1919 letter to Colonel Langhorne, Captain Matlack described J.J.'s difficulties with the pink bollworm in Candelaria. "Recently this district was declared to be in the non-cotton zone due to the pink boll worm and the Kilpatricks were directed by agents of the Agriculture Department to destroy or dispense of their cotton seed according to regulations at once. Kilpatricks immediately failed to do so and in spite of orders against planting cotton, they immediately made arrangements and planted a large crop of cotton at Pilares (Porvenir), Texas violating both State and Federal law". Then evidencing paranoid tendencies, the King of Candelaria accused Captain Matlack of covertly planting pink boll worms in his fields in an attempt to ruin his crops.[341]

The Kilpatrick feud reached its highest point on the night of August 15, 1919, when the war of words erupted into gunfire. J.J. recorded his account of the incident in his journal in an entry titled, "The Attempt to Assassinate Me and My Grey-Haired Wife." The day began with a frightening discovery. During the night, someone poisoned all of Kilpatrick's dogs. Not much is known about the killing of the dogs except it should be understood that the killing left the Kilpatrick home without the numerous watch dogs that usually protected the place. That evening, after darkness fell and the dogs had been silenced, J.J. and Lula Kilpatrick sat at the dining table in their Candelaria home. A gunman outside crept up to the northeast side of Kilpatrick's house to a point where he could see the couple eating supper through a large dining room window. The assassin fired a shot shattering the window glass. J.J. wrote, "At the crack of the rifle I instinctively knew its meaning and instantly whirled to my left and placed a solid adobe wall between me and whoever it was that fired the shot, and yelled to my wife, 'Blow out the lights!' Coolly informing me to blow them out myself, she got up after some twenty-five or thirty seconds to call the rangers. As she passed through an adjoining room directly in line with the assassin's fire, a second shot rang out, the ball fanning her cheek and shattering a mirror in a wardrobe just in front of her." Apparently Lula was slightly wounded by the bullet grazing her cheek or by flying glass. J.J. continued, "Thinking the assassin had gone, I squatted down a few seconds before my wife got up and peeping between the jamb and a column of books piled on the sill of the window where I had been standing, distinctly saw a medium size man with a soldier hat on and over all pants..." The gunman then disappeared into the darkness. Kilpatrick found two 30-30-rifle casings in his yard and the matching bullets in the walls of his house. According to Kilpatrick, Captain Matlack dismissed shooting by saying, "No soldier did this for there is not a man in my troop who is such a poor shot. Also according to J.J. a little Mexican girl saw two U.S.

soldiers running from scene of the shooting. In addition Kilpatrick wrote that the next day, Captain Matlack "took his troop to the target grounds" for nighttime practice, an event previously unobserved by the King of Candelaria. J.J. summed the shooting attempt by saying, "It was especially in the interest of Matlack to silence my tongue. The only way to do this was to make me a citizen of the spirit world whose inhabitants hold no communication with sub-lunar mortals except by the doubtful means of the ojiuja boards." Although J.J. took his charges of attempted murder to a Presidio County grand jury, no indictment was returned against Captain Matlack.[342]

After the shooting and the suspicious demise of his dogs, J.J. replaced his poisoned watchdogs with peacocks. The peacocks lived in the trees and on the roof of the house and store or perched atop the cotton gins. Sharp eyed and incredibly noisy when anyone approached, the birds proved to be superior to watch dogs. An approach by anyone day or night to Kilpatrick's residence brought about a very loud screeching response from the watchful birds. The peacocks guarded the Kilpatrick store and house for the next eighty years.

"We used to contend with the Comanches every light moon. We knew what we were going up against when we seen [sic] a bunch of Comanches; there were two things to do, fight or run. You meet a bunch of Mexicans and you don't know what you are going up against; whether they are civilized or not."

Sam H. Neill

The Brite Ranch Raid

Chapter 7

On Christmas Day, 1917 , eleven months after Pershing's troops withdrew from Chihuahua and went to the trenches of Europe, Mexican bandits resumed their attacks on U.S. soil striking in the upper Big Bend at a ranch owned by one of the region's best-known residents, L. C. Brite. The raid at the Brite Ranch demonstrated that the border troubles were far from over and that Pershing's campaign in Chihuahua had failed to bring an end to border raids. Lucas Charles (Luke) Brite came to rugged northwest Presidio County from Frio County, Texas, in 1885, and established his ranch at the foot of Capote Peak. Brite found the abundant highland grasses some thirty miles west of Marfa to be a "cattle heaven." It was here, fifteen miles east of the Rio Grande and Mexico, that Brite built his 125,000-acre empire, a spread nearly half the size of the state of Rhode Island.[343]

Luke Brite became a wealthy and influential rancher. In 1904 he registered the Bar Cross Brand and began breeding Hereford cattle. During the decade between 1910 and 1920, Brite sold some ten thousand bulls for breeding purposes. Brite whiteface Herefords became known across the country, winning prizes in stock shows in Kansas City, St. Louis, Fort Worth, Phoenix, and Albuquerque. Luke Brite helped organize the Highland Hereford Breeders Association and served as president of the Panhandle Southwest Cattle Raisers Association from 1917 to 1920. He was also a philanthropist, giving $25,000 in 1911 to endow the Brite College of the Bible at Texas Christian University, where he was a trustee from 1914 until his death in 1941.[344]

Because of the remote location of his ranch, Brite opened a general merchandise store in 1914 to serve some forty to sixty ranch employees and residents.[345] A post office operated in the store from 1916 until 1926, as the ranch community of Brite grew.[346] The store manager and postmaster, Pierre Guyon, bragged to the Marfa *New Era* newspaper in 1915 that the Brite store would sell "anything from a toothpick, a plug [of] Battle-Axe tobacco to a traction engine."[347] The location of the Brite store near the border made it one of the few centers of trade in the remote, sparsely populated upper Big Bend.[348] Except for frequent livestock thefts, the Brite community remained isolated from the revolution in Mexico until Christmas Day, 1917. The ranch, along with its well-stocked store and remuda of fine horses, made a tempting target for Mexican raiders.[349] On the day of the raid, Luke Brite was at his home in Marfa, leaving ranch foreman, Van Neill, in charge. Neill's father, Sam H. Neill, a U.S. Customs inspector in the Big Bend district and a cowman along with his wife were house guests at the ranch. The Neills expected guests from Marfa and Valentine for a noontime Christmas dinner.[350]

An early riser, Sam Neill was awake when the raiders attacked at dawn. The elder Neill sat drinking coffee about 7:30 a.m. in the kitchen of his son's house, when he looked down the Candelaria road and saw six horseman riding fast in his direction from the southwest.[351] When the riders drew their guns and started shooting at the house, Neill spread the alarm, found his revolver and rifle, and ran outside to fight back. He took a position in the yard behind a protective corner of the ranch house and started shooting at the raiders. Meanwhile, some forty odd other raiders took up positions around Brite.[352]

In the shooting which followed, a bullet creased the elder Neill's nose; he was again wounded in the right leg a few minutes later. Amid cries of *Mueran los gringos*! (Death to the Americans!), one of the raiders, dressed in a Carrancista officer's coat, galloped up to a fence surrounding the Neill house. Although he was wounded, Sam Neill shot the Mexican from his horse, killing him instantly. Subsequently, the Neills wounded four other raiders. The wounded and dead were carried off by their compatriots.[353]

The raiders captured Thomas Sanchez, who was milking a cow when the fight began, and sent him to the Neill house with a message demanding the surrender of the besieged inhabitants along with the keys to the Brite store. The Neills declined to surrender, and they said that the keys were in the possession of Pierre Guyon, the store manager, who lived a few hundred yards away. Sanchez then went to the Guyon house, where he got the keys, and let the raiders into the store.[354]

Inside the store, the raiders found plenty of loot. They dumped sacks of corn and beans on the floor and filled the empty sacks with hats, ammunition, coats, overalls, bolts of cloth, canned goods, and Hamilton Brown brand shoes. They then dressed themselves in new clothing and took forty dollars from a cash drawer. Lacking explosives, they tried to batter open the store's safe with new axes taken from the merchandise. The door of the safe, however, withstood the bashing. Thomas Sanchez led some of the raiders to a nearby remuda of saddle horses, hoping to distract them and prevent further bloodshed. In all, they took about $1500 worth of supplies and twenty saddle horses.[355]

After the raiders became occupied with looting the store and rounding up the horses, the gunfire died down. About that time, a telephone in the Neill ranch house began ringing. Thinking there was an opportunity to call for help, Mrs. Van Neill ran to the telephone, only to discover it was the bandits ringing the house from the store. They had cut the telephone lines to Marfa, making it impossible to call the outside world. Meanwhile, Crecencia Natividad, another Brite employee, braved bandit gunfire by going outside the ranch house to beg in Spanish for the Neills' lives during the siege.[356]

A little later, Christmas dinner guests began to arrive at the Neill house, unaware the raid was in progress. The Reverend H. M. Bandy, the preacher at the First Christian Church in Marfa, his wife, and two women passengers pulled up in front of the Neill house at 9.00 a.m. in a touring car. The raiders surprised Bandy, who expected only a quiet holiday meal. Just as the raiders were about to open fire on the terrified minister and his passengers, Van Neill sent out a Mexican boy to tell the bandits not to kill Bandy, as he was a *padre* (priest). In response, the bandits allowed the preacher and his passengers to enter the ranch house safely.[357]

Bandy recalled the scene when he entered the Neill house:
"Sam Neill was standing in the door with his face all bloody. During the siege, Sam got very shaky and was trembling. He asked his son Van for some liquor, but I advised against giving it to him. Neill then appealed to my wife. She thought the old man needed it and gave it to him. After he drank it, his nerves became steady."[358] The preacher, "a splendid shot," offered a prayer before picking up a gun to defend a section of the ranch house.[359]

A short time later, other Christmas guests began to arrive. Van Neill's brother-in-law, Hodge Hunter, a merchant from Valentine, arriving with two women passengers, stopped his car in front of the Guyon house. Like the Bandy party, Hunter and his passengers were unaware the raid was in progress since the shooting had died down. The store manager called a warning to Hunter, who then saw the bandits and quickly sped away to Valentine for help.[360] Meanwhile, James Cobb, a neighbor who lived several miles from the Brite headquarters, heard gunfire. Cobb walked within sight of the raid before he saw the bandits carrying loot from the store. When he realized what was happening, he ran back to his house and phoned for help.[361]

Cobb and Hunter fortunately escaped the notice of the raiders, but other arrivals were less fortunate. Sometime between nine and ten o'clock, Mickey Welch drove his mail hack into Brite on his regular mail route from Candelaria to Valentine. He carried two Mexican passengers, one a clock repairman, the other a Carrancista paymaster fleeing Pancho Villa's army after the Carrancista defeat at Ojinaga. As the mail hack approached the store, the raiders opened fire, killing Welch's two passengers. They took Welch prisoner, forcing the hot-tempered Irishman to unharness his mules and sit in his mail hack while other raiders continued trying to batter open the safe in the store.[362]

With the well-practiced vehemence of a border mule driver, Welch loudly cursed his Mexican captors for stealing his mules. Once, the angry mail driver's captors allowed him to walk unmolested toward Guyon's house, but Welch stubbornly turned back and tried to retrieve his mules.[363] It was a fatal mistake for the mail driver. Two of the raiders grabbed Welch, dragged him into a back room of the store, and hung the struggling mailman from the rafters. To finish the job, they cut Welch's throat and wiped their blades clean on his shirt before letting the body fall to the floor.[364] They departed, leaving the slain mailman lying in a large pool of blood.[365]

Time was running out for the bandits, however, as news of the raid reached Marfa and Valentine. At about 12:30 p.m. the raiders, laden with stolen loot, began leaving the store. They headed across the steep Candelaria rim rock riding for Los Fresnos, Chihuahua, a crossing point on the Mexican side of the Rio Grande southwest of the Brite ranch. News of the raid shattered an otherwise peaceful Christmas morning in Marfa. To celebrate the holiday, the U.S. troops stationed at Fort D. A. Russell took the day off. Word about the Brite raid came as cavalry troopers ate a special noon Christmas dinner in the mess hall of the army camp. Responding quickly, some cavalrymen dashed to nearby trucks or caught rides in automobiles, while others saddled their horses to ride the thirty miles to Brite. An automobile posse, led by Sheriff Ira Cline, joined about a hundred cavalrymen in a wild ride to Brite. Slower, mounted cavalry followed behind. Word spread to the border outposts of the 8 th Cavalry at the Candelaria, Holland, and Evetts Ranch camps by telephone. Mounted troops from these border outposts rushed to intercept the raiders before they made good their escape to Mexico.[366]

It took the posse and the cavalrymen about an hour to get to Brite from Marfa. Their guide was Grover Webb, an U.S. Customs inspector, who was familiar with the rough upper Big Bend river country. Webb recalled that the raiders were still in sight when the first vehicles from Marfa arrived at Brite. Fleeing over the rim rock of the rugged Sierra Vieja Mountains, three miles west of the Brite headquarters, the raiders left a clearly marked trail of dropped loot and dead bodies. The horseless cavalrymen and posse gave chase in their automobiles to the edge of the rim rock. Four hundred yards beyond the store, the pursuers discovered the bodies of Mickey Welsh's two Mexican passengers. About two miles further, they found the partially buried body of the first raider killed by Sam Neill.[367] When the troopers and the posse reached the summit of the rim rock, their pursuit was blocked by the steep cliffs of the Candelaria Rim.[368] Only horses could negotiate the path to the Rio Grande valley below the rim rock, but during the raid most of the horses and mules at Brite had been stolen, handicapping those in pursuit. It was some time before the mounted cavalrymen from Marfa were able to catch up with the automobiles at the rim and continue the chase. The dismounted cavalrymen and posse had to content themselves by firing a few long distance shots with high-power rifles as the bandits, unaffected by the shots, disappeared from sight in the valley far below. On the trail descending the face of the rimrock, the bandits dropped much of their loot and gear, including a Carrancista officer's sword and officer's coat.[369]

The raiders rode hard to the Los Fresnos ford and crossed into Mexico safely. Later in the afternoon, Troops M and G of the 8 th Cavalry, some two hundred men, crossed the Rio Grande at Los Fresnos and continued the chase on Mexican soil.[370] The American column, commanded by a U.S. Army captain named Fisk, followed the raiders around the north slope of the Sierra La Ventana. On December 26th about 1:00 p.m., the American troops engaged about fifteen of the raiders at a point four miles from the Rio Grande. The running fight between the retreating Mexicans and the American troops ended in a canyon in the Sierra Pilares not far from the village of Pilares, Chihuahua. The American troops killed ten raiders and recovered a considerable amount of loot taken in the raid, including food, clothing, ammunition, and several horses and mules. Another five or more of the bandits escaped into the mountains. The cavalry had only one casualty: Pvt. John F. Kelly was wounded in the fight.[371] That evening, Fisk's command withdrew from Mexico with the recovered Brite property.[372]

The withdrawal of the army from Mexico did not bring an end to the repercussions of the raid, as a whirlwind of Anglo indignation swept the upper Big Bend. News of the Brite raid spread panic as far away as Marfa, and rumors of an impending attack by Mexican raiders circulated. Armed residents began automobile patrols of Marfa, Valentine, and the surrounding roads. Women and children sought the protection of the hastily fortified Presidio County courthouse.[373] Feelings continued to run high, and citizens called for official response to the Brite raid. On 29 December 1917 a group of about 200 cowmen, rangers, river guards, and citizens met at the Stockman's Club in Marfa. Lt. Col. George T. Langhorne and Texas Ranger Jim Gillette spoke to the crowd about the continuing border troubles. The group decided to form a vigilance committee to register and disarm the Mexican population of Brewster, Presidio, Jeff Davis, Culberson, and Hudspeth counties. Suspicious Mexicans were to be watched and their activities reported to the committee. The committee also sent a telegram to the adjutant general of Texas requesting that a cavalry regiment consisting of "men accustomed to our rough country and border conditions" be formed to give the vigilantes official status.[374]

While the identity of the Brite raiders has never been clearly established, unsubstantiated reports that link Pancho Villa to the attack do exist. Contemporary newspaper accounts of the raid are sketchy and conflicting at best. Following the raid, all sorts of rumors circulated as to who might have been responsible. The El Paso Times of December 28th 1917 reported that Lt. Col. George T. Langhorne, commander of the Big Bend military district, had information that the raiders were Villistas impersonating Carrancista forces by dressing in Carrancista uniforms in an attempt to discredit the de facto Mexican government. On January 4th 1918, the *El Paso Morning Times* ran a photo of the bandit killed by Sam Neill and identified the body as that of Antonio Avila. According to the *Times*, Avila was the leader of the raiders and on the body authorities found the identification papers of a Carrancista officer. Also the body was clad in a Carrancista officer's uniform and hat. Another theory about the identity of the Brite raiders came from Harry Warren, who interviewed the Reverend H. M. Bandy in April 1925 and wrote an unpublished manuscript about the raid. According to Warren, Villa himself ordered the Brite raid and on the day of the attack was not far away, awaiting the return of his men just across the border from Brite on the Mexican side. Warren wrote that the leader of the raiders was Placido Villa Nueva, a Villista colonel, whom he described as a "big man with big whiskers and somewhat spotted." The Reverend Mr. Bandy recalled seeing a man matching this description who appeared to be the leader of the bandits on the day of the raid. Warren went on to say that Villa and some of his followers awaited the return of the Brite raiders in a canyon called "de los Siete Alamos," near where the American troops engaged the fleeing raiders. It is equally possible that the raiders acted on their own and were simply bandits out to steal whatever came their way. During the waning years of the revolution, banditry became a common occurrence. Many bandits had former ties with various revolutionary factions, making it extremely difficult to assess their rather confused political loyalties.[375]

"...every time a bunch of these same bandits get over here on a marauding tour and our boys has[sic] to deal with them, they are no doubt reported as being a bunch of the leading citizens of Mexico, murdered in cold blood by our officers and citizens."

Texas Ranger Capt. W. M. Hanson

Massacre at Porvenir

Chapter 8

By 1918, the revolution in Mexico and the war in Europe had left Texas authorities with a military situation along the Rio Grande for which they were unprepared. When it became apparent that no additional help in maintaining order would be forthcoming from the United States Army, whose top priority at the time was World War I, Texas authorities struck out on their own. The adjutant general of Texas, James A. Harley, organized a state guard from a selective draft of eligible young men. More than fifteen thousand strong, the guard consisted of two cavalry brigades and a single brigade of infantry. The 35th Texas Legislature appropriated $400,000 for the Border Service Fund and expanded the size of the state Ranger force. In addition, the Loyalty Rangers, a volunteer secret service branch of the Texas Rangers, gathered information on Mexican revolutionary activities on both sides of the border. Loyalty Rangers investigated cases of draft evasion, desertion, cattle stealing, and anti-American activities. Special Rangers, made up of cattlemen, also patrolled the Rio Grande.[376]

The final responsibility for border protection rested with Ranger Captains who had to deal with the border troubles on a day-to-day basis. For example, Ranger Company B Captain J. M. Fox faced a difficult, if not impossible assignment of protecting more than four thousand square miles of wide-open border in Marfa. Badly undermanned, Company B consisted of Fox and eleven regular Ranger privates. About 200 cattlemen served as volunteers. Some were duly sworn Special Rangers like Sam Neill and O. C. Dowe, but the majority of Company B held informal appointments. As Fox searched for an appropriate response to the Brite raid, his attention focused on the bad reputation of the

Mexicans at Porvenir given him by local ranchers. The ranchers agreed with Fox that Porvenir was a bandit nest that needed to be cleaned out. These feelings had a strong racial overtone aggravated by the murders of Mickey Welch, Jack Howard, and Rangers Sitters and Hulan, as well as by the rancher's view that the Porvenir Mexicans were squatters and thieves living on previously open rangeland.[377]

Isolated from the outside world by the Sierra Vieja, the tiny ranch community of Porvenir, Texas, became the target of Anglo retaliation shortly after the Brite raid. The village lay on the Rio Grande, a few miles upriver from Pilares, Chihuahua, in northwest Presidio County. Ironically, though the town's name means future in Spanish, Porvenir offered no future to the some 140 Mexicans living there in 1918. They scratched out subsistence living by farming and raising goats and cattle. Many came to Texas to escape the civil war that consumed Chihuahua in 1910. By 1918, Porvenir had a school but no post office or store; the nearest store was on the Texas side of the Rio Grande, at Brite, a hard day's horseback ride distant. [378]

In late January 1918, Captain Fox ordered Ranger Bud Weaver to lead a group of Company B Rangers to Porvenir. On the 23rd, Rangers Andy C. Barker, Clint Holden, Boone Oliphant, Max Herman, Allen Cole, and others drove by automobile to the John Pool ranch on the Candelaria rim rock where they got horses to cross into the rough river country. The following day, more ranchers joined the force at the Pool ranch including John Pool, his brother Buck Pool, Tom Snyder, and Raymond Fitzgerald. The Americans, some forty in number, rode to Porvenir, arriving there after midnight on the twenty-fourth. The Americans, some wearing masks, surrounded Porvenir and at 1:00 A.M., roused the sleeping Mexicans. The pitiful residents were rounded up and held at gunpoint while the Rangers searched their *jacales*, the crude mud huts housing most of the villagers. In one *jacal*, they found two rifles and a shotgun. They found a holstered pistol hanging near a cot in the house of John Bailey, the lone Anglo living in Porvenir. The Rangers confiscated all of the guns. Following the search, they released all the villagers except Roman Nieves, Eutimio Gonzales, and Manuel Fierro. The Rangers held the trio for questioning because they wore Hamilton Brown shoes, a type carried by the Brite store and stolen during the raid.[379]

After leaving Porvenir, the Rangers took their prisoners to a camp in an abandoned railroad tunnel near the San Carlos coal mine, a few miles distant, where they questioned the Mexicans about the Brite raid before releasing them the following day. Making a fateful decision, Nieves and Gonzales returned to Porvenir. Fierro went back to his home in Mexico.[380] But the Rangers were not finished with Porvenir. On the afternoon of the twenty-seventh, the Rangers went to Camp Evetts, an 8 th Cavalry border outpost located not far from Porvenir, where they received an unenthusiastic welcome. One of the troopers, Cpl. Robert F. Keil, described the arrival of the lawmen and recalled that considerable friction existed between the Rangers and the cavalrymen. Rangers frequently extorted money from off-duty soldiers in Marfa. Pairs of Rangers would catch cavalrymen alone and charge them with various offenses; the Rangers would, for twenty dollars, forget the offense and promise to "take the money to the judge in the morning." The money, of course, never went further than the Rangers' pockets and the troopers never forgot the swindle. According to Keil, on one payday the Rangers victimized fourteen cavalrymen from one troop.[381]

As Troop G lounged around the mess hall, the Rangers were directed to Capt. Henry H. Anderson's tent, where they presented Anderson with a letter from his commanding officer, Col. George T. Langhorne, requesting army assistance to the Rangers in going to Porvenir and subduing the village. Suspicious of the Rangers' mission because he knew the Porvenirans were innocent and peaceful, Anderson placed a telephone call to his commanding officer to verify the Ranger request. When Marfa confirmed the Rangers' letter, Anderson assembled his men in the mess hall and told them to prepare for a mission to Porvenir.[382]

Before they left camp, Anderson ordered his men to surround the village, see that no one escaped, and seize all firearms and weapons. At about 10:30 p.m. the Rangers and some forty Troop G cavalrymen left Camp Evetts bound for Porvenir. The uneasiness between the troopers and the Rangers continued as the Rangers rode separately from the cavalrymen. Heavily armed, the Rangers each wore two forty-five Colt pistols with ammunition hanging from crossed cartridge belts. They appeared nervous and jumpy, not stopping to loosen their saddle cinches and taking occasional drinks of whiskey to calm their nerves.[383]

The night was bitterly cold when the Americans surrounded Porvenir just after midnight. Not a light showed from any of the *jacales* in the village. The troopers awakened the sleeping villagers and led them outside into the freezing night while the soldiers searched for weapons. Guarded by a detail of troopers, the shivering Mexicans huddled around a fire. The cavalrymen found one old gun with no shells and a few knives that were overlooked in the previous search of the village. The second search of Porvenir did not turn up any stolen Brite property.[384]

Some of the troopers tried to reassure the frightened Mexicans as they huddled by the fire, explaining that they were with the Rangers looking for bandits. They promised when the search of the *jacales* had been completed, the people could go back to bed. But the people would not be comforted; the mention of the word Ranger brought a look of fear to every Mexican face. The lawmen remained apart, standing a short distance away, watching. Finally, after the search was completed, the Rangers requested that Captain Anderson withdraw his troops. The lawmen said they wanted to question the prisoners in their native tongue. Anderson agreed to withdraw his men but added that he knew all of the Mexicans and that he was sure there were no bandits among them. Troop G withdrew a short distance up the road to Camp Evetts and waited.[385]

The Rangers started separating the men from the women and children. Sensing danger, some of the women and children began to scream and cry pleading for the lives of the prisoners. The Rangers selected 15 men between the ages of 16 and 72 and marched them off into darkness to a rock bluff about a mile south of Porvenir where they unceremoniously shot the Mexicans to death. The sound of the gunfire produced instant pandemonium, and as soon as the Rangers finished their bloody deed, they mounted their horses and quickly rode away, shouting drunken, Comanche-like yells. The women and children began wailing, and the startled cavalrymen rode back to a pitiful scene as the grief-stricken survivors recognized the dead.[386]

The 8th Cavalry troopers were caught in a totally unexpected situation. Captain Anderson ordered a guard placed around the survivors because the Rangers had told the women they would return and kill them all. While most of the troopers returned to Camp Evetts, the captain sent for a priest in Candelaria, leaving only a small patrol behind. Sometime before daylight, the survivors of the massacre abandoned Porvenir, fleeing across the river to Mexico where they sought refuge in Pilares. During the night, one of the women gave birth to a baby girl as the newborn's father lay dead across the river in Texas.[387]

The Rangers orphaned forty-two children that night. The fifteen murdered Mexicans were mostly poor tenant farmers with large families. There is no hard evidence linking any of the villagers to the Brite raid. Several had lived in Porvenir for a number of years; Eutimio Gonzales, for example, had been there since 1890. Some were former residents of Porvenir who had the misfortune of visiting relatives in the village when the Rangers struck.[388]

The dead men included Macedonio Huertas, a thirty-year-old father of two children. Another victim, Tiburcio Jaquez, was a fifty-year-old father of seven children who had lived in Porvenir since 1910. Longino Flores, about forty-four years old, left a wife, three children, and two grandchildren. A respected member of the Porvenir community, Flores had farmed on the river with his family for about three or four years. Harry Warren described Flores as being "highly esteemed by U.S. Customs officers and a great assistant and favorite" of the officers. Manuel Morales, forty-seven, another longtime resident of the village, left a wife and seven children, including a daughter born the night of her father's murder. Eutimio Gonzales, one of the men taken to the San Carolos railroad tunnel by the Rangers, was a longtime resident of Porvenir, forty-three years old, married and the father of nine children. The other man taken to the tunnel, Roman Nieves, was an American citizen and longtime Porvenir resident, who left a wife and seven children. The oldest man killed by the Rangers was Antonio Castanuedo, about seventy-two, from Pecos, Texas. A previous resident of the village, Castaneudo appeared on the 1910 Census of Porvenir. The youngest victim of the massacre was sixteen-year-old Juan Jimenez. The unmarried men included Alberto Garcia, thirty-five, and Severiano Herrera, eighteen, also from Pecos, who was visiting relatives in Porvenir. Pedro Jimenez, twenty-seven, and Vivian Herrera about twenty-three, were also both unmarried. Little is known about Zarapio Jimenez, only that he was twenty-five years old when he met his death, as was Pedro Herrera, about twenty-five, also from Pecos. The men from Pecos had come to Porvenir to teach their relatives how to farm cotton at Porvenir.[389]

Twelve-year-old Juan Flores, son of Longino Flores, watched in horror that night as his father was shot and killed before his eyes. The little boy had been taken with the doomed men to the bluff but had been somehow become separated from the group in time to save his life. Terrified at what he had witnessed, little Juan ran weeping to his father's body that lay face down on the rocky ground. When the child turned the corpse over, he discovered that in addition to many terrible wounds his father had suffered, most of his face had been blown away. It left the child with such terrible memories that scarred him for life. Despondent over the loss of her husband, Juan's mother later took her own life. Juan recalled in an interview done for a documentary film in 2002 that in addition to the rangers, several ranchers and at least one soldier took an active part in the killing. He remembered a particular rancher who had planned the murders and went so far as to select the rock bluff where the victims were shot to death. After the killings, the youngster saw this rancher, his clothes covered in blood, smiling about his awful deed. Juan Flores kept silent about what he had seen. He realized that no Anglo lawman would believe him and if any did Juan's own life would be in great jeopardy. It was a secret even his family did not know until he told them about it more than eighty years later. After the massacre, Juan Flores had terrible nightmares frequently awakening his family with his screams in the night.[390]

Sometime before dawn, news of the massacre reached Harry Warren, Porvenir's schoolmaster, who lived about a mile north of the village. The news brought grief to the Warren household because one of the Porvenirans killed was the father of Warren's wife, Juliana. In addition to the death of his father-in-law, the schoolmaster almost lost one of his sons in the massacre. Warren's boy had been rounded up in Porvenir by the Rangers but luckily was sent with the women because one of the ranchers recognized him and pleaded for the youth's life. The Rangers also spared the life of John Bailey, the only Anglo living in the village.[391]

Bailey and Warren went to Porvenir, arriving there just before sunrise, and found the village abandoned except for a few soldiers standing guard over the bodies of the slain Mexicans. Warren became suspicious when the soldiers told him that they had no idea who had killed the Porvenirans and that the troopers had only just ridden up and found the bodies. There was no one to dispute the story, since the Porvenir survivors were now in Mexico. They were not alone, for word of the massacre spread panic among the Mexican population of the upper Big Bend. Fearing the Rangers were coming to wipe out them out, hundreds of Mexicans living near Candelaria on the Texas side bolted across the Rio Grande to Mexico, some taking only their families, hurriedly leaving their possessions and livestock behind.[392]

Early in the morning, an old Mexican woman crossed the river from Pilares and asked the American troopers to load the Porvenir dead on to her cart so that they might be buried in Mexico. The soldiers loaded the bodies and permitted the old woman to take her grisly load to the graveyard near Pilares. The bodies were buried in a mass grave. A few days after the massacre, some soldiers from Camp Evetts came to Porvenir, then knocked down and burned the abandoned *jacales* the Porvenir Mexicans once called home.[393]

An army cover-up of the murders kept word of the massacre out of the newspapers. In his official report of the incident, Captain Anderson said that one of his patrols found the fifteen bodies the morning of the twenty-ninth and that no one knew how they were killed. Since the bodies had been buried in Mexico, no physical evidence of the murders existed. Even Henry Warren had not actually witnessed the incident. Warren ran into a stone wall of opposition when he tried to reveal the news to the outside world. After Captain Anderson denied any knowledge of the massacre, Warren complained to Col. George T. Langhorne, commander of the Big Bend Military District in Marfa. The colonel stuck with Captain Anderson's version and wrote Warren that "I don't believe you are the kind of man who should be in a position of influence and instructing others."[394] When army authorities continued to disavow any knowledge of the massacre, Warren decided to take legal action and began collecting power of attorney from the victims' families to file a case before the United States Court of Claims.[395]

The victims' families had good reason to trust Harry Warren with their case, for while he was not a lawyer, he was an educated man, who had lived, in the upper Big Bend for a number of years. The schoolmaster was born July 17th 1859, in Waterford, Mississippi. He graduated from the University of Mississippi in 1881 with a bachelor's degree in philosophy. The following year, he came to Eagle Pass, Texas, and became an elementary teacher. In 1902 he was elected justice of the peace for Presidio County. In 1910 Warren bought a ranch near Porvenir and married Juliana Jaquez.[396]

Since Porvenir had been destroyed and his pupils gone, Warren closed his school and moved his family to Candelaria to seek employment. He hoped to teach in the Candelaria school but ran afoul the American military, who considered him a troublemaker for continuing to speak out about the Porvenir affair. When Warren arrived in Candelaria, the colonel kept him under surveillance. The Candelaria camp commander, Lt. Leonard F. Matlack, telegraphed Colonel Langhorne requesting that "Mr. Warren of Porvenir be moved from the vicinity of the river. He is a dangerous man in that he agitates among the Mexicans on both sides of the river and keeps the situation at the boiling point. The man is trying to get in communication with Mexicans across the river to have them give him power of attorney to institute a suit against the United States government for the people who were killed at Porvenir. Mr. Warren is now in Candelaria and I have forbidden him to talk to the Mexicans across the river until this matter can be adjusted."[397]

The "adjustment" meant the rejection of Warren's teaching contract by the county school superintendent, who wrote the embattled teacher that it would not be renewed because "...the military authority will not stand for your remaining in Candelaria for reasons I suppose well known to you." When Warren could not find work in Candelaria, he went to Jeff Davis County in 1919 where he worked as a deputy sheriff for a short time. He left West Texas and moved to Arizona, remaining there until the army left the Big Bend a few years later.[398]

Harry Warren was not alone in trying to bring the Porvenir massacre to light. Candelaria merchant and justice of the peace, J.J. Kilpatrick, and his wife Lula also deplored the murders and were vocal about the army cover-up. In a letter to United States Rep. Thomas L. Blanton, Kilpatrick wrote: "From the best information we can obtain, none of the fifteen dead Mexicans had anything to do with the Brite raid. And now the general belief is that the Mexicans were killed in order to strike terror into the hearts of bandits and thieves for the purpose of putting an end to the raids and the stealing."[399]

In a letter to the War Department, Mrs. Kilpatrick wrote of the massacre and Warren's troubles: "The killing of those fifteen Mexican farmers broke up Professor Henry Warren's school and turned him out of house and home. He came down here and through sympathy for the old teacher and because we considered it right, we gave the old man a small school so that he could finish out his school term. However, the County Superintendent would not approve his new contract, informing me that Colonel Langhorn had told her in case we gave Warren a school down here that he, Langhorn, would chase the old school master out of the country."[400]

Several months passed before the outside world learned the

truth about the massacre. Initially, a version of the Porvenir killings that had been fabricated by Captain Fox, found its way into the newspapers of the day. In his official report to the adjutant general, the Ranger captain painted a completely different picture of the murders at Porvenir. Captain Fox, who was not present at the massacre, asserted that his men came under gunfire and the fifteen were killed when the Rangers returned fire. Fox also falsely reported that the Rangers found stolen property, including Joe Sitter's saddle and goods from the Brite raid, at Porvenir.[401]

When the Ranger captain attempted to whitewash the story of the massacre, the Porvenir survivors challenged Fox's story in a Mexican court of inquiry. The inquest, conducted in Ojinaga on February 2, 1918, by the Carrancista commander, the mayor of the town, and a municipal judge, heard eight Porvenir survivors, some of whom were Mexican-American citizens, give statements describing the massacre. All said the victims were innocent of any crimes and were brutally murdered by American Rangers. They noted the American army was nearby but did not participate in the killings. The court sent copies of the sworn statements to Gen. J. C. Murguia, the Carrancista commander in Cuidad Chihuahua, to the Mexican ambassador in Washington, and to Texas Ranger W. M. Hanson, captain of the Loyalty Ranger Force. The Mexican ambassador in Washington sent a letter of protest to the Wilson government.[402]

Responding to the Mexican protest, Texas Ranger Captain Hanson traveled to Marfa to look into the Mexican charges. Placed in command of the Special Ranger force statewide, the newly appointed Hanson was the logical choice. He had a long career of law enforcement, having been a deputy sheriff and United States marshal before joining the Texas Rangers. He was familiar with Mexico, having worked for several years as a member of the Mexican secret service of Porfirio Diaz.[403] While in Marfa, the Ranger captain had other tasks to perform. Hanson spent most of his time determining how many political supporters new Texas Gov. William P. Hobby had in the Big Bend. Only six months earlier, Hobby had become governor after the impeachment of James E. Ferguson. As 1918 was an election year, Ferguson, even though he had just been impeached, ran against Hobby in the July primary elections. The captain remained loyal to Hobby politically and had no ties with the Ferguson crowd.[404]

Hanson discovered Hobby had considerable political support, particularly among the influential ranchers who were members of the Stockman's Club. He heard rumors that Captain Fox was a still a Ferguson supporter and had distributed some Ferguson literature around Marfa. But Hanson found that Fox also enjoyed great popularity at the Cattlemen's Club; the ranchers liked Fox and thought he was doing a good job in the face of considerable odds. Hanson talked to several club members, among them Raymond Fitzgerald, one of the ranchers present at the massacre. In reporting to Adj. Gen. James A Harley, Hanson said that he felt Fox supported Hobby and that the ranchers were quite satisfied with the work of Captain Fox in teaching the river Mexicans a lesson.[405]

As the Texas election approached, some details of the Porvenir massacre became public after a U.S. Army special inspector looked into the charges made by Warren and Kilpatrick and the story reached the newspapers. In his investigation of the Porvenir killings, Col. W. J. Glascow found that the Rangers were guilty of killing the Porvenir victims and that they had been guided to the village by Troop G. The investigation caused Governor Hobby to disband Ranger Company B on 6 June 1918, and fire Rangers A. C. Barker, Max Herman, Bud Weaver, Allen Cole, and Boone Oliphant. Captain Fox resigned, claiming he had been discharged for political reasons.[406]

In an open letter published in the *Brownsville Herald* of July 12, 1918, Texas Adjutant General Harley disputed Fox's charges of politics being behind his dismissal: "As you know fifteen Mexicans were killed while in the custody of your men after they had been arrested and disarmed. This is verified by all proof. The troublemaker and lawless Ranger has no place on the border where international complications can be brought on that will involve our nation in trouble that will hamper its progress in Europe. You know as all peace officers should know, that every man whether he be black, yellow or brown has the constitutional right to trial by jury and that no organized band operating under the laws of this state has the right to constitute itself judge, jury and executioner. You were not forced to resign by the governor for political reasons but your forced resignation came in the interest of humanity, decency, law and order."[407]

Nor did the matter stop there. In January 1919, J.T. Canales, a fiery forty-two-year-old Brownsville state representative, presented eighteen charges of Ranger corruption and abuse of Mexican citizens before a joint committee of the Texas Senate and House investigating the state Ranger force in Austin. The charges included cases of murder, flogging and torture of prisoners, drunkenness, and assault. The Porvenir massacre was the single most serious case before the committee.[408]

Canales took the floor to describe the condition of the Texas Rangers: "There are now and have been for some time, in the state Ranger force men of desperate character, notoriously known as gunmen, their only qualification being they can kill a man first and then investigate afterward. The character of these men is notorious and well known and the Adjutant General is either negligent in the selection of his men or else it his policy to have such characters in the Ranger force to terrorize and intimidate the citizens of the state."[409]

The result of the Canales investigation was the complete reorganization of the Texas Rangers. They were reduced from twelve to four companies not to exceed fifteen privates, a sergeant, and a captain in each. The Texas Legislature passed a law stating that any person could make charges against a state Ranger and that the adjutant was required to begin legal action if the evidence was sufficient. The committee, however, closed its investigation without hearing any of the Porvenir evidence when it ran short on time and adjourned.[410]

The public reprimand and dismissal, however, were the only actions taken against Fox and the Company B Rangers, no criminal charges were filed. This is probably because the Rangers had a great deal of support in the Anglo community of West Texas. During the Canales investigation, a large group of ranchers from Terrell, Brewster, Jeff Davis, Presidio, Hudspeth, Culberson, and El Paso counties traveled to Austin to ask that the Ranger force be increased to a thousand men in the border country to protect them from more raiding.[411]

While the army, the State of Texas, and most Anglo Texans wanted to forget the atrocity at Porvenir, Harry Warren would not let the matter rest. The aging teacher continued to pursue the Porvenir massacre case before the United States Court of Claims until his death in 1932. Although the Porvenir case remained pending until 1946, the court never heard it. The Porvenir massacre is one of the better-documented examples of the reign of terror imposed on the Mexican population living along the Rio Grande between 1915 and 1920. Within weeks, a Mexican reprisal for the innocent blood spilled at Porvenir would strike at the Neville Ranch as the violence continued.[412]

"When I got back I found that my son had been shot all to pieces. There was a hole in his forehead. You could drop a hen egg through this hole.... He had been beat with rifles and a stick, and he was black and blue all over his face and head...The Mexican woman was dead in the kitchen. Everything in the house was torn upside down, scattered all over, and everything gone. Nothing was there except some empty boxes, empty trunks, old bedsteads; everything else was carried away".

Ed Neville

The Neville Ranch Raid and the Burning of Pilares

Chapter 9

If the Rangers thought intimidation of border Mexicans would end the raiding, they were sorely mistaken, for the Porvenir massacre only provoked more trouble in the upper Big Bend. Two months after the event, a group of Mexican raiders, including several relatives of the murdered Mexicans at Porvenir, retaliated by attacking the northern Presidio County ranch of Ed Neville.[413]

When Edwin Watts (Ed) Neville purchased a new 1917 Liberty truck to haul supplies to his out-of-the way ranch on the Mexican border, the forty-nine-year-old rancher anticipated remaining on the Rio Grande in spite of the continuing trouble. The ranch extended northward, along the Rio Grande from Presidio County, into Jeff Davis County and southern Hudspeth County. While large, Neville's ranch was not nearly as prosperous as Luke Brite's spread atop the Candelaria rim rock, several miles away. Neville's ranch lay in the rugged desert river country, much different from the rolling grassland of the Brite ranch. After the Brite raid, Neville moved his wife and two daughters to the safety of Van Horn while he and his son, Glen, continued to live on the lower part of their border ranch. Located about a hundred yards from the Rio Grande, Neville's crude ranch house lay six miles upriver from Porvenir.[414]

On Neville's place, water was scarce; the Rio Grande provided the only surface water. To alleviate his water shortage, he trapped rainwater by damming dry washes or arroyos, creating an earthen reservoir called a tank. Neville built a number of tanks on his ranch; in early 1918 he was building one near his ranch house to provide irrigation water for farming vegetables and raising hay. The rancher hired Mexican workers from Porvenir and Pilares who returned to their homes at the end of each week. Several of the men employed by Neville escaped being murdered by the Rangers at Porvenir because they were away working on the Neville tank when the massacre occurred.[415]

When Neville's Mexican workers learned of the massacre at Porvenir, they demanded their wages from the rancher, saying they intended to go back to Mexico and join Pancho Villa's army. Neville made a special trip to town and returned with the payroll for his men. The Mexicans thanked Neville for their pay and told him that they did not blame him for the murders at Porvenir. The workers, with the exception of Adrian Castillo and his wife and son, lcft for what was described by one source as a Villista camp just across the river.[416]

Ed Neville never completed his dam and irrigation project. Two months after the massacre at Porvenir, on March 25, 1917, Neville went to Van Horn on his monthly supply trip and met an American cavalry patrol. The soldiers told the rancher about a report of an impending raid that had been passed on by some river Mexicans. Neville became concerned about the rumor and left Van Horn about 10:30 that morning, reaching his ranch before sundown. He ate supper and talked with his son Glen about what he had heard. Glen told his father that everything had been quiet at the ranch. As the two discussed the rumor, they heard the tramp of feet outside the ranch house. Ed Neville went down the hall, looked out through the screen door, and saw some fifty Mexican raiders, who started shooting at the house. The bullets easily penetrated the walls, forcing the elder Neville to run outside for the cover of a ditch some three hundred yards distant. As he ran, he called for his son to follow. When Glen charged out the door of the ranch house, the raiders shot the young man, mortally wounding him. Additionally, the raiders beat the dying cowboy with rifle butts when they stormed into the house.[417]

Meanwhile, with bullets flying all around, the elder Neville reached the safety of the ditch where he hid. He wandered through the darkness until early the next morning, occasionally hearing the raiders talking and looting the house before their departure about 3:30 A.M. He recognized one of the raiders as Jesus Nieves, a twenty-four-year-old Mexican from San Antonio, Chihuahua. Shortly after the raiders concluded the attack and escaped back across the border, the cavalrymen of Troop G, led by Major Anderson, arrived at the Neville ranch.[418]

One of the troopers, Cpl. Bob Keil, one of the troopers who had been present at the Porvenir bloodletting, recalled later that they heard Ed Neville calling from the darkness as the patrol rode up. They found Glen Neville shot in the head and knee, moaning deliriously near the door of the ranch house.[419] According to Cpl. Keil, the troopers carried the dying youth into the house, they came upon a grisly scene. Also according to Keil, after murdering the cook, Rosa Castillo, by shooting her in the head and the chest, the raiders mutilated the woman by cutting off her breasts and laying them on the floor on both sides of her body, which they left sitting in an upright position against a wall of the ranch house. The soldiers found the woman's small son, Jose, standing near his mother's body and crying. The child had a serious head wound and had probably been left for dead by the raiders. The woman's other two young children were also in the kitchen. They had not been wounded but had witnessed their mother's death. Nineteen-year-old Glen Neville died of his wounds at 6:00 A.M. It should be noted that Cpl. Keil's account of the multination of Rosa Castillo was disputed by her son, Jose. "My mother, Clara, was accidentally killed. She was not disfigured as some reported." 420

By dawn, the cavalry troopers found a well-marked trail left by the raiders; it led to the Rio Grande through several cut barbed wire fences. Since the G Troop patrol had only 31 men, Major Anderson waited for reinforcements before crossing the border in pursuit of the bandits. When word of the raid reached Marfa, Colonel Langhorne dispatched the men of A Troop, along with their mounts and gear. The troopers rode railroad cattle cars to Valentine and, proceeding from there on horseback, arrived at Neville's ranch at 3:00 P.M. These reinforcements included several expert trackers, a pack train, and a machine gun troop, some ninety men in all. They crossed the Rio Grande in pursuit of the raiders on the evening of the twenty-fifth. The American column proceeded west, across the Sierra Pilares, camping for the night on the T. O. Ranch at Alto Puerto, Chihuahua.[421]

At 4:00 a.m. the following day, the Americans again picked up the trail, which led back through the Sierra Pilares to the small village of Pilares, Chihuahua, on the Rio Grande. Pilares consisted of about a dozen squalid adobe huts. When the cavalrymen were about 800 yards away, Mexican riflemen in the village and atop some steep cliffs behind it began shooting. The Americans established a firing line, deployed the machine gun squad armed with Browning automatic rifles, and charged the village.[422]

Upon seeing the charge of the Americans, most of the Mex i-cans, including a number of women and children, fled in terror to the nearby mountains. The riflemen also retreated as the Americans poured into the village, and a fierce gunfight took place. The cavalrymen chased the Mexicans out of the village and pursued some as far as eleven or more miles into the mountains, killing thirty-three and wounding eight others. One American trooper, Pvt. Carl Alberts, died in the cavalry charge when he was shot from his horse.[423]

After the fight, the Americans searched the huts in Pilares, where they found a considerable number of German-made Mauser rifles, plus ammunition and dynamite, some of which was being made into bombs or grenades of the type employed by the Villista cavalry at Ojinaga. Among the dead, the troopers found the body of the leader of the raiders, Jesus Urias, who by one account was a Villista. Another of the dead Mexicans wore Glen Neville's chaps, another the murdered cowboy's boots. Two or three of Ed Neville's horses also turned up in Pilares, as well as some jewelry recognized as having belonged to Neville.[424]

Some evidence surfaced at Pilares linking the dead raiders to the Brite raid, including letters and postcards stolen from Mickey Welch, the mail driver killed at Brite. Many of the dead bandits wore some sort of Carrancista military apparel or insignia; this may have indicated that they wished to implicate Carranza in the raid but more likely, they were willing to wear any clothes that came their way. The cavalrymen then burned Pilares, leaving one adobe hut, occupied by a Mexican woman and her child who pleaded that their home be spared.[425]

The troops did not remain in the smoking ruins of Pilares for long. By the time the column crossed the border in pursuit of the raiders, the Carrancista commander in Ojinaga, General Murguia had protested the intrusion of U.S. troops on Mexican soil and sent some five hundred cavalrymen to stop the Americans. When the Americans burned Pilares, these Carrancista cavalrymen were not far away, and the approach of the Mexican troops prompted Major Anderson to order his men back across the Rio Grande shortly before sundown on the 26th. The cavalrymen returned to Camp Evetts after having been in the saddle for fourteen hours; they covered seventy-two miles in the day's pursuit.[426]

Who were the Neville raiders? Initial army reports named only three of the thirty-three dead, but further investigations tied twenty-four other Mexicans to the attack. According to the army, several Neville raiders were former residents of Porvenir or had close relatives killed by the Rangers during the massacre. Eighteen-year-old Francisco Gonzales, for example, was the son of Eutimio Gonzales, whom the Rangers took to the San Carlos railroad tunnel before murdering him at Porvenir. Another Neville raider, Luis Jimenez, may have been related to one of the three members of the Jimenez family, including the youngest Porvenir massacre victim, sixteen-year-old Juan Jimenez. One other former Porvenir resident named as a Neville raider was Juan Sanchez who, although he lost no family in the massacre, lost his home at Porvenir. A final raider identified by army intelligence was Juan Rodriquez, who had worked on the building of Neville's dam before the raid.[427]

One explanation for the Neville raid, therefore, is that it was an act of vengeance carried out by relatives of victims of the Porvenir massacre and that Ed Neville's ranch was simply the most convenient target. Robbery likely could not have been a prime motive in the raid, for the rancher had little to steal. The cruel murder of Rosa Castillo in front of her children and the battering of Glen Neville appear to be acts designed to terrorize those living on the Texas side and provoke an emotional response. Some of the raiders were clearly motivated by the murders at Porvenir.[428]

Again, as at the Brite raid, possible political motivations of the raiders are difficult to access. Some evidence indicates that the bandits might have been Villistas; however, the proof is far from conclusive. Revenge for the Porvenir massacre appears to be the prime motivation for the raid. The possibility of Carrancista involvement in the Neville raid is remote. 8 th Cavalry Capt. J.S. Tate, who accompanied Major Anderson on the American expedition, noted, "There is absolutely no evidence that there were any Carrancista soldiers implicated in the raid on Neville's ranch, nor in the engagement at Pilares, Chihuahua."[429]

In November 1918, following the Neville raid, special orders r egarding American military pursuits on Mexican territory were issued to the 8 th Cavalry, changing earlier policies. American troops under the command of commissioned officers could now cross the Rio Grande in pursuit of bandits or livestock thieves in an area from Ojinaga to Pilares. These orders permitted a surge of American crossings, many of which resulted in tragic clashes with the Mexican civilian population. These American crossings in the upper Big Bend continued until August 1919, when the last American punitive expedition crossed into Mexico at Candelaria.[430]

These military forays did little to satisfy Ed Neville's desire for revenge. After the raid Neville buried his son, sold his river ranch, and moved to Marfa where he operated the Long Horn Cafe for many years. Neville, however, could not put the loss of his son behind him and, following his appointment as a Special Texas Ranger began hunting down Mexicans he suspected of participating in the raid. His vendetta became an "intimate part of Neville's life," one that continued for many years. He went out nights, after he had closed his restaurant, searching Mexican houses in and around Marfa for different men he suspected. On many of these searches, he went with Texas Ranger Jeff Vaughn and others. Neville's daughter recalled that her father kept a black book with some sixty names in it and over the years until his death in 1952, he scratched out many of the names in the book. Marfa is a small town, so it is highly unlikely that no one knew of Neville's vigilante campaign. The fact that his behavior was tolerated says much about the hatred and fear Anglo border communities had for the flood of Mexicans who came across the Rio Grande fleeing the revolution.[431]

"The waters of the Rio Grande in the upper Big Bend, as they flow to the sea, are ever murmuring the funeral dirge of innocent human beings cruelly slain; and in the soughing of the night winds among the rock hills, or in the lonely valleys, their sepulchral voices are heard pleading for common justice... These poor creatures were taken unresisting from their homes and murdered. Some were shot in the back; one in the belly, one in the head and one riddled with lead. Some were killed pleading for their lives; others shot down, begging for time to pray, trying to kiss, with their blood stained lips, the feet of their executioners. Oh God of mercy, how they groaned and writhed while dying, their staring eyes fixed on those who were killing them."

J.J. Kilpatrick Sr., 1919

Sotol, Ransom, And The Last American Punitive Expedition Into Mexico

Chapter 10

The Great War in Europe came to an end on Armistice Day, November 11,1918, and American troops began to filter back across the Atlantic. Meanwhile the 8th Cavalry continued to guard the border in the upper Big Bend. Border duty for the cavalrymen became monotonous and lonely, as the troopers conducted routine drills, marches, and constant patrols of the Rio Grande. World War I demonstrated the obsolescence of the mounted horseman in an effective fighting force. Only in the rugged terrain of the Mexican border did mounted troops continue to be of use to the U.S. Army, and that use was to be short-lived. Border duty was a dreary, unpleasant assignment for the troopers, many of them members of the National Guard who had been pressed into the cavalry because they were farm boys with knowledge of horses. The hero prestige enjoyed by the returning European veteran reduced the once-proud American horse soldier to a second-class status. This erosion of status, combined with the loneliness of border duty, made the cavalry ripe for trouble.[432]

In these last days of the mounted cavalry much new military technology came to the border, reviving the horse soldiers' military effectiveness. When the American troops came home from

Europe, so did the fledgling American air corps, which was soon to be assigned to border duty. In June 1919 the 20th Aero Squadron, consisting of twenty-nine flying officers and twelve De Haviland DH-4 airplanes and their ground crews, arrived at Fort Bliss in El Paso, Texas, to begin daily air patrols of the border from Nogales, Arizona, to Boquillas, Texas. When they returned from Europe, the 12th, 96th, and 104th Aero Squadrons also joined the border patrol at Fort Bliss, forming the First Surveillance Group of the United States Army Air Corps.[433]

The air patrol brought much change to cavalry operations in the Big Bend military district. A DH-4 could fly from Marfa to the border in forty-five minutes over the same rugged terrain that took mounted cavalrymen more than a day to cover. The airplanes were also more versatile. They could be used for patrol, surveillance, scouting, and carrying messages that were dropped from the planes to the cavalrymen below.[434]

While military use of the airplane proved to be a tremendous technical advance, aviation was in its infancy. The border air patrol experienced many problems when it brought its DH-4s to the desert environment of the upper Big Bend. The DH-4, not famous for rugged construction, became known as a "flaming coffin" by those hearty individuals brave enough to fly them. The 440 horsepower V-12 Liberty engines in the DH-4 were water cooled, and many times they overheated when flying at low altitudes over the desert. Since there was no satisfactory oil for the Liberty at that time, the engine would not withstand sustained flying; frequently the main bearings in the engine seized, causing the engine to burn up. Dirt in gasoline also frequently caused the Liberty engine to stop running, often with disastrous results. In the upper Big Bend, there were few airfields, and a forced landing in the rocky terrain invariably ended in a fiery crash. In part, this resulted from the plane's design. The DH-4's axle, or spreader bar between the wheels of the landing gear, had less than a foot of ground clearance. In forced landings in the rough terrain of the border, rocks taller than the spreader bar flipped the airplane up on its nose or over on its back with disastrous results.[435]

In spite of the many problems the army experienced with the primitive DH-4, the First Surveillance Group managed to patrol two thousand miles of international border on a daily basis by 1919. The river patrol flights were a welcome sight to Americans living in remote areas and served as a demonstration of the military might of the United States to Villista bands roaming the other side of the river.[436]

American pilots had orders that prohibited their flying over the border, but as one flyer recalled: "Officially, we were not to fly across the border, but if we were curious about the terrain or inspired by any other reason that might occur to a young pilot flying over that isolated area, we did sometimes fly over to investigate. No reports were made of these deviations unless the sightings obtained were considered important."[437]

In June 1919, the U.S. Army drove Pancho Villa from the city of Juarez, in his last major military defeat. Rumors circulated that he had again retreated to the upper Big Bend. Therefore, the top priority of the fledgling border air patrol was to locate Villa in the mountains of the Chihuahuan Desert. On the ground, the troopers of the 8 th Cavalry also looked for Villa. Restrictions against American troops crossing into Mexico in the upper Big Bend had been relaxed to allow the army to pursue horse and cattle thieves into Mexico even if they had not committed raids on United States soil. This relaxation of the rules prohibiting border crossings were a result of the Brite and Neville raids and of the end of World War I. Thus, with the war in Europe over, the U.S. Army was again prepared to intervene in Mexico.[438]

In addition to looking for Villa and cattle rustlers, the American cavalry hunted smugglers. From the time the Rio Grande was made an international boundary, the upper Big Bend area had been a haven for smugglers. Contraband ranged from weapons and stolen cattle to illegal liquor. Shortly before passage of the Volstead Enforcement Act and national prohibition in 1920, the U.S. Army set out to stop the smuggling of sotol, a fiery and potent liquor made from the bulb of the sotol cactus. It had good reason to do so because the sotol smugglers found considerable demand for their liquor among the American troopers stationed at the border outposts.[439]

After numerous incidents of drunkenness among the American soldiers, the Big Bend Military District adopted a prohibition against the drinking or possession of sotol by troopers, with offenders subject to court-martial. As problems with drunken men increased at border outposts, the army dealt sternly with repeat offenders by rank reduction and transfer. For example, in an investigation of sotol drinking by Troop M, stationed at Ruidosa in September 1918, Capt. Lester A. Sprinkle said that five cavalrymen, among them the cook, were being transferred because the men were “addicted to the use of sotol and apt to cause trouble in the future." The army tracked down the smuggler selling sotol to the soldiers at Ruidosa; a few days later he died in a gunfight with an 8 th Cavalry lieutenant in Barrancas, the Mexican border town across from Ruidosa.[440]

Sotol drinking similarly plagued the cavalry post at Candelaria. In spite of army prohibitions, members of Troop K continued to carry on a lively sotol trade from several saloons across the Rio Grande in San Antonio, Chihuahua. According to J. J. Kilpatrick, smugglers made regular trips to the army camp bringing sotol for the soldiers. When two youthful Mexican smugglers crossed the river near the cavalry camp, they were ambushed and murdered.[441]

Kilpatrick said he discovered the bodies in the river near several bottles of sotol after he heard a fusillade of shots about 9:30 P.M. June first. The following morning, in the wet sand of the river bank, the King of Candelaria found a number of spent shell casings from a government issue forty-five caliber automatic pistol and the tracks of two persons who wore army boots with the distinctive "double E" soldier-shape, the kind worn by the cavalry troopers. Kilpatrick concluded that American soldiers had killed the Mexican youths, one fifteen and the other twenty-one years old.[442]

The murder of the two Mexicans created a great outpouring of grief across the river in San Antonio, Chihuahua. As Kilpatrick described it: "Their bodies were taken to the Mexico side where a small crowd of excited men, women and children gathered. The men were protesting against the injustice and wrongs of *Los Americanos*. The women were weeping, and the children crying. A white-haired-old squaw, when she recognized the older of the boys, crossed her bosom and uttering a loud scream, fell in a faint by the side of the corpse. A woman with several small children hanging to her shabby dress and howling, came wringing her hands and sat down by the body of the younger boy, and taking it, all muddy and wet in her arms, she cried as if her heart would break. It was his mother and kissing his lifeless lips, she exclaimed, *O Muchacho mio*, why did the *Gringos malos* (villains) kill you, dear. You who never harmed anyone? Surely they had no pity and no mercy for the *Mexicanos Pobres* (poor people) and are worse than *los banditos* (the bandits), who rob us but spare us the lives of our children."[443]

According to Kilpatrick, the Mexicans of San Antonio believed the boys were murdered to steal their sotol. However, Kilpatrick conjectured, "...two or more soldiers might have committed the deed thinking their superior wished it done to stop the smuggling of sotol. Lieutenant Turner himself hinted to me that this might have been the real explanation of the killing. Anyway, if true, such a drastic method did not stop the happy liquor sprees of the soldiers; for according to Mexican testimony, some of them slipped over the river and got themselves the fiery stuff trading it when they had no money, for blankets, shirts, etc."[444]

If Kilpatrick's story is credited, the killings happened when Capt. Leonard F. Matlack, commander of Troop K at Candelaria, was away from the camp. When the captain returned and learned of the incident, he ordered Troop K to the banks of the Rio Grande and sent a message for the people of San Antonio to assemble immediately on the opposite river bank. Fearing reprisals if they did not obey, the Mexicans of San Antonio came to the river, where the American captain gave them a stern lecture on selling sotol. Matlack did not speak fluent Spanish, so he used an interpreter to tell the Mexicans that if they did not stop selling sotol to his men, the army would destroy San Antonio. This was a threat the Mexicans did not take lightly, since American troops previously had burned the nearby village of Buena Vista to the ground; the Mexicans also remembered the Porvenir and Pilares retaliations. According to Kilpatrick, a drunken Mexican yelled to the interpreter, "Tell the Captain I'll sell sotol to whom I please--even to President Wilson were he to come over here and want to buy it." But as the merchant recalled, the fellow had second thoughts after his defiant talk and "...thinking his life wouldn't be worth a tortilla if this Gringo Captain got hold of him, he took cold feet and fled to parts unknown." But Matlack's warnings went unheeded, the American soldiers continued drinking sotol, and the San Antonio saloons supplied the demand. If Kilpatrick can be believed, Matlack's threat to destroy San Antonio reflected an increasingly aggressive attitude on the part of local army officers toward border Mexicans as relations between the two groups worsened.[445]

Trouble between Troop K and the Mexicans persisted and soon led to open clashes between American troops and Mexican irregulars known as *defensas sociales*. The *sociales* were volunteer corps loyal to Carranza; Carranza gave them arms and support in return for their patrolling frontier areas outside the reach of regular *Carrancista* troops and fighting against Villa. Given official sanction by Mexican law in 1922, the *sociales* were employed extensively in Chihuahua as popular support of Villa began to erode after 1915 and he resumed guerrilla tactics. The community defense by the *sociales*, who fought off Villista as well as Carrancista attacks on their villages, was not understood by Americans, who saw any armed Mexican irregular as a bandit or outlaw.[446]

In 1919 the *defensas sociales* operating near San Antonio, Chihuahua, were led by Chico Cano, a revolutionary leader with a somewhat questionable reputation. American lawmen and army officials branded Chico Cano as a bandit and cattle thief and made numerous attempts to apprehend him. Official U.S. Army records state that he and one of his men, Placido Zapata, had taken part in the Neville raid. Cano's problems with American authorities began in 1912 when he and nine of his men smuggled a herd of horses and mules into Texas and ran into trouble with American lawmen. Mexican revolutionaries frequently financed their military operations by selling stolen *hacienda* cattle and horses in the United States. In 1913 U.S. Customs Inspectors Jack Howard and Joe Sitters spotted Cano in the United States and arrested him for smuggling livestock into the country. The following day, as the lawmen escorted their prisoner to Marfa, the party was ambushed by a group of Mexicans seeking to free Cano. The fight left Howard dead and Sitters badly wounded while Cano escaped unharmed.[447]

Following the ambush, Chico Cano became a hunted man while he continued to be involved in the fighting in Mexico. During the revolution, he was loyal to several different factions beginning with Pascual Orozco and the dreaded "red flaggers." Sometime after Villa's victory at Ojinaga in 1914, Cano joined the Villista cause. During the early part of 1917, he and Gen. Jose Ynez Salazar commanded two Villista forces operating near Ojinaga. U.S. Army intelligence reported in May of 1917 that a serious break between the two took place. According to these reports, Salazar's men took part in several rapes and other crimes that outraged Cano. Cano had relatives and friends living along the river in the upper Big Bend and did not approve of such conduct. When he learned that Salazar planned to attack Candelaria, Cano sent word to Salazar that he would assist the Americans by attacking the Villistas from the rear. Cano also warned the American military of Salazar's plans. Salazar made no attack on Candelaria and when his supplies ran low, his men deserted, many of them joining Cano's forces. Following the break with Salazar, Cano became anxious to make friends with the Carrancistas as well as the Americans.[448]

Cano's efforts to patch things up with the Americans failed, and the army continued to try to capture him. In late June 1919 Troop K and Troop M, commanded by Captain Matlack, crossed into Mexico, ostensibly in pursuit of cattle thieves. The mission, however, soon turned into a deadly manhunt. When the captain and his men rode into San Antonio, they questioned the people as to the whereabouts of Cano. They learned that Cano and his men were heading up the Rio Grande, north of San Antonio. Beginning pursuit, the Americans split up, Troop M crossing the Rio Grande to continue the search in Texas and Troop K riding up the Mexican side. Later, a small detachment of Troop K, under the command of Lieutenant Turner, came to the Melendez house, near San Antonio, where they found Esmenegilde Dominguez, another suspected Neville raider. When the lieutenant attempted to arrest Dominguez, the Mexican, who was drunk, resisted. A couple of the troopers attempted to lasso him, and when he tried to escape into the house, a soldier drew his pistol and shot Dominguez in the back. The bullet passed through his body, severely wounding him and striking a young child standing in the doorway of the house. The severely wounded Mexican man was arrested and carried back to the Candelaria camp. The Americans left the badly wounded child behind after rendering medical aid. Back in the United States, Dominguez was tried, convicted of being a Neville raider, and sent to jail.[449]

Meanwhile, Chico Cano and his patrol headed upriver at a slow pace, unaware of the American troops in pursuit. At noon the following day, Cano and his men stopped at El Comedor on the Rio Grande to cook and eat dinner. Following their usual custom, the Mexicans pulled off their boots, spurs, and bandoleers and lay down to take a siesta. Shortly thereafter, Captain Matlack and his scout, Jesus Cabezuela, leading Troop K, rode up to the Mexicans. One of Cano's men awoke, saw the Americans, and in panic fired a shot. The cavalrymen were as surprised as the aroused *sociales*, but the fight was on. In a quick but decisive skirmish, Troop K swept Cano's camp with machine-gun fire, killing five of his men. Cano and three others escaped into the thick mesquite along the riverbank. In his flight into the brush, Cano left his boots and spurs and found himself barefoot.[450]

The following day, his feet badly bruised and cut, Cano came to the riverbank near Candelaria to buy a pair of shoes. He related to J. J. Kilpatrick his surprise at the American attack: "I had no idea that Captain Matlack was after us. Had I known it, my men and I, on leaving Boquillas, where we spent the night, would have scattered, taken to the hills, and made for the mountainous Gordo Trail, where one man could hold back a hundred. I had been down the river on a scout the day before Captain Matlack passed through San Antonio, and was on my way to Pilares to confer with Jim [Kilpatrick] in regards to the re-settlement of the farms on the Mexican side. Captain Matlack himself had requested my co-operation in inducing the people to return to their abandoned homes along the river."[451]

According to the Kilpatrick account, Cano recalled his previous relationship with the American captain. "It seemed, that while I was a Villista I had no difficulty in getting along with the Captain. He and I were great friends. Several times he invited me over to his camp and watered [sic] and dined me, making numerous presents from the United States Government's storeroom. From the many things he said to me, I inferred that he wanted me to act as chief spy on the Mexican side of the river. More than once, I was warned to be on my guard against this cunning officer. Not believing, however, that a captain in the United States Army was other than what he seemed to be I paid little attention to the friendly admonition."[452]

"Since turning Carrancista, it appears, Captain Matlack lost his friendship for me, and finally fell upon me with a hundred men to eight, and made a desperate attempt to assassinate me, yet I am the same person I was when he used to water [sic] and dine me and introduce me to his officer friends. Why the Captain wanted to take my life, I do not know, for I have never harmed a single American or committed any crime on the soil of the United States."[453]

Cano's bewilderment over the American attack after he lost his usefulness as a spy for American intelligence was shared by others. The municipal president of San Antonio, Chihuahua, sent a report of the attack on Cano's men to the governor of the state, protesting the killing and proclaiming the innocence of the dead. The Mexican official said he saw the bodies of Placido Zapata, Roman Segura, Pedro Salas, and Carlos Levario at El Comedor after they had been killed by the Troop K and that no witnesses could be found to explain the reason for their deaths. The incident caused "great indignation" against Troop K on the Mexican side of the river as tensions between the two countries increased. The Mexico City *El Excelsior* newspaper echoed the Mexican outrage over the American attack of the *sociales* patrol.[454]

In Washington, the crossing into Mexico by Troop K and the Mexican outcry over the killings touched off discussions in both houses of Congress. New Mexico Sen. Albert B. Fall seized the opportunity to try to discredit the Carranza government on the floor of the United States Senate by blaming the Mexican president for the troubles on the border. Hoping to link Carranza to the upper Big Bend raids, Fall inaccurately charged that since the Brite Raid of December 1917, more than a dozen Carrancista officers and men had been killed by American troops in the upper Big Bend. He included in his list of Carrancista raiders the dead Villista shot by Sam Neill and the members of Cano's *sociales* patrol killed by Troop K in Mexico. The senator wanted to bring about a U.S. military intervention in Mexico. He personally owned extensive mining interests in northern Mexico and the revolution had caused him to lose a great deal of money on his investments. Supported by American investors and oil men who were frightened by Carranza's nationalism and by the 1917 Mexican Constitution, which declared all of the subsoil mineral rights to be the property of the nation, Fall wanted to overthrow Carranza and place a more sympathetic leader in the Mexican government.[455]

Senator Fall's supporters included the membership of the National Association for the Protection of American Rights in Mexico. Made up of some of the largest American investors in Mexico, the association represented businessmen who were engaged in agriculture, banking, mining, and petroleum. Some of the more prominent members were the Chase National Bank, J.P. Morgan and Company, The Texas Company, Standard Oil of New Jersey, and the Pan-American Petroleum and Transport Company headed by Edward L. Doheny. Doheny was later accused of bribing Fall in the infamous Teapot Dome oil scandal. Although a jury found Doheny not guilty of giving a bribe, Fall went to prison for accepting $100,000 for federal oil leases he administered as Secretary of the Interior in the Harding administration.[456]

Texas Company subsidiaries alone controlled over 4.5 million acres in northeast Mexico. By 1919 the association, through Senator Fall, had demanded that northern Mexico be annexed to the United States or that a protectorate over the entire country be established following a U.S. military invasion. Other activities of the association included the monitoring of newspapers, labor groups, Socialists, suspected Bolsheviks, and other individuals who challenged Senator Fall's calls for intervention or the aims of the organization.[457]

J. J. Kilpatrick ran afoul of the association when he began to write inflammatory articles and letters to newspapers criticizing Senator Fall and the anti-Carranza U. S. Senate *Investigation of Mexican Affairs.* In response, Charles H. Boynton, executive director of the association, wrote the Bureau of Investigation (later the Federal Bureau of Investigation) that the Kilpatrick family, whom Boynton called "the nucleus of all deviltry in that country," should be "closely watched." The Bureau of Investigation took no action against Kilpatrick although Matlack made a number of serious charges.[458]

Meanwhile, Brig. Gen. James B. Erwin, commander of the El Paso Military District, also challenged Senator Fall's charges against the Carranza government. Erwin, whose command extended from Columbus, New Mexico, to Fort Hancock, Texas, stated that his troops had found no evidence to suggest a Carrancista involvement in any of the border raids. In Candelaria, Kilpatrick expressed similar feelings by writing, "I must say the truth of Rio Grande history in the Big Bend demands that Senator Fall's statements should be challenged and the flimsy and false evidence upon which they are founded exposed."[459]

While Senator Fall and the Association for the Protection of American Rights in Mexico hoped to engineer an intervention, one came about for other reasons. At 9:30 A.M. on Sunday, 10 August, two American flyers took off from the Marfa airfield in a DH-4 on a routine border patrol flight. Lt. H. G. Peterson, the pilot, and Lt. Paul H. Davis, the observer-gunner, flew to Lajitas on the Rio Grande, and turned upstream heading for Bosque Bonito. When the Americans flew over Presidio, Texas, they mistook the swollen Rio Conchos, which flows into the Rio Grande at Ojinaga, for the Rio Grande and flew into Mexico.[460]

At 11:30 a.m. the two Americans noticed a railroad bridge that did not appear on their map, and realized they were lost. A short time later, while flying over a mountain range, the rigging on one of the wings collapsed, forcing the plane down. At 12:30, Peterson crashed the DH-4 atop a mesa. The two flyers were uninjured but they were completely lost in Mexico and more than one hundred miles from the border.[461]

The railroad bridge that Peterson and Davis saw was actually the only railroad bridge crossing the Rio Conchos in the area at Falomir, Chihuahua. Taking a compass and a canteen, the pair struck out walking for the bridge at 1:30 P.M. After walking for two hours in the heat of the day, they ran low on water and abandoned their trek to the bridge to look for water in the river-bed. After several hours they found a small pool of water in a worn rock in the river bottom and drank all of it. Unable to sleep because of their thirst, the two flyers walked most of the night before finding a ranch house where they bought water, tortillas, and coffee.[462]

A Mexican at the ranch house directed the two Americans back to the Rio Conchos, and they tried to head downriver through the rough desert mountains. At one point, they attempted to swim down the river but were unable to do so because of the swift current. By Monday morning, August 11th, the aviators reached the irrigation settlement of Sabaco, Chihuahua, on a crude raft they had constructed. Peterson described their progress: "It was the roughest kind of going. Often we had to pull ourselves over cliffs by our hands. At 5:30 o'clock, airships passed over us. We did our best to attract their attention, but owing to the clouds, they were compelled to fly over the mountains and unable to see us. We estimated that we swam 28 miles. Peterson was so hungry that he ate several buckeye nuts which later made him sick.... While swimming down the river, we were sucked under twice by eddies, so we decided it was unsafe to continue, so we went to sleep with a rock for a bed. Peterson nearly grabbed a rattlesnake in groping his way among the rocks and I came within several feet of another one."[463]

After the two flyers left Sabaco, Peterson and Davis found themselves surrounded by six armed Mexicans who took them prisoner. Peterson and Davis were led away from the Rio Concho and into the mountains, where the group traveled north for the next two days, stopping to get food at ranches; they headed to San Antonio.[464] Peterson and Davis had fallen into the hands of Jesus Renteria, a Mexican whom Kilpatrick described as "an all around thief, with a predilection for horse stealing." Renteria once worked for a railroad in Kansas where he was involved in an accident in which he lost his right arm and leg. Because he was maimed, he was also called "Mocho" or "Corkleg," referring to his wooden leg. In place of his right hand Renteria was said to have had a hook, further adding to his fearsome appearance.[465] During the days that followed, Peterson established something of a relationship with his captor by talking to Renteria, who spoke English, about Kansas. Mocho took a liking to the young American and sometimes allowed him to ride without a guard. On several occasions, Peterson boldly argued with Renteria about his capture, only to have the bandit repeatedly reply "Do you want to die now?" Peterson then judiciously turned the conversation back to talk about Kansas which seemed to bring out Renteria's less violent side.[466]

On August 17 th, a week after their crash, the two captives reached the mountains near San Antonio. From a hiding place near the village, Renteria wrote a note addressed to Dawkins Kilpatrick, the Candelaria storekeeper and son of J. J. Kilpatrick, demanding a ransom of $15,000 for the aviators' release. Renteria also permitted the two flyers to write notes to be telegraphed to their parents. Peterson wired his mother in Hutchinson, Minnesota: "Davis and myself had forced landing in Texas on Border. Were captured by Villistas, Mexican bandits, and are being held for $15,000 ransom to be paid to Dawkins Kilpatrick, storekeeper in Candelaria, Texas, not later than August 18 or we will be killed. Correspond with Secretary of War, Major Walton, First Bombing Group, El Paso, and Dr. Warren Davis, Strathmore, California. I am in good health and spirits as I am sure the War Department will meet ransom. If not, goodbye, as they mean business. Love and don't worry."[467]

Although Renteria's ransom note was addressed to Dawkins Kilpatrick, a messenger delivered it to Captain Matlack at Camp Kenney. The following day, the younger Kilpatrick responded to Renteria, saying that he needed more time to raise the money, and setting in motion a series of negotiations. Upon learning the ransom demands, Washington sent a strongly worded telegram to the Carranza government demanding Mexican help in obtaining the release of the pilots. Carranza replied personally, promising to cooperate by dispatching troops to the upper Big Bend. In Washington, the War Department authorized the payment of the ransom, but getting the cash to Candelaria in time to meet Renteria's demands was another matter. Fortunately, a group of ranchers attending the Bloys Camp Meeting, an annual revival, pledged the money to be delivered by the First National Bank in Marfa to Captain Matlack at Candelaria.[468]

Once the captain got the ransom money, he set out to free the hostages. Renteria insisted that the money be brought to him in Mexico before he would deliver the aviators. The captain refused to do so because he feared the kidnappers would kill the hostages. In turn, Matlack proposed several plans to deliver the ransom that were rejected by Renteria. On the afternoon of August

18 th, H. N. Fennell of the Marfa National Bank, accompanied by an 8 th Cavalry officer, arrived with the $15,000. The same afternoon, Matlack and Fennell took the money to San Antonio to show it to agents of Renteria. Negotiations between Renteria and Matlack concerning the delivery of the aviators and the payment of the ransom continued through the day and into the night.[469] About midnight, August 19 th, the captain sent a message to Renteria that the time was up and if any harm befell either aviator, Matlack would hold the entire population of San Antonio responsible: Renteria must act within an hour. This was not an idle threat, for some two hundred American cavalrymen stood assembled under the cover of darkness, waiting for orders to charge into San Antonio. Renteria sent back word that he could find no messenger he could trust, but if Matlack would bring half the money into Mexico, his agents would meet him with one aviator, who would be released. The exchange was to begin when a signal flare was lighted on a mountain west of San Antonio. Renteria failed to send the signal, and after waiting a short time, Matlack rode into Mexico down an old trail from the ford to San Antonio. On this trail, Matlack met one of Renteria's agents and made an exchange for Lieutenant Peterson. After taking Peterson safely to the army camp, Matlack again returned to Mexico with the balance of the money to rescue Davis.[470]

Matlack traveled the same trail he had used previously, but when he arrived at the place where he expected Davis to be delivered, he found no one there. The captain waited a short time before he saw Davis and a mounted guard emerge from a nearby cornfield. When Matlack approached, he whispered to Davis to jump up behind him and draw one of his pistols, since the captain had no intention of paying a second ransom. Matlack showed the money to the bandit and, as soon as Davis jumped on the horse behind him, drew his pistol and told the bandit to tell Renteria to "go to hell" before riding off into the darkness with the astonished flyer. Matlack and Davis soon reached Candelaria unharmed by taking a different route to avoid ambush.[471]

With the safe return of Peterson and Davis, the U.S. Army was free to retaliate, thus beginning the last American punitive expedition into Mexico early on the morning of August 19th. After receiving orders from Colonel Langhorne, three columns of troops including Troops C and K, commanded by Captain Matlack, crossed the river at Candelaria in pursuit of Renteria and his accomplices. Simultaneously, Troop A, 5 th Cavalry, and Troop E, 8 th

Cavalry, commanded by Maj. James P. Yancey, crossed at Ruidosa, while Troop C, 5th Cavalry, and a machine-gun troop entered Mexico at Indio. In addition to the troops, Pack Trains 6, 11, 13, and 26 joined the expedition. Each man carried two field rations and one emergency ration; the mules carried two days' grain with three days' reserve rations.[472]

The army thought Renteria and his band would flee south into the mountains, moving as rapidly as possible away from the border to Coyame, Chihuahua, where Renteria had relatives; one of the flyers heard Renteria say that he was going to Coyame to spend his share of the ransom money. The three American columns planned to march to Carrizo Springs, Chihuahua and unite there on August 20 before advancing to Coyame.[473]

Peterson and Davis rode horseback with Troop K, to try to lead the Americans back over the route they had covered the previous week as captives. Texas Rangers, U.S. Customs inspectors, and several civilians joined the expedition as scouts, among them D. D. Kilpatrick, O. C. Dowe, H. B. O'Neill, C. C. Hurst, John Carr, and Pablo Chaves. As the Ruidosa column rode into Barrancas, Chihuahua, it arrested five Mexicans who were wanted in the U.S. as draft evaders and sent them under guard to the Texas side where they were jailed. Because water was scarce, the Candelaria and Ruidosa columns marched to the T. O. Tanks, twenty miles from the border, where they camped for the night. The Indio column camped at the El Toro Tank several miles to the south.[474]

At 5:30 a.m. August 20th, Troop K, led by Captain Matlack, and Troop A, commanded by Capt. J.K. Cowell, marched from T. O. Tanks toward the settlement of Carrizo Springs, Chihuahua, eighteen miles to the south. At 8:00 a.m., the column sighted the village, which consisted of two or three adobe huts. In a scene of fast and scattered action, the Americans charged. Capt. C. R. Neal and ten men rode at a gallop into Carrizo Springs to prevent escape. Meanwhile, the inhabitants of the village, including several women and children, scattered into the hills when they saw the Americans. The civilian scouts pursued two mounted Mexicans over a nearby ridge. About forty-five minutes later, Captain Neal's patrol returned to the main American column with three dismounted Mexican prisoners. Another Mexican was taken prisoner in one of the adobe huts of Carrizo Springs. When the civilian officers accompanying the expedition saw the four prisoners, they identified three of them as criminals on the run from Texas. The prisoners so identified were Jesus Jiner, wanted in United

States for stealing livestock from the Brite Ranch; his son, Francisco Jiner, wanted for breaking his father out of jail; and Jose Fuentes, wanted for the murder of the brother of the expedition's scout, Pablo Chavez. When Chavez recognized his brother's murderer, Major Yancey was told, "Watch Pablo Chavez, he might try to do something to this man." Yancey, however, took no precautions for the safety of the prisoners.[475]

Major Yancey headed the expedition in the direction of Coyame, leaving a patrol under Maj. Paul Frank to watch the village and look for more Mexicans who might try to return that night. The Mexican prisoners, under guard, followed the column on foot. After leaving Carrizo Springs, Yancey ordered Sgt. Ernest (Cook) Fields, one of the cavalrymen escorting the prisoners, to turn them over to the Rangers. The Rangers took charge of the nervous Mexicans and lagged behind the army column a short distance. Suddenly, without warning, the Rangers started shooting their prisoners. When the gunfire started, some of the prisoners broke and ran for their lives but were quickly cut down. Upon hearing the shots, a few of the cavalry troopers riding in the rear guard whirled their horses around in time to see the running prisoners being killed by the Rangers. The commotion caused the column to halt briefly, but Major Yancey ordered the troops to proceed. Later the Rangers rejoined the troopers, but nothing was said about the killings; none of the troopers wanted the Rangers to know they were witnesses.[476]

The expedition left the bodies of the four prisoners where they lay and proceeded on to the Paradero Tank to camp for the night. After establishing a camp, the soldiers discovered a nearby sotol still and obtained two kegs of the liquor. Practically the entire command got roaring drunk, including the expedition's commanding officer, Major Yancey. Only Captains Matlack and Cowell abstained, and they watched as their commanding officer "excelled in libationess." Following an all-night binge, the expedition did not resume until ten o'clock the next morning when the hungover major had to be assisted onto his horse. A short time later, Major Yancey's horse stumbled, pitching the officer, backside first, into a sharply thorned *Pitahayas* cactus. Two army doctors riding nearby "rushed up and stood the warrior on his head" and picked the thorns out before "replacing him in the saddle."[477]

At this point the American army, anxious to avoid a confrontation with Carrancista troops, decided to withdraw. While Carranza had initially indicated that he would help the Americans capture the bandits, the Mexican president's patience quickly wore thin when it appeared the American forces might stay in Chihuahua longer than a few days. On August 21, Carranza protested the continued presence of the American troops to the U.S. State Department. As the American expedition approached Coyame, a sizeable force of Carrancista regulars, dispatched from Ojiniga and Chihuahua, converged on the village from the opposite direction. The *El Paso Times* reported that in San Pedro, Chihuahua, Hipolito Villa had assembled a force of Villistas to fight the Americans.[478]

The troopers were fifteen miles from Coyame when a DH-4 flew over the column and dropped a message from Colonel Langhorne, ordering the expedition to return to Texas. Yancey's command had now been in Mexico three days and had been authorized to remain only if on a hot trail. After a short consultation among the officers, who had heard a report that Renteria was hiding in Coyame, Major Yancey, acting against orders decided to ignore the new command and ride on to Coyame in "hot pursuit," though the trail had long since grown cold. Although Yancey acted against his orders, Colonel Langhorne did not question the major's decision to advance to Coyame.[479]

When the American troops arrived at Coyame, they stayed outside the town and sent Dawkins Kilpatrick, who knew many of the villagers, to talk to the mayor. The mayor asked Kilpatrick who had given the Americans permission to be in Mexico, and Kilpatrick replied that they were in pursuit of bandits and had permission from the Carrancista commander at Ojinaga to do so. The mayor pointed to a place outside the village where the Americans could camp and, after Kilpatrick took his leave, telephoned Gen. Antonio Pruneda, commander at Ojinaga, to check out the story. While in Coyame, Kilpatrick learned that some twelve hundred Carrancista troops were fast approaching and he relayed the information back to the American expedition.[480]

News of the approaching Carrancista troops caused Yancey to lead the expedition back to Texas. The troops crossed the border at 1:00 A. M. 25 August. Their departure from Mexico was just in time to avoid a clash with the Carrancistas. A few hours after the Americans left Coyame, the Carrancistas rode into town and arrested eight men in a dance hall who the Carrancistas claimed were part of Renteria's band. The prisoners were sent to Chihuahua City where the Carrancistas executed them. While President Carranza protested the presence of the American expedition in

Mexico, local Carrancista officials, particularly Gen. Antonio Pruneda, tried to cooperate with the Americans in apprehending Renteria.[481]

This time American and Carrancista armies did not clash, and an international incident was averted. While the intervention caused considerable excitement along the border, as well as in Washington and Mexico City, it came to nothing. The American expedition failed to capture Jesus Renteria, who according to some sources, lived in Coyame until he died of old age during the 1970s.[482]

Five days after the American expedition withdrew from Mexico; a letter purportedly written by Jesus Renteria was mailed to the *Douglas Dispatch* in Douglas, Arizona. It read: "It caused me great surprise when I read in your newspaper of Tuesday 26th, saying that I had been killed and that seeing that the notice had been confirmed, and seeing that such notice is absurd, I wish, therefore that you would let me relate some facts about it that will convince you that I am alive." According to the letter, after Renteria got the ransom money and learned that U.S. troops had crossed into Mexico in his pursuit, he and his men crossed back into Texas, went to El Paso, and then on to Douglas "with plenty United States money left."[483]

As at the Porvenir massacre, the Army officers involved in Renteria's pursuit denied any knowledge of the killing of the prisoners. In his official report of the expedition, Major Yancey didn't mention the capture of prisoners nor that he had turned them over to the Rangers. Contemporary newspapers carried the American military's version of the events obtained from Army press releases. The *El Paso Times* reported that when the expedition took Carrizo Springs, "the bandits fought desperately" from an adobe blockhouse, though no such reckless fight had taken place.[484]

The cover-up of the killings by the Rangers did not escape the attention of J.J. Kilpatrick,the King of Candelaria, who again created a controversy by challenging the army's version of the events in a series of articles published by the Marfa *New Era* newspaper. The outspoken Kilpatrick wrote the War Department about the killing of the prisoners taken at Carrizo Springs.[485] As a result of Kilpatrick's outcry about the murder of the prisoners on the punitive expedition, the army, in 1920, tried Major Yancey before a court-martial at Fort Sam Houston, Texas. The charges against the major included turning over his prisoners from Carrizo

Springs to the Texas Rangers and making a false report of the expedition. Yancey plead not guilty to the charges of contributing to the death of the prisoners, though he entered a plea of guilty to charges of falsifying his report.[486]

The court-martial found Yancey guilty of turning over the prisoners to the Rangers and of falsifying his report of the expedition. Judge Advocate Maj. E. C. McNeill called the Yancey case, "as aggravated a case of false official statement as I have ever come in contact with." However, in view of "the conditions of border service, and the previous excellent record efficiency of this officer," and the fact that Yancey was "closely connected with the most prominent people in Rappahannock County, Virginia," acting Judge Advocate Gen. E. A. Kreger urged clemency for Yancey. President Woodrow Wilson confirmed the findings on January 26, 1921, commuting Yancey's sentence to a reprimand and a restriction to the limits of his post for six months, and a forfeiture of fifty dollars a month of pay for the same period. Yancey resigned his commission, evading this light sentence. Since the murders were committed in Mexico, none of the Rangers stood trial, although the Yancey case determined that the lawmen had murdered the prisoners.[487]

Following the last American punitive expedition into Mexico, the army withdrew from its frontier outposts on the Rio Grande and the Big Bend settled down. The death of Pancho Villa in 1923 brought an end to his arms-for-cattle trade, and the border raids ceased. To the great relief of the Kilpatricks and their Mexican neighbors, Troop K left Candelaria within months of the final expedition and the camp was soon abandoned. Because of the considerable violence that has taken place in the Big Bend, the area has been called the "Bloody Bend." The region's remote and rugged desert topography contributed considerably to making it a haven for lawlessness. But to say that the events that took place there during the revolution in Mexico were unique is to ignore the historical record. Countless Mexicans fleeing to Texas met with similar repression all along the border. For example, a like situation existed in the lower Rio Grande Valley of Texas where, according to William G. B. Morrison, a Cameron County attorney: "The enemies of the Rangers accuse them of killing from one hundred to five thousand, and we know that during our troubles down there that there were a great many fights in which both the citizens and the Rangers took part and I am inclined to believe the citizens and the Rangers killed probably some innocent people in the excitement. We were almost terror stricken down there, and of these innocents, I should imagine the citizens killed just as many as any Ranger."[488]

The King of Candelaria's vendetta against Captain Matlack continued well after the captain left Candelaria. As a result of Kilpatrick's unceasing animosity for the captain, Matlack's wartime commission, as an officer was not renewed. He resigned his captain's commission after J.J. Kilpatrick journeyed to Washington D.C. to "protest Matlack's permanent commission as captain." According to one source Matlack did not contest the demotion to save his retirement benefits. Leonard Matlack was honorably discharged on November 30, 1920 "by reason of convenience of the government, his services no longer required as a Captain United States Army." Matlack continued his military service however. The following month, he again enlisted at Fort Bliss as a master sergeant. He served as the chief bugler at Fort Bliss. In August 1927 Matlack finally retired as a master sergeant. Following his retirement he returned to Kentucky. During World War II, Matlack worked as a guard at a defense plant. The gallant old horse soldier died November 22, 1950. [489]

In 1927, Jim Kilpatrick journeyed to Ojinaga, Chihuahua. He spent the night in the Mexican border town on his way to check on his cattle ranch located on the *Rio Concho* southwest of *Ojinaga*. That evening Jim got drunk on *sotol*. He went to bed smoking a cigarette and caught the bed on fire. By the time Kilpatrick realized the danger, the room had filled with smoke. He tried to escape but tragically fumbled his way into a closet thinking it was the door to the outside. He didn't make it; Jim Kilpatrick died of smoke inhalation that night. When J.J. and Dawkins learned of the death, they went to *Ojinaga* to retrieve the body. One account states that J.J. and Dawkins placed Jim's body in the back seat of their Reo touring car propping him up between J.J. and Dawkins. They put his hat on his head and bribed the Mexican border guards to allow them to cross the border. When they reached the Texas side, U.S. Customs officers ask them what was wrong with Jim. J.J. replied that Jim was just drunk again and they were taking him home. No further questions were asked and Jim's father and brother took him to Marfa where the family buried him.[490]

J.J. Kilpatrick Sr., "died suddenly" of an apparent heart attack while on a trip to Washington, D. C. in 1935. Dawkins Kilpatrick continued to farm cotton and operate the store until his death in

1947. The Kilpatrick store continued to be the heart of the Candelaria community until it ceased doing business in 1995. As of this writing, Kilpatrick's store and home is located on private property and is not open to the public.[491]

List of Abbreviations

ABB-Archives of the Big Bend, Sul Ross State University, Alpine, Texas

BBD-RG393-Big Bend District, 1914-1915 and 1917-1920; Records of the United States Army Continental Commands, 1821-1920; Record Group 393; Washington National Records Center, Suitland, Maryland.

DAR-RG393-Records of fort D. A. Russell, Texas, 1914-46, Records of the United States Army Continental Commands, 1821-1920; Record Group 393; National Archives, Washington, D.C.

AGP-Biennial Reports of the Adjutant General of Texas

EPH-*El Paso Herald*

EPT-*El Paso Times*

FSIMA-United States Senate *Investigation of Mexican Affairs*

HWP-Harry Warren Papers, Archives of the Big Bend, Sul Ross State University, Alpine, Texas

ICFFBI-RG65-Investigative Case Files of the Bureau of Investigation, 1908-1922, Records of the Federal Bureau of Investigation, RG-65

NYT-*New York Times*

TSA-Texas State Archives, Austin

USGS-United States Geological Survey

USMU-RG391-Records of United States Army Mobile Units 1821-1942, Record Group 391; National Archives, Washington D. C.

NOTES

[1]. Herbert Eugene Bolton ed., *Spanish Exploration In The Southwest: 1542-1706* (New York: Charles Scribner's Sons, 1916), 144-45, Bustamente took part the Chamuscado-Rodriguez *entrada* of 1581-1582 resulting in the first detailed descriptions of the Jumano Indians following Cabeza De Vaca's writings of his encounter with the "cow people"; C.C. Smith, G.A. Davies and H.B. Hall, *Lagenscheidt's Standard Dictionary of the English and Spanish Languages* (Berlin : Langenscheidt, 1966), 179; James M. Daniel, "The Spanish Frontier in West Texas and Northern Mexico" *Southwestern Historical Quarterly* (Austin: Texas State Historical Association, 1968), 71:482.

[2]. Texas State Historical Association *Handbook of Texas* (Austin: Texas State Historical Association, 1952), 1:262, (hereafter cited TSHA).

[3]. Donald E. Chipman, "In Search of Cabeza De Vaca's Route Across Texas: An Historiographical Survey" *Southwestern Historical Quarterly 91*) (October, 1987).

[4]. Cyclone Covey ed., *Cabeza* De Vaca'*s In The Unknown Interior of America* (Albuquerque: University of New Mexico Press, 1990), 15; Victor J. smith, "Early Spanish Exploration In The Big Bend of Texas" (Alpine: West Texas Historical and Scientific Society Publications, 1928), 60-62.

[5]. Ibid, 115-116; Note: assuming a Spanish league tobe 2.63 miles, De Vaca's distance of 50 leagues (about 131 miles) to the buffalo hunting grounds of the plains of West Texas is a reasonable estimate for the sixteenth century.

[6]. Covey, 116; Note: *The American Heritage Dictionary of the Engllish Language*, On Line Edition, 1992, states that a calabash is "An annual vine having white flowers and smooth, large, gourds."; J. Charles Kelly, Jumano *and Patarabueye Relations at* La Junta *de los Ri´os* (Ann Arbor: Museum of Anthropology, University of Michigan, 1986), 16-17.

[7]. Covey, 115; Danny Martin Young, "Identification of the Jumano Indians" MA Thesis (Alpine: Sul Ross State Univerisity, 1970), 3; Kelly "Jumano and Patarabueye", 139-140.

[8]. J. Charles Kelly, "The Historic Indian Pueblos of La Junta De Los Ri´os", *New Mexico Historical Review*, (Albuquerque: *New Mexico Historical Review*, 1952), XXVII:277; Young, 8-9.

[9]. Kelly, "Jumano and Patarabueye", 119-120: Carlos E. Castaneda, *Our Catholic Heritage in Texas, 1519-1936*, (Austin: Von Boeckmann-Jones, 1936), III:226; Enrique rede Madrid, trans., *Expedition to* La Junta *de los Ri´os, 1747-1748: Captain Commander Joseph de Ydoiaga's Report to the Viceroy of New Spain*, Special report 33 (Austin: Texas Historical Commission, 1992), 55.

[10]. Kelly, "Jumano and Patarabueye", 120-121.

[11]. Ibid.

[12]. Kelly, "Jumano and Patarabueye", 123-125.

[13]. Covey, 124-125; TSHA Handbook, I:347, II:281.

[14]. J. Lloyd Mecham, "The Second Spanish Expedition To New Mexico", *New Mexico Historical Review 1* (Albuquerque: *New Mexico Historical Review, 1926*, 270-271.

[15]. Mecham, 270-271, 288.

[16]. TSHA Handbook, I:572; J. Lloyd Mecham, "Antonio De Espejo And Hist Journey To New Mexico, *Southwestern Historical Quarterly* 30 (Austin: Texas State Historical Society, 1927), 114, 120-121.

[17]. Herbert Eugene Bolton, *Spanish Exploration In the Southwest: 1542-1706*, (New York: Charles Scribner's Son's, 1916), 172-173. The population estimate of 10,000 seems exaggerated but apparently Espejo must have seen a large number of Indians at La Junta. Hoping to gain recognition from the Spanish Crown Espejo, wanted to make his efforts appear as grand as possible.

[18]. Ibid. Note, the humpbacked cows described by Espejo are bison. His reference to the *Rio Del Norte* is the first reference to that name and he is credited with naming the river. See TSHA Handbook, I:572; Kelly, "The Historic Indian Pueblos", 265.

[19]. Nancy P. Hickerson, "The Visits Of The "Lady in Blue": An Episode In The History Of The South Plains, 1629", *Journal of Anthropological Research* (Albuquerque: University of New Mexico, 1990) 46:81.

[20]. Hickerson, "The Visits", 88-91; Mrs. Edward E Ayer: *The Memorial of Fray Alonso De Benavides 1630.* (Albuquerque: Horn and Wallace, 1965), 59.

[21]. Ibid.

[22]. Benavides, 273; J. Charles Kelley, "Juan Sabeata and Diffusion in Aboriginal Texas", *American Anthropologist* 57 (Menasha: American Anthropological Association, 1955), 984: TSHA Handbook, II:522; Frederick Webb Hodge, ed., *Handbook of American Indians North of Mexico*, (New York: Rowman and Littlefield, 1971) 2:400; Ayer, 273.

[23]. TSHA Handbook, II:81, 172.

[24]. Castaneda I:312; Bolton, 321-322.

[25]. Castaneda, I:317; Bolton, 325.

[26]. Castaneda, I:317-318; Howard G. Applegate and C. Wayne Hanselka, La Junta *de los Ri´os Del Norte y* Conchos, (El Paso: Texas Western Press, 1974), 17, 20.

[27]. Ibid; Claude Dooley and Betty Dooley and the Texas historical Commission, *Why Stop? A Guide to Texas Historical Roadside Markers,* (Houston: Gulf Publishing Company, 1978), 405.

[28]. Castaneda, I:320-321; Bolton 330.

[29]. Bolton, 331-332.

[30]. Bolton, 336.

[31]. Kelly, "Juan Sabeata", 981; *On Line Grolier*; Hickerson, "The Visits", 82-83.

[32]. Bolton, 340; Castaneda, I:274-275.

[33]. Kelley, "Juan Sabeata", 985; Bolton, 340; Charles Wilson Hackett, ed., *Hisorical Documents Reating to New mexico, Nueva Vizcaya, and Approaches Thereto, to* 1773. (Washington: Carnegie Institution Of Washington, 1926) II: 241-243. Note The Indians described French ships as, "wooden houses" where the Frenchmen, "slept at night on the water."

[34]. Hankett, "Historical Documents", II:257-259, 265.

[35]. TSHA Handbook I:54, 385; Elizabeth A. A. John, "Spanish-Indian Relations in the Big Bend Region", *The Journal of Big Bend Studies 3* (Alpine: Sul Ross State University, 1991), 72.

[36]. John, "Spanish-Indian Relations," 72; Ralph A. Smith, "Bounty Power Against The West Texas Indians", *West Texas Historical Association YearBook*, (Abilene: West Texas Historical Association, 1973), and 49:41-42, 46-47.

[37]. George B. Eckhart, "Spanish Missions of Texas: 1680-1800", *Journal of the Arizona Archaeological & Historical Society*, Number 3 (Arizona Archaeological & Historical Society, 1967), 32:7, 18.

[38]. Enrique Rede Madrid, trans., *Expedition to* La Junta *de los Ri´os, 1747-1748: Captain Commander Joseph de Ydoiaga's Report to the Viceroy of new Spain,* Office of the State Archaeologist Special Report Series, No. 33, (Austin: Texas Historical Commission, 1992), xi, 63-65; Applegate and Hanselka, 16.

[39]. Madrid, 50, 63.

[40]. Madrid, 63-64.

[41]. Madrid, 64.

[42]. Kelly, "*The Historic Indian Pueblos of* La Junta *De Los Ri´os*", 50-51.

[43]. Kelly, 29-31, 37: Madrid, 47.

[44]. William Burton Mitchell, "My First Trip To The Big Bend 1885" MS in the W. B. Mitchell Collection, Museum of the Big Bend Archives, Sul Ross State University, Alpine, 1-2; *San Angelo Standard Times*, December 24, 1979.

[45]. Ibid.

[46]. Eighth Census of the United States: 1860 Population, Presidio County, Texas, Fort Leaton, 75 Note: Misspellings on these hand written documents are not uncommon; Ninth Census of the United States: 1870 Population, Presidio del Norte, Presidio County, Texas, 126; Tenth Census of the United States: 1880 Population, Milton Faver Ranch, Presidio County, Texas, 15; Barry Scobee, "Don Milton Faver: Founder of a Kingdom" *True West* (Austin: Western Publications, 1962), 18.

[47]. J. Evetts Haley, *Jeff Milton: A Good Man with a Gun* (Norman: University of Oklahoma Press, 1982). 75.

[48]. TSHA, 1:587; J. E. Gregg, "Additional History Of Presidio County" *Voice of the Mexican Border* (Marfa, 1934), 281.

[49]. Gregg, "Additional History", 286; Jack Shipman, ed., "Don Milton: Milton Faver, the Big Bend's First American Cattle King" *Voice of the Mexican Border*, (Marfa, 1933), 22.

[50]. "Big Bend Mystery Man Recalled" *San Angelo Standard Times*, November 27, 1958, Gregg, "Additional History", 286.

[51]. Ibid.

[52]. Leavitt Corning, Jr., *Baronial Forts of the Big Bend: Ben Leaton, Milton Faver and Their Private Forts in Presidio County* (Austin: Trinity University Press, 1969), 121; Shipman, "Don Milton: Milton Faver, the Big Bend's Frist American Cattle King" , 22; *San Antonio Express-News*, December 9, 1978.

[53]. Shipman, "Don Milton: Milton Faver, the Big Bend's First American Cattle King",22-23; Gregg, "Additional History", 286.

[54]. Shipman, "Don Milton: Milton Faver, the Big Bend's Frist American Cattle King",23-24; Corning, 59.

[55]. Barry Scobee, "Don Milton Faver: Founder Of A Kingdom" Sul Ross State College Bulletin Vol.XLIII No. 3 (Alpine, 1963), 41.

[56]. Scobee, "Don Milton Faver", 44; Jack Lafferty, "Don Milton Faver...Texas First Cattle King" *Texas Parade* (1956), 24; "Big Bend Mystery Man Recalled" *San Angelo Standard Times*, November 27, 1958; J. E. Gregg, "The History of Presidio County" MA Thesis (Austin: University of Texas, 1933), 125.

[57]. Gregg, "Additional History", 286; *Big Bend Sentinel*, September 1, 1950; Scobee, "Don Milton Faver", 44; Robert M. Utley, "The Range Cattle Industry in the Big Bend of Texas" *Southwestern Historical Quarterly* (Austin: Texas State Historical Association, 1966) LXIX: 427.

[58]. Barry Scobee, "Don Milton Faver: Founder of a Kingdom", *Big Bend Sentinel*, September 1, 1950; Corning, 44; *True West*, June, 1962, 53.

[59]. Corning, 52.

[60]. TSHA, 2:841; Clifford B. Casey, *Mirages, Mysteries and Reality: Brewster County, Texas The Big Bend Of The Rio Grande* (Seagraves: Pioneer Book Publishers, 1974), 22; Gregg, "The History of Presidio County", 85-86.

[61]. TSHA, 2:408-409; Gregg, "History of Presidio County", 87, 92.

[62]. Gregg, "History of Presidio County", 75, 107.

[63]. Ibid, 79, 80, Note: Gregg made this observation in the early 1930's.

[64]. Ibid, 84, 88, 89.

[65]. Ibid, 93, 96.

[66]. Ibid, 102, 108, 109; Oren Arnold, *Irons in the Fire: Cattle Brand Lore*, (London: Abelard-Schuman, 1965), 48-49 Note: A wagon bolt was the long bold securing the end gate to the wagon.

[67]. Gregg, "Additional History", 288.

[68]. Ibid; *San Antonio Express-News*, December 9, 1978.

[69]. *Big Bend Sentinel*, September 1, 1950.

[70]. Ibid; Cecilia Thompson, *History of Marfa and Presidio County, Texas 1535-1946*, (Austin: Nortex Press, 1985), 1: 267.

[71]. Utley, 433-434.

[72]. F. A. Mitchell, "The Stampede At Robbers' Roost", *Voice of the Mexican Border*, (Marfa, October 1933), 90.

[73]. Ibid.

[74]. Thompson, 266-267; *San Angelo Standard Times*, November 27, 1958; Tommy D. Wood, interview with author, October, 1994.

[75]. TSHA, 1:315, 800-801; *On Line Grolier;* Boyd Chambers, interview with author, December, 1994.

[76]. *Dallas News*, Feb. 21, 1887.

[77]. Bill Knight, interview with author, August 2000; Ilene Harrison, "Spear-Cross Lawman" undated notes; Karen Brown, "They Moved West With Destiny" 1965 notes.

[78]. Ibid

[79]. Ibid.

[80]. Ibid

[81]. T. D. Wood interview.

[82]. Irwin May, Jr. "Welfare And Ranchers: The Emergency Cattle Purchase Program And Emergency Work Relief Program in Texas, 1934-1935" *The West Texas Historical Association Year Book* (Abilene: West Texas Historical Association, 1971) XLVII:3: *On Line Grolier.*

[83]. Ibid.

[84]. May, 6, 10-11.

[85]. Ibid, T. D. Wood interview; Boyd Chambers interview.

[86]. Boyd Chambers interview.

[87]. Robert Allen, "The Silver Heart Of Chinati" *Voice of the Mexican Border* 1 (February-March 1934), 278.

[88]. State Department of Highways and Public Transportation, *General Highway Map of Presidio County, Texas* (Revised 1985); A. H. Belo Corporation, *Texas Almanac: 1990-91* (Dallas: A. H. Belo Corp., 1989), 298.

[89]. Paul Carlson, "The Discovery Of Silver in West Texas," *West Texas Historical Association Year Book* LIV (1978): 55; Clyde P. Ross, *Geology and Ore Deposits Of The Shafter Mining District Presidio County, Texas* (Washington: United States Department of the Interior, 1943) 49.

[90]. Dorthy Davenport, "John W. Spencer" MS in the Barker Texas History Center, Austin, 1.

[91]. Davenport, 2; Roy L. Swift and Leavitt Corning, Jr., *Three Roads to Chihuahua: The Great Wagon Roads That Opened The Southwest 1823-1883* (Austin: Eakin Press, 1988), 31; Carlson, "The Discovery of Silver," 57.

[92]. Carlson, "The Discovery of Silver," 58.

[93]. TSHA, 1:624; 2:595.

[94]. TSHA, 2:595, 596.

[95]. Paul H. Carlson, *"Pecos Bill" A Military Biography of William R. Shafter* (College Station: Texas A&M University Press, 1989), 3.

[96]. TSHA, 2:841; Jerry Korn, ed. *The Great Chiefs* (Chicago: Time Life Books, 1975), 80; Carlson, "*Pecos Bill*", 118; Carlson, "The Discovery of Silver," 59.

[97]. Robert Wooster, *History of Fort Davis* (Santa Fe: Southwest Cultural Resources Center National Park Service, 1990), 315; *Presidio Mining Co. V. Bullis and Others* Supreme Court of Texas, June 25, 1887 (see *Southwestern Reporter* 68 Tex.581), 862.

[98]. Robert M. Utley, *Fort Davis National Historic Site, Texas* (Washington: United States Department Of The Interior National Park Service, 1965), 59; Lowell D. Black and Sara H. Black, *An Officer And A Gentleman: The Military Career of Lieutenant Henry O. Flipper* (Dayton: The Lora Company, 1985), 106-107; TSHA, 3:299.

[99]. Carlson, "The Discovery of Silver," 60-62; *Presidio Mining Co. V. Bullis and Others*, 862; John W. Clark, Jr., *Archaeological Investigations At The Ramon Castelo Outbuilding Shafter, Presidio County, Texas* Report No. 37 (Austin: Texas Department of Highways and Public Transportation, 1988), 15; Ross, 50.

[100]. Ibid.

[101]. Charles Deaton, *Texas Postal History Handbook* (Houston, 1981), 140, Ross, 117, United States Geological Survey, *Shafter, Tex.* 1:24,000 (1983).

[102]. John Earnest Gregg, "The History of Presidio County" MA Thesis (Austin: University of Texas, 1933), 144-145.

[103]. Clark, 15; Ronald C. Brown, *Hard-Rock Miners: The Intermountain West 1860-1920* (College Station: Texas A&M University Press, 70.

[104]. Brown, 70-71.

[105]. Ibid; Clark, 20.

[106]. Ibid; Twelfth Census of the United States: 1900-Population, Shafter Village, p. 13-23.

[107]. Twelfth Census, 12-23; Clark,15,22.

[108]. Clyde P. Ross, *Geology And Ore Deposits Of The Shafter Mining District Presidio County, Texas* (Washington: United States Department Of The Interior, 1943), 50, 56, 112, 117-119.

[109]. Ross, 49; Thomas E. Evans, *Gold and Silver in Texas* (Austin: Bureau of Economic Geology University of Texas, 1975), 31; Note: In *Hard-Rock Miners: The Intermountain West 1860-1920* author Ronald C. Brown defines a stope as, "excavations at the vein or ore deposit and are the holes through which ore is initially removed" ; U. S. Government Printing Office, *General Map of the Presidio Mine (1942).*

[110]. Tracy Hammond Lewis, *Along the Rio Grande* (New York: Lewis Publishing Company, 1916), 81-83.

[111]. Ibid.

[112]. Ibid.

[113]. Clark, 17; Ross, 49.

[114]. Clark, 17, Ross, 51; A. H. Belo Corporation, *Texas Almanac and State Industrial Guide 1939*, 115; *Texas Almanac 1949-1950*, 119.

[115]. Clark, 19.

[116]. Ibid; Clark, 20; *San Angelo Standard Times*, March 1, 1981; *Dallas Morning News*, February 11, 1980.

[117]. P. H. Pruett, Co. C. 10th Arkansas Infantry, Compiled Service Records of Military Units in Confederate Organizations, Records of Confederate Movements and Activities, RG-109, National Archives and Records Administration, General Reference Branch, Washington, D. C. (hereafter cited as Pruett Compiled Service Records); Pruett, Jessie A., "Life of Philip Halker Pruett Written From Memories of Jessie A. Pruett," MS, 1:16-17.

[118]. Pruett, 1:16-17.

[119]. John H. Worsham, *One of Jackson's Foot Cavalry: His Experience and What He Saw During the War 1861-1865* (New York: The Neale Publishing Company, 1912), 292.

[120]. Worsham, 293.

[121]. Dyer, Ser. II, VII:18-19.

[122].Pruett, 1:23-24.

[123]. Ibid.

[124]. Pruett, 1:27.

[125]. Ibid; John D. Unruh, The Plains Across: The Overland Emigrants and the Trans-Mississippi West 1840-1860 (Urbana:University of Illinois Press, 1979) 408-409.

[126]. Pruett, 1:24-25, 27.

[127]. *The American Encyclopedia*, On Line Edition, Grolier Electronic Publishing, Danbury,Ct., 1991.

[128]. Pruett, 1:24-25, 27.

[129]. Ibid., 1:29; *The American Peoples Encyclopedia*, 19:259; *The American Encyclopedia.*

[130]. Athern, Robert G. *Union Pacific Country* (Chicago: Rand McNally & Company, 1971), 170.

[131]. Pruett, 1:30.

[132]. Ibid., 1:33.

[133]. Ibid., 1:32-34.

[134]. Ibid., 1:33.

[135]. *The American Peoples Encyclopedia*, 6:682 & 685; *The American Encyclopedia.*

[136]. Pruett, 1:35.

[137]. Ibid., 1:36-38.

[138]. Ibid; *The American Peoples Encyclopedia,*, 17:238.

[139]. Pruett, 1:42-44.

[140]. Ibid., 1:50-51.

[141], *The Handbook of Texas*, 2: 79.

[142]. Pruett, 1: 51; Note: Durham cattle are today known as Shorthorns.

[143]. Ibid., 1:53-54.

[144]. Ibid. 1:39.

[145]. Ibid. 1:40-41.

[146]. Pruett, 1:55.

[147]. *El Paso Times*, February 14, 1993.

[148]. Ibid., 1:56-58; Haley, J. Evetts. *Charles Goodnight: Cowman and Plainsman*, (Norman: University of Oklahoma Press, 1983), 234.

[149]. Pruett, 1:57-59.

[150]. Leckie, William H. *The Buffalo Soldiers: A Narrative of the Negro Cavalry in the West*, (Norman: University of Oklahoma Press, 1978), 156-57.

[151]. Pruett, 1:59; *The Handbook of Texas*, 2:355.

[152]. Pruett, 1:61-62.

[153]. Ibid., 1:62-63.

[154]. Ibid., 1:65.

[155]. Ibid., 1:66-67.

[156]. Schultz, Marvin E.,"Last Hunt: The Killing of the Buffalo in the Concho Region, 1876-1878.", 133-134.

[157]. Ibid., 135.

[158]. Utley, Robert M., *Frontier Regulars: The United States Army and the Indian: 1866-1891*. (New York: Macmillian Publishing Co., Inc.), 123, 421.

[159]. Schultz,137-141.

[160]. *The Handbook of Texas*, 1:145 Note: San Angela later became known as San Angelo; Clements, Gus. *The Concho Country*. (San Antonio: Mulberry Avenue Books, 1981), 92.

[161]. Ibid., 59.

[162]. Ibid., 64, 115.

[163]. Pruett, 2:1-5.

[164]. Ibid., 2:5.

[165]. Ibid., 2:7.

[166]. Schultz, 139.

[167]. *The Handbook of Texas*, 1:315-316.

[168]. Pruett, 2:8.

[169]. Ibid, 2:8-9.

[170]. Ibid, 2:10.

[171]. Ibid, 2:12, 16.

[172]. Ibid,, 2:14.

[173]. Ibid., 17-18.

[174]. Ibid., 19-21.

[175]. Clements, 93; Pruett, 2:25.

[176]. Mrs. Leander Glenn Jackson, interview with Glenn Justice, December 3, 1992; Leander Glenn Jackson, "Untitled Family History," MS,; Melancthon Glenn Jackson, interview with Mrs. Leander Glenn Jackson, undated notes; *The American Encyclopedia*.

[177]. Pruett, 2:26-28, Jackson, "Untitled Family History."

[178]. Pruett, 2:29-30.

[179]. Ibid., 2:30-31.

[180]. Ibid., 31-32.

[181]. Barkes, J. M., *Major and Historical Springs of Texas*, (Austin: Texas Water Development Board, 1975), 60; Melancthon Glenn Jackson, interview with Mrs. Leander Glenn Jackson, undated notes.

[182]. Pruett, 2: 35-36.

[183]. Ibid.

[184]. Daggett, Marsha, ed., *Pecos County History*, (Fort Stockton: Pecos County Historical Commission, 1984.), 1:87; *The Handbook of Texas* 2:355.

[185]. *The Handbook of Texas*, 1:387, 839, 2:355; Haley, *Charles Goodnight: Cowman and Plainsman*, 134.

[186]. Williams, Clayton. "The Pontoon Bridge of the Pecos, 1869-1886", (Odessa: The Permian Historical Annual, 1978), XVIII, 3-10; *The American Encyclopedia*.

[187]. Pruett, 2:40-41.

[188]. Williams,12,15.

[189]. Pruett, 2:42-43.

[190]. Ibid.

[191]. Ibid., 2:44-45; Note: Jessie Pruett's account of fording the Pecos at Pontoon Crossing paints a remarkable picture of a forgotten but once important Pecos River ford.

[192]. Pruett, 2:47-48

[193]. Dagget, 1:20; Barkes,57-58.

[194]. According to *Dorland's Illustrated Medical Dictionary*, a felon is an extremely painful abcess usually caused by a pathogenic microrganism.

[195]. Leckie, *The Buffalo Soldiers*, 26.

[196]. *The Handbook of Texas*, 1:54-55.

[197]. Dee Brown, *Bury My Heart At Wounded Knee* (New York: Simon and Schuster, 1981) 374-375.

[198]. Ball, 28.

[199]. James B. Gillett, *Six Years With the Texas Rangers 1877-1881* (Lincoln: University of Nebraska Press, 1976), 161; Jerry Korn, ed., *The Great Chiefs* (Chicago: Time Life Books, 1975), 80; *The Handbook of Texas*, 2:840.

[200]. W. W. Newcomb Jr., *The Indians of Texas: From Prehistoric to Modern Times* (Austin: University of Texas Press, 1984), 103.

[201]. William H. Leckie and Shirley A. Leckie, *Unlikely Warriors: General Benjamin Grierson and His Family* (Norman: University of Oklahoma Press, 1984), 260; Wayne R. Austerman, *Sharps Rifles and Spanish Mules: The San Antonio-El Paso Mail 1851-1881* (College Station: Texas A&M University Press, 1985) 299-300; Robert Wooster, *History of Fort Davis, Texas* (Santa Fe: National Park Service, Deptartment of the Interior, 1990) 239.

[202]. Major General E. T. Conley, Adjutant General, U. S. Army to Mr. S. M. Swearingen, Pres. Marfa Chamber of Commerce, 15 February 1938, "Record of Old Fort Davis Texas Military Post", Fort Davis Archives.

[203]. Leckie, *Unlikely Warriors*, 260; Colonel B. H. Grierson, Tenth Cavalry, to Assistant Adjutant-General, Department of Texas, San Antonio, Subject: Report of Operations Against Victorio, 20 September 1880, Records of the War Department, Adjutant General's Office, Record Group 94, National Archives, Washington D.C., 14, (hereafter cited *Grierson's Report on Operations Against Victorio.*)

[204]. Pruett, 2:49, 55; State Department of Highsways and Public Transportation, *General Highway Map of Jeff Davis County Texas* (Revised 1985), Southwest Parks and Monuments Association, *Map of the Military District of the Pecos Dept. of Texas* (Revised 1878, 1879, 1880).

[205]. Pruett, 2:53; Tenth Census of the United States: 1880-Schedule 1, Fort Davis, Presidio County; USGS, *Marfa* map, 1:250,000 (Revised 1959), USGS, *Van Horn* map, 1:250,000 (Revised 1954); Ball, 12.

[206]. Wooster, 3.

[207]. Ibid.

[208]. Albert D. Richardson, *Beyond the Mississippi* (New York: Bliss & Co., 1867) 225.

[209]. Pruett, 2:58-60.

[210]. Pruett, 2:62-63.

[211]. Tenth Census of the United States: 1880-Schedule 1, Fort Davis, Presidio County.

[212]. Douglas C. McChristian, ed., *Garrison Tangles in the Friendless Tenth: The Journal of First Lieutenant John Bigelow, Jr. Fort Davis Texas* (Bryan: J. M. Carrol & Company, 1985) 8, 44.

[213]. Tenth Census of the United States: 1880-Schedule 1, Fort Davis, Presidio County.

[214]. Barry Scobee, *Fort Davis Texas, 1583-1960* (Fort Davis: Barry Scobee, 1963), 130-131.

[215]. Pruett, 2: 66.

[216]. Ibid, 2: 67-68; Scobee, *Fort Davis Texas,*141.

[217]. *Grierson's Report on Operations Against Victorio,* 15.

[218]. Ibid, 16.

[219]. Ibid.

[220]. Robert K. Grierson, "Journal Kept on the Victorio Campaign in 1880," Fort Davis Archives.

[221]. Ibid.

[222]. Grierson to wife, Aug 2, 1880, Grierson Papers, Illinois State Historical Library.

[223]. Robert M. Utley, *Frontier Regulars: The United States Army And The Indian:1866-1891* (New York: Macmillan Publishing Co., Inc., 1973) 372; *Record of Old Fort Davis Texas Military Post,* Compiled by Frank M. Temple and Barry Scobee from the Fort Davis Historical Society, 1955, 71956, R-23, Fort Davis Archives.

[224]. Pruett, 71; Will F. Evans, *Border Skylines Fifty Years of "Tallying Out" on the Bloys Round-Up Ground: A History of The Bloys Cowboy Camp Meeting* (Dallas: Cecil Baugh, 1942) 208.

[225]. Pruett, 72; Scobee, *Fort Davis Texas,* 142.

[226]. Ibid; Evans, 208.

[227]. Utley, 373; *Frontier Times,* Vol 8. No. 12, September 1931, 560; Ball, 100.

[228]. Wooster, 248.

[229]. Pruett, 2:70.

[230]. Pruett, 2:73-74.

[231]. Barry Scobee, *Old Fort Davis* (Fort Davis: Old Fort Davis Company, 1947) 47, 88.

[232]. Betty Dooley and Claude Dooley, *Why Stop? A Guide to Texas Histroical Markers* (Houston: Lone Star Books, 1985) 175; Pruett, 2:75; Scobee, 129; Clifford B. Casey, Mirages, Mysteries, and Realiy Brewster County Texas (Seagraves: Pioneer Book Publishers, 1974) 59.

[233]. Pruett, 2:76-77; Clayton W. Williams, *Texas Last Frontier: Fort Stockton and the Trans-Pecos, 1861-1895* (College Station: Texas A&M University Press, 1982) 268.

[234]. Pruett, 2:78.

[235]. Williams, 268; Walter Prescott Webb, *The Texas Rangers: A Century of Frontier Defense* (Austin: University of Texas Press, 1982) 410.

[236]. Pruett 2:79; Scobee, *Old Fort Davis* 141-142. The quoted account was written by Barry Scobee and agrees essentially with Jessie Pruett's memories. Scobee cited his source as, "Jesse Anderson Pruett to me in 1952. Much of the Pruett family data in this book came to me from him and his sister, Mrs. Andrew. G. (Ora) Prude of Fort Davis, in pleasant talks at various times."

[237]. Pruett, 2: 80-81; Scobee, *Old Fort Davis,* 141-142.

[238]. Pruett, 2:83; Dooley, 175.

[239]. Pruett, 2:85.

[240]. Pruett, 2:75.

[241]. Pruett, 2:86.

[242]. Ibid, 2:87.

[243]. Ibid, 2:88.

[244]. Ibid, 2:89.

[245]. Leckie, *Unlikely Warriors*, 84, 99.

[246]. Wooster, 315.

[247]. Pruett, 2:89.

[248]. Scobee, *Old Fort Davis,* 129. Although Scobee does not cite his sources but presents the land transaction between Grierson and Pruett as a quote. It agrees essentially with Jesse Pruett's writings about the sale of the land; Pruett, 2:91.

[249]. Pruett, 2:102.

[250]. Pruett, 2:101; http://www.ppri.usu.edu/locoweed.htm.

[251]. Pruett, 2:108, 109.

[252]. Pruett, 2:113, 114.

[253]. James W. Wilkie, *The Mexican Revolution: Federal Expenditure and Social Change Since 1910* (Berkeley: University of California Press, 1973), 299; Alan Knight, *The Mexican Revolution,* (Cambridge University Press, 1986), 1:15, 21.

[254]. Knight, 1:77, 78, 115.

[255]. Knight 1:176, 186, 194, and 203.

[256]. Charles C. Cumberland, *Mexican Revolution: Genesis Under Madero* (Austin: University of Texas Press, 1952), 170, 241.

[257]. Knight, 2:170, 493.

[258]. Mark Wasserman, *Capitalists, Caciques, and Revolution: The Native Elite and foreign Enterprise in Chihuahua, Mexico 1854-1911* (Chapel Hill: University of North carolina Press, 1984), 1, 2, 110.

[259]. Ibid, 6, 7, 59, 110.

[260]. Ibid, 100, 101, 104, 110.

[261]. *El Paso Times* hereafter cited *EPT*, December 25, 1917.

[262]. *EPT*, December 28, 1917, January 1, 1914.

[263]. *EPT*, January 1 and 5, 1914.

[264]. *EPT*, January 6, 8, and 10, 1914.

[265]. *EPT*, January 10, 1914.

[266]. *EPT*, December 13, 1913.

[267]. *EPT*, January 6, 1914.

[268]. Martin Luis Guzman, *Memoirs of Pancho Villa* (Austin: University of Texas Press, 1975), 132.

[269]. District Intelligence Officer to Department Intelligence Officer, Smuggling in the Big Bend District, January 14, 1918; Villista Activities; 201 File, Big Bend District, 1914-15 and 1917; Records of the United States Army Continental commands, 1821-1920; Record Group 393, Washington National Records Center, Suitland, Maryland (hereafter cited as BBD-RG93).

[270]. Pvt. Alfred L. Cooper to Lt. Milton N. Glosser, June 4, 1919; Director of Military Intelligence to Intelligence Officer, Marfa, Texas, June 27, 1919; BBD-RG93.

[271]. Col. J. A. Gaston to Commanding General, Southern Department, March 2, 1917, BBD-RG93.

[272]. ; Alan Knight, *The Mexican Revolution* (Cambridge: Cambridge University Press, 1986), II: 343-345.

[273]. Clarence C. Clendenen, *The United States and Pancho Villa: A Study in Unconventional Diplomacy* (Ithaca: Cornell University Press, 1961), 206.

[274]. Ibid, 33, 42, 59.

[275]. Ibid, 210-11.

[276]. Friedrich Katz, "Pancho Villa and the Attack on Columbus, New Mexico," Friedrich Katz, "*The American Historical Review* (February 1978): 116, 128; Fredrich Katz, *The Secret War in Mexico: Europe, the United States and the Mexican Revolution* (Chicago: University of Chicago Press, 1981), 32.

[277]. Clarence C. Clendenen, *Blood on the Border: The United States Army and the Mexican Irregulars* (New York: Macmillan, 1969), 279, 280; Ronnie C. Tyler, *The Big Bend* (Washington, D. C.: National Park Service Office of Publications, 1975), 168; Authur R. Gomez, "The Glenn Springs-Boquillas Raid Reconsidered: Diplomatic Intrrigue on the Rio Grande,"*The Journal of Big Bend Studies* 4 (1992), 97-113.

[278]. Tyler, 169; Clendenen, 281.

[279]. Clifford B. Casey, *Mirages, Mysteries and Reality: Brewster County Texas The Big Bend of the Rio Grande* (Seagraves: Pioneer Book Publishers, Inc., 1974), 132.

[280]. Clendenen, 287, 289-90; Col. Frank Tompkins, *Chasing Villa: The Story Behind the Story of Pershing's Expedition Into Mexico* (Harrisburg: Military Service Publishing Co., 1934), 228; G.G. Raun, "The National Guard on the Border and One Soldier's Viewpoint," *The Journal of Big Bend Studies* 6 (1994), 123-135.

[281]. Harry Warren, "Harry Warren Papers 1835-1932," hereafter cited HWP; ABB; J.J. Kilpatrick, Jr., to Harry Warren, March 1925; *EPT*, November 7, 14, and 18, 1917.

[282]. *EPT*, November 7, 1917.

[283]. *EPT*, November 15, 1917.

[284]. *EPT*, November 17, 1917 and December 12, 1917.

[285]. *EPT*, December 1 and 13, 1917.

[286]. Station Report, Big Bend District, August 1919, BBD-RG93.

[287]. U. S. Army Map of Presidio, Texas, March 27, 1911, Historic Map Collection, Barker Texas History Center, Austin; General Orders 18, August 4, 1919, Records of Fort D. A. Russell, Texas 1914-46 *Records of the United States ArmyContinental Commands, 1821-1920;* Record Group 393; National Archives, Washington, D. C. (Hereafter cited as DAR-RG393.)

[288]. Return of Casualties, Troop K, 8th Cavalry, December 1, 1917, Records of United States Army Mobile Units 1821-1942, Record Group 391, National Archives, Washington, D. C. (hereafter cited USMU-RG391); J.J. Kilpatrick Sr., Value of Evidence Collected by the Fall Senate Committee: An Examination of the Exaggerated and Fabricated Testimony of Some of the Witnesses," MS, Barker Texas History Center, Austin, 5.

[289]. Ruidosa Camp and Telephone File, DAR-RG393.

[290]. Gaston to Captain Mitchell, July 19, 1916, Copy Telegram, BBD-RG93; Return of Troop K, August 1919, USMU-RG391.

[291]. Return of Casualties, Troop G, 8th Calvary, March 1918, USMU-RG391.

[292]. General Orders 20, December 11, 1929, DAR-RG393.

[293]. Telephone file, DAR-RG393.

[294]. Maj. R. B. Woodruff to District Intelligence Officer, February 27, 1920, BBD-RG93; Extracts AEF, Monterrey, District Intelligence Officer File, BBD-RG93.

[295]. Macon M. Kilpatrick to Glenn Justice, email correspondence, January 4, 2001; *Civil War Times Illustrated*, April 1963, 15.

[296]. Ibid; William H. Kilpatrick to Mrs. J.E. Walker, July 1, 1943.

[297]. Ibid.

[298]. Undated newspaper clipping titled, "J.J. Kilpatrick" J.J. Kilpatrick Collection, Archives of the Big Bend, Sul Ross State University.

[299]. Ibid; note: J.J. Kilpatrick named one daughter Lula Livingston, born May 12, 1890 and another daughter Margret Huxley born November 11, 1898.

[302]. USGS, Marfa Map 1:250,000 ; Fred I. Massengill, *Texas Towns*, 1936, 34; J. Charles Kelley, *Candelaria, Presidio County, Texas, Water Improvement System: An Archaeological and Historical Survey*, 1991, *With Apprasial and Recommendations;* http://www.tsha.utexas.edu/handbook/online/articles/view/CC/hnc6.html; http://.rootsweb.com~txpost/presidio.html.

[303]. Mark Wasserman, *Capitalists, Caciques, and Revolution: The Native Elite and Foreign Enterprise in Chihuahua Mexico 1854*-1911 (Chapel Hill: University of north Carolina Press, 1984), 1-2, 110; Thirteenth Census of the United States: 1910 Population, Candelaria, Precinct; *El Paso Times*, hereafter *EPT*, 10 January 1914.

[304]. William H. Kilpatrick to Mrs. J.E. Walker, July 1, 1943; Mary Kilpatrick Howard, "Kilpatrick Cotton Farms Candelaria Texas", undated notes in the possession of the author; Thompson, 12, 24.

[305]. *San Angelo Standard Times*, April 8, 1928.

[306]. Notes from Marian Walker, 1986.

[307]. Pat H. green, taped interview with the author, August 5, 1984; Department of Justice Bureau of Investigation to Lt. J.C. White, District Intellingence Office, Marfa, Texas, 6 May, 1918; BBD-RG93.

[308]. Manual A. Machado, Jr., "The Mexican Revolution and the Destruction of the Mexican Cattle Industry" *Southwestern Historical Quarterly LXXIX*, No. 1 (July, 1975) p. 1-7.

[309].http://www.tsha.utexas.edu/handbook/online/articles/view/GG/jcgdu.html; undated *El Paso Herald article.*

[310]. Return Of The 8th Regiment of Cavalry, November, BBD-RG393; General Services Administration National Archives and Records Service Washington, DC to Glenn Justice, 15 October 1982, Subject Leonard F. Matlack; National Archives, Washington DC to Glenn Justice, 4 August 1987, Subject Leonard F. Matlack; Col. G.T. Langhorne to Mr. J. D. Jackson, Alpine, Texas, 2 September 1918, BBD-RG393.

[311]. Ibid; http://bible.gospelcom.net/; J.J. Kilpatrick Jr., "Nunez Ranch Raid and the Killing of Bandits on Telephone Wires", MS, Barker Texas History Center, Austin.

[312]. Headquarters Big Bend District, Camp Alberts, Marfa, Texas, General Orders No. 26, August 29, 1919; DAR-RG393.

[313]. Greene Interview; Hq. Eighth Cavalry, Marfa, Texas to Commanding General Southern Department, May 22, 1918, BBD-RG393; Headquarters, Big Bend District, Marfa, Texas, to Mr. T. B. White, May 5, 1918, BBD-RG393.

[314]. Headquarters Big Bend District, Marfa Texas, March 25, 1917 General Orders No. 12, BBD-RG93.

[315]. Greene Interview.

[316]. Ibid.

[317]. Ibid; Commanding Officer, Camp Ramer, Valentine, Texas to Comanding Officer, 5th. Cavalry, Marfa, Texas, Subject Recommendation of Scout, November 3, 1919, BBD-RG393.

[318]. *Marfa New Era* , February , 1914,

[319]. J. S. Ayers, Special Inspector, Treasury Department, United States Customs Service, Port of El Paso, Texas to Pat Kelly, 1st Lieut, Cavalry Headquarters, Eighth Cavalry, Marfa, Texas, April 16, 1918,

[320]. Office of the Special Agent Treasury Department to Pat Kelly, 1st Lieut, Cavalry, Headquarters Eight Cavalry, Marfa, Texas, April 16, 1918, BBD-RG393.

[321]. Greene Interview; undated notes, Manual Carrasco to Glenn Justice.

[322]. Ibid.

[323]. Ibid; O. C. Kirven, Clerk of the Court of Criminal Appeals of Texas, May 13, 1918, "J.J. Kilpatrick Jr. Murder Case", BBD-RG393.

[324]. Ibid.

[325]. Commanding Officer, Troop K, 8th Cavalry to Commanding Officer, Big Bend District, Marfa, Texas, 21 September, 1919; Records of the United States Army continental commands, 1821-1920; Record Group 393; Washington National Records Center, Suitland, Maryland; hereafter cited BBD-RG93.

[326]. Ibid.

[327]. Leonard F. Matlack, 1st. Lieut. Cavalry to C. O. Big Bend District, Marfa, Texas, May 18, 1918, BBD-RG93.

[328]. Hq. Eighth Cavalry, Marfa, Texas, May 22, 1918 to Commanding General, Southern Department, Fort Sam Houston, Texas; J.J. Kilpatrick Sr. to Senator Morris Shepard, Washington D. C., August 24, 1918; BBD-RG93.

[329]. Matlack at Candelaria to Col. Langhorne, Signal Corps United States Army Telegram, January 25, 1918; BBD-RG93.

[330]. Commanding Officer, Troop K, 8th Cavalry to Commanding Officer, Big Bend District, Marfa, Texas, Subject: History of the Kilpatrick Family at Candelaria, Texas, September 21, 1919, BBD-RG93.

[331]. Ibid; "Military Information Digest, Marfa Sector"Jan. 20, 1931; BBD-RG93,

[332]. District Intelligence Officer to Department Intelligence Officer, Hq. So. Dept., Fort Sam Houston Texas, Subject Dawkins Kilpatrick, October 4, 1918, BBD-RG93.

[333]. J.J. Kilpatrick to Hon. T.W. Gregory, Washington, D. C., April 22, 1918, BBD-RG93.

[334]. Matlack to Col. Langhorne, Signal Corps., United States Army Telegram, Jan. 21, 1918.

[335]. G. T. Langhorne, Colonel, 8th Cavalry to Commanding General, Southern Department, Fort Sam Houston, Texas, May 22, 1918, BBD-RG93.

[336]. Charles Brite, correspondence, Aug. 12, 1918, BBD-RG93.

[337]. Greene Interview.

[338]. Ibid; Mrs. J.S.H. Howard to American Red Cross, Marfa, Texas, 1918 correspondence, BBD-RG93.

[339]. Commanding Officer, Troop K 8th Cavalry to Commanding Officer, Big Bend District, Marfa, Texas, Subject: History of the Kilpatrick Family at Candelaria, Texas, September 21, 1919, BBD-RG93.

[340]. Greene Interview.

[341]. Commanding Officer, Troop K 8th Cavalry to Commanding Officer, Big Bend District, Marfa, Texas, Subject: History of the Kilpatrick Family at Candelaria, Texas, September 21, 1919, BBD-RG93.

[342]. J.J. Kilpatrick, "The Attempt to Assassinate Me and My Grey-Haired Wife", MS, Barker Texas History Center, Austin, 1-20.

[343]. Texas State Historical Association, *Handbook of Texas*, (Austin: Texas State Historical Association, 1952), 1:218, hereafter cited TSHA; Noel L. Keith, *The Brites of* Capote (Fort Worth: Texas Christian University Press, 1952), 1-5, 45; United States Geological Survey, Marfa map, 1:250,000 (rev. 1975); General Land Office State of Texas, *Acreage in Texas by Counties* map.

[344]. TSHA, 1:218.

[345]. Keith, 257.

[346]. Charles Deaton, *Texas Postal History Handbook*, 2nd. Ed. (Houston, 1981), 78.

[347]. Marfa *New Era* 12-23-15; according to the *Oxford English Dictionary*, a traction engine is a stationary engine sometimes used for agricultural purposes such as the threashing of grain or pumping of water.

[348]. Presidio County had only 5,218 residents in 1910, *Abstract of the Thirteenth Census of the United States 1910*, "Number and Distribution of Inhabitants," 590.

[349]. W. D. Smithers, "Army Supply Routes To Border Outposts In the Upper Part of Presidio County Of the Big Bend District of Texas 1916-21," Archives of the Big Bend, Sul Ross State University, Alpine, Texas (hereafter cited as ABB).

[350]. United States Senate, *Investigation of Mexican Affairs*, "Preliminary report and Hearings of the Committee on Foreign Relations United States Senate Pursuant to Senate Resolution 106," testimony of Sam H. Neill, 2:1040-52 (hereafter cited as FSIMA).

[351]. Keith, 110; EPT December 27, 1917.

[352]. FSIMA, testimony of Sam H. Neill, 2:1040-52; Keith, 114.

[353]. Ibid.

[354]. EPT, December 27, 1917.

[355]. Ibid; FSIMA, testimony of Sam H. Neill, 2:1040-52, Keith, 114.

[356]. Ibid.

[357]. Ibid; H. M. Bandy to Henry Warren, April 10, 1925, "Harry Warren Papers 1835-1932," ABB (hereafter cited as HWP).

[358]. H. M. Bandy to Henry Warren, April 10, 1925, HWP.

[359]. Keith, 114.

[360]. Warren, "The Raid On Luke Brite's Ranch, Presidio County, Texas, On Xmas Day, 1917," HWP.

[361]. Ibid.

[362]. Ibid; EPT, December 27, 1917.

[363]. Warren, "The Raid on Luke Brite's Ranch."

[364]. Ibid; Testimony of Grover Webb 2:1526-29.

[365]. Ibid.

[366]. Ibid; EPT December 22 and 27, 1917.

[367]. Testimony of Grover Webb, 2:1526-29; Keith, 113.

[368]. Ibid; USGS, *Marfa* Map 1:250,000; Pat Greene, "Taped Interviews Pat Greene to Glenn Justice," July 28, 1984.

[369]. Testimony of Grover Webb, 2:1526-29.

[370]. Ibid; Testimony of Sam Neill, 1040-52; USGS, *Marfa* map; Smithers, "Army Supply Routes."

[371]. EPT, December 27, 1917.

[372]. FSIMA, testimony of Capt. Leonard L. Matlack; 2:1627-61; *San Antonio El Bravo* H13-5, *Carta Topografica* 1:250,000 *Chihuahua Y Texas.*

[373]. *EPT* December 27, 1917.

[374]. Ibid.

[375]. EPT, December 29, 1917; Warren, "The Raid on Luke Brite's Ranch," 6.

[376]. EPT, January 1917, "Baker Approves Hobby's Plan to Patrol the Border"; Annual Report of the Adjutant General of Texas for the Year Ending December 21, 1918, TSA, Austin.

. [377]. Ibid; Montly Returns Company B, ranger Force, State of Texas for the Monthing Ending January 31, 1918; Biennial reports of the Adjutant General of Texas 1911-1918, general correspondence June 4, 1918.

[378]. USGS, *Marfa* map, 1:250,000; *Detenal carta Fopografia, San Antonio el Bravo* H13-5 1:250,000 *"Chihuahua y Texas"* map 1978; state department of Highways and Public Transportation, hereafter cited TDHP, *General Highway Map of Presidio County, Texas* (rev. 1983) Thirteenth Census of the United States: 1910-Population, Pilares Village, Precinct 8, pp. 316-21.

[379]. Harry Warren, "The Porvenir Massacre in Presidio County Texas on January 28, 1918" MS in the "Harry Warren Papers 1835-1932," Archives of the Big Bend, Sul Ross State University, Alpine, hereafter cited as HWP; TDHP, *General Highway Map of Presidio County, Texas.*

[380]. Warren, "The Porvenir Massacre," HWP; Walter Prescott Webb, *The Texas Rangers: A Century of Frontier Defence* (Austin: University of Texas Press, 1935), 502.

[381]. Robert H. Keil to Mrs J. E. Walker, personal correspondence December 31, 1961. Keil witnessed the Porvenir massacre as a young cavalry corporal.

[382]. Ibid; Proceedings of the Joint Committee of the Senate and the House in the Investigation of the Texas State Ranger Force, January 13, 1919, Investigation of the El Porvenir Fight, Statement of Cesario Huerta, pp. 1600-02.

[383]. Warren, "The Porvenir Massacre," HWP; Robert H. Keil to Mrs J. E. Walker, personal correspondence December 31, 1961.

[384]. Robert H. Keil to Mrs J. E. Walker, personal correspondence December 31, 1961, Walker papers in the J.J. Kilpatrick Collection, Archives of the Big Bend, Sul Ross State University, Alpine, Texas.

[385]. Ibid.

[386]. Ibid.

[387]. Ibid.

[388]. Ibid; Warren, "The Porvenir Massacre," HWP.

[389]. Ibid; Taped Interview, "Juan Flores to Goad Davis For The Documentary Film, *American Lynching: Strange and Bitter Fruit*" August 6, 2002.

[390]. Ibid.

[391]. Ibid.

[392]. Warren, "The Porvenir Massacre," HWP.

[393]. Ibid.

[394]. Ibid; Col. W. J. Glasgow, Special Investigator to the Commanding Officer Big Bend District, May 7, 1918; Big Bend District, 1914-15 and1917-20, Record Group 393, Washington National Records Center, Suitland, Maryland (hereafter cited as BBD-RG393); Commanding Officer, Troop K, 8th Cavalry to Commanding Officer, Big Bend District, February, 6, 1918, BBD-RG393.

[395]. Warren, "The Porvenir Massacre," HWP.

[396]. "Biographical Data Sheet of Harry Warren," HWP.

[397]. Ibid; Lieutenant Matlack to Commanding Officer Big Bend District, undated, Kilpatrick 201 file, BBD-RG393.

[398]. Alice R. Brown, County School Superintendent, to Harry Warren, March 23, 1918, Kilpatrick 201 file, BBD RG393; "Biographical Data Sheet of Harry Warren," HWP.

[399]. J.J. Kilpatrick to Hon. Thomas Blanton, March 6, 1918, Kilpatrick 201 file, BBD-RG393.

[400]. Lula D. Kilpatrick to the Adjuntant General, War Department, August 11, 1918, Kilpatrick 201 file, BBD-RG393.

[401]. J. M. Fox to General Harley, January 30, 1918, General Correspondence, Biennial Reports of the Adjutant General of Texas 1911-1918.

[402]. Proceedings of the Joint Committee of the Senate and the House in the Investigation of the Texas State Ranger Force, January 13, 1919, "Investigation of the El Porvenir fight," pp. 1602-5.

[403]. FSIMA, testimony of W. M. Hanson, 3223.

[404]. *Brownsville Herald,* July 12, 1918, as cited in the HWP; Biennial reports of the Adjutant General of Texxas 1911-1918.

[405]. W. M. Hanson to Jas. A. Harley, February 2, 1918; General Correspondence.

[406]. General Order 5, June 4, 1918, Biennial reports of the Adjutant General of Texas 1911-1918, General Correspondence.

[407]. *Brownsville Herald,* July 12, 1918, HWP.

[408]. Webb, 515; Proceedings of the Joint Committee of the Senate and the House in the Investigation of the Texas State Ranger Force, January 13, 1919, pp. 3-5, 145-48, 164.

[409]. Webb, 516.

[410]. Proceedings of the Joint Committee of the Senate and the House in the Investigation of the State Ranger Force, January 13, 1919, 966.

[411]. Ibid.

[412]. "Biographical Data Sheet of Harry Warren" HWP, H. L. McCune, Jr. to Dr. Clifford B. Casey, July 3, 1946, HWP.

[413]. District Intelligence Officer to Commanding Officer Big Bend Distrct, January 6, 1920; see also Neville Ranch Raid file in Correspondence of the District Intelligence Officer, BBD-RG393; Robert H. Keil to Mrs. J.E. Walker correspondence, December 31, 1961.

[414]. Lois Neville Kelly to Dr. Clifford Casey, September 9, 1972, Clifford B. Casey Collection 1882-1981, Archives of the Big Bend, Sul Ross State University, Alpine, Texas (hereafter cited as ABB).

[415]. Ibid.

[416]. Ibid.

[417]. Preliminary Report and Hearing of the Committee on Foreign Relations United States Senate, *Investigation of Mexican Affairs*, testimony of Ed Neville, 2:1511; *Van Horne Advocate*, March 30, 1918.

[418]. Ibid; District Intelligence Officer to Commanding Officer Big Bend District, January 6, 1920, Henry H. Anderson, Major, 8th Cavalry to Commanding Officer, Big Bend District, Marfa, Texas, Subject: Neville Raid, May 31, 1918, BBD-RG393.

[419]. Robert H. Keil to Mrs. J. E. Walker, December 31, 1961; Joyce E. Means, *Pancho Villa Days at Pilares*, (Tucson: Joyce E. Means, 1994), 211.

[420]. Ibid; Anderson, "Neville Raid."

[421]. Capt. J. S. Tate, 8th Cavalry, U.S.A., to W. J. Glasgow, Department Inspector, and Subject: Resume of Neville's Ranch Raid and Pursuit of Raiders, May 1, 1918, BBD-RG393.

[422]. Ibid.

[423]. Ibid; Harry Warren, "The Raid on Nevil's [sic] Ranch in Presidio County in 1918," MS in the Harry Warren Papers, 1835-1932, ABB (hereafter cited as HWP).

[424]. Keil to Walker, December 31, 1961; J.J. Kilpatrick, "Value of the Evidence Collected By the Fall Senate Committee: An Examination of the Exaggerated and Fabricated Testimony of Some of the Witnesses," p. 10, undated (probably written in 1919) MS, J.J. Kilpatrick Paper Collection, Barker Texas History Center, Austin, Texas; Statement of capt. J. S. Tate, 1st Lt. D. Minard, 1st Lt. T E. Boundinot, 2nd Lt. G. B. Shombers, 1st Sergeant Goehring, Headquarters Eighth Cavalry Marfa, Texas, April 25, 1918, BBD-RG393.

[425]. Capt. J. S. Tate, 8th Cavalry, U.S.A., to Col. W. J. Glasgow, Department Inspector, Subject: Resume of Neville's Ranch Raid and Pursuit of Raiders, May, 1, 1918, BBD-RG393; Warren, "Neville Raid," HWP.

[426]. Tate, "Resume of Neville's Raid," BBD-RG393.

[427]. District Intelligence Officer to Commanding Officer Big Bend District, January 6, 1920, BBD-RG393.

[428]. Keil to Walker, December 31, 1961.

[429]. Capt. J. S. Tate, 8th Cavalry, U.S.A., to Col. W. J. Glasgow, Department Inspector, Subject: Resume of Neville's Ranch Raid and Pursuit of Raiders, May 1, 1918, BBD-RG393; Kilpatrick, "Value," 10.

[430]. Department Adjutant, Fort Sam Houston, Texas, to Commanding Officer, Big Bend District, Marfa, Texas, Subject: Mexican Situation, May 13, 1918, November 11, 1918, BBD-RG393.

[431]. Lois Neville Kelly to Dr. Clifford Casey, September 9, 1972, Clifford B. Casey Collection 1882-1981, ABB.

[432]. *NYT*, November 11, 1918; Return of the Eight Regiment of cavalry, September 1917 to December 1919, *Records of the United States Army Continental Commands*, 1821-1920, Record Group 393, washington National records Center, Suitland, Maryland (hereafter cited as BBD-RG393); Robert H. Keil to Mrs. J. E. Walker, December 31, 1961.

[433]. Stacey C. Hinkle, *Wings Over the Border; The Army Air Service Armed Patrol of the United States-Mexican Border 1919-1921*, Southwestern Studies no. 26 (El Paso: Texas Western Press, 1970) 6-8; Hinkle, *Wings and Saddles: The Air and Cavalry Punitive Expedition of 1919*, Southwestern Studies no. 19 (El Paso: Texas Western Press, 1967), 3-4.

[434]. Hinkle, *Wings and Saddles*, 6-9; W. D. Smithers *1,932.90 Miles of Line and Rio Grande Boundary Was Flown Daily By Army Pilots From the Bases On Or Near The U. S.-Mexican Border In Late 1918 and 1919, In DeHavilands*, map, ABB.

[435]. Hinkle, *Wings Over the Border*, 6-8.

[436]. Ibid, 8-9.

[437]. Stacey C. Hinkle, quoted in *Wings Over the Border*, 11.

[438]. Ibid; By Order of Colonel Langhorne, November 12, 1918, Memorandum; Headquarters Big Bend District, BBD-RG393.

[439]. *NYT*, January 16, 1920; General Orders, 43, December 9, 1919, BBD-RG393.

[440]. General Orders, no. 43, December 9, 1919, Subject: The Killing of Sotol Smuggler, September 14, 1918, Lester A. Sprinkle, capt. 8th Cavalry, USA to Commanding Officer, 8th cavalry, Marfa, Texas, Subject: Investigation of drinking of sotol and crossing the river by members of Troop M, 8th Cavalry, at Ruidosa, Texas, September 2, 1918, The Commanding Officer Troop M, 8th Cavalry to the Commanding Officer Big Bend District, BBD-RG393.

[441]. J.J. Kilpatrick, Sr., "Fall Reiterates Charges That Carrancista Soldiers are Slain by Pursuing U.S. Troops: An Examination Into the Truth of These Charges and an Account of the Killing of Two Youthful sotol Smugglers and of Gregorio Renteria", MS, Barker Texas History Center, Austin, 5, 13-14.

[442]. Ibid, 13-14.

[443]. Ibid.

[444]. Ibid.

[445]. Ibid.

[446]. Ibid; 3-6; *Excelsior*, June 22, 1919; Alan Knight, *The Mexican Revolution* (Cambridge: Cambridge University Press, 1986), 2:331, 332, 359, 394.

[447]. J.J. Kilpatrick, Jr., "Nunez Ranch Raid and the Killing of Bandits on Telephone Wires," MS, barker Texas History Center, Austin; Inspector Luke Dowe to Collector of customs, Eagle Pass, Texas, February 15, 1913, see J.J. Kilpatrick file, barker Texas History Center. J.J. Kilpatrick, again in oppostition to army sources presents a different picture of Cano and captain Matlack's pursuits of him, one that is given credence by contemporary Mexican sources and recent scholarship such as Knight.

[448]. From the District Intelligence Officer, District Intelligence Office Headquarters, Big Bend District, to Commanding Officer, Subject: Names and descriptions of Mexicans who raided Neville's Ranch, January 6, 1920, BBD-RG393; Col. J. A. Gaston, 6th Cavalry, to the Commanding General, Southern Department, Subject: Weekly Report, May 18, 1917, BBD-RG393; Inspector Luke Dowe to the Collector of Customs, Eagle Pass, Texas, February 15, 1913; see J.J. Kilpatrick file, Barker Texas History Center.

[449]. *Excelsior,* June 22, 1919; Kilpatrick, "Nunez Ranch Raid."

[450]. Ibid, 9-11.

[451]. Ibid.

[452]. Ibid, 15.

[453]. Ibid; Return of Troop K, June 1919, USMU-RG-391. Troop K had 75 to 100 men in June 1919.

[454]. *Excelsior,* June 22, 1919.

[455]. J.J. Kilpatrick, "Value of The Evidence Collected By The Fall Senate Committee: An Examination of the Exaggerated and fabricated Testimony of Some of the Witnesses," MS, Barker Texas History Center, Austin, 2-3; *EPT* July 21, 1919; Francis Russell, *The Shadow of Blooming Grove: Warren G. Harding in His Times* (New York: McGraw-Hill Book Co., 1968), 266; Mark T. Gilderhus, *Diplomacy and Revolution: U.S.-Mexican Relations Under Wilson and Carranza* (Tucson: University of Arizona Press, 1977), 96-99.

[456]. *Bulletin of the National Association for the Protection of American Rights in Mexico,* 1 (February 9, 1920): 9, Investigative Case Files of the Bureau of Investigation, 1908-1922, Records of the Federal Bureau of Investigation, RG-65 (hereafter ICFFBI-RG65) available on microfilm from the National Archives, see roll no. 874); Russell, 638, 641.

[457]. John Mason Hart, *Revolutionary Mexico: The Coming and Process of the Mexican Revolution* (Berkeley: University of California Press, 1987), 155; ICFFBI-RG65, roll no. 874.

[458]. John Suter, Bureau of Investigation, Washington, D. C., From Charles Boynton, October 16, 1919, ICFFBI-RG65, roll no. 874.

[459]. *EPT,* July 21, 1919; Kilpatrick, "Value," 2-3.

[460]. *San Antonio Express*, August 25, 1919.

[461]. Ibid.

[462]. Ibid.

[463]. Ibid.

[464]. Ibid; Kilpatrick, "Nunez Ranch Raid," 27.

[465]. Ibid.

[466]. *San Antonio Express*, August 25, 1919.

[467]. *El Paso Herald*, August 18, 1919.

[468]. *NYT*, August 18, 1919.

[469]. Capt. Leonard F. Matlack, 8th Cavalry, to Commanding General, Southern Department, Ft. Sam Houston, Texas, Subject: Report on payment of ransom for aviators, August 27, 1919, BBD-RG393.

[470]. Ibid.

[471]. Ibid.

[472]. Commanding Officer, U. S. Troops, Punitive Expedition to Mexico, to Commanding Officer, Big Bend District, Marfa, Texas, August 24, 1919, BBD-RG393.

[473]. Ibid; Harry Warren, "The Punitive Expedition to Mexico" MS, HWP, ABB, 3-4; Testimony of Sgt. Joseph Reuth, Rocord of the Trial by General Court-Martial of Capt. James P. Yancey, Cavalry, 75-84, Office of the Judge Advocate, the Pentagon, Washington, D. C.

[474]. Ibid; Warren, "Punitive Expedition to Mexico."

[475]. Testimony of Sgt. Joseph Reuth, Rocord of the Trial by General Court-Martial of Capt. James P. Yancey, Cavalry, 75-84, Office of the Judge Advocate, the Pentagon, Washington, D. C.; Warren, "Punitive Expedition to Mexico."

[476]. Ibid.

[477]. Warren, "Punitive Expedition to Mexico," J.J. Kilpatrick, "Border History: The Late Punitive Expedition Into Mexico," 5, 16-18; MS, Barker Texas History Center, Austin; Kilpatrick and Warren both described the "sotol spree" of the cavalrymen but their sources are unclear. Warren failed to name his sources and Kilpatrick said, " My information comes from several United States Soldiers and especially from an Army Officer, all of whom were present." Kilpatrick's son, Dawkins, served as a scout for the expedition and likely provided some of the information. No reference to the event is made in the official army records but in view of the prohibitions against the drinking of sotol, this does not seem surprising.

[478]. Warren, "The Punitive Expedition to Mexico," 5-8; *EPT* August 24, 1919.

[479]. Ibid.

[480]. *EPT, August* 23, 1919; Warren, "The Punitive Expedition to Mexico," 5.

[481]. *EPT,* August 23, 1919; Hinkle, *Wings and Saddles,* 37, *NYT* August *25, 1919.*

[482]. Mrs. J. E. Walker, interview with author, August 1987; Jose hernadez, interview with author, undated notes made about 1981.

[483]. *EPT,* August 29, 1919.

[484]. Commanding Officer, U. S. Troops, Punitive Expedition to Mexico to Commanding Officer, Big Bend District, Marfa, Texas, August 24, 1919, BBD-RG393; Marfa *New Era,* March 27, 1920; *EPT,* August 21, 1919.

[485]. P. H. Greene, To Whom it May Concern, April 8, 1918, BBD-RG393.

[486]. E. C. McNeill, Major, Judge Advocated, Memorandum re Clemency for Capt. J. P. Yancey, November 10, 1920, BBD-RG393.

[487]. Ibid.

[488]. General Court-Martial Orders, no. 6, War Department, Washington, February 1, 1921, Office of the Judge Advocate, the Pentagon, Washington, D. C.

[489]. Mrs. J. E. Walker, interview with author, Åugust 1987; http:userdb.rootsweb.com/ky/death/ search.cgilast=matlack&first=leonard.

[490]. Greene Interview; Mrs. J. E. Walker, interview with author, Åugust 1987

[491]. William H. Kilpatrick to Mrs. J.E. Walker, July 1, 1943.

BIBLIOGRAPHY

Allen, Robert. "The Silver Heart of Chinati" *Voice of the Mexican Border,* March 1934.

Applegate, Howard G. and C. Wayne Hanselka. *La Junta de los Rios Del Norte y Conchos,* El Paso: Texas Western Press, 1974.

Arnold, Owen. *Irons in the Fire: Cattle Brand Lore,* London: Abelard-Schuman, 1965.

Ayer, Mrs. Edward E. *The Memorial of Fray Alonso De Benevides 1630,* Albuquerque: Horn and Wallace, 1965.

Batchelder, Roger. *Watching and Waiting on the Border.* Boston: Houghton Mifflin, 1917.

Braddy, Haldeen. *The Paradox of Pancho Villa.* El Paso: Texas Western Press, 1966.

Brown, Karen. "They Moved West With Destiny" 1965 notes.

Black, Lowell D. and Sara H. Black. *An Officer and a Gentleman: The Military Career of Lieutenant Henry O. Flipper,* Dayton: the Lora Company, 1985.

___________. *Pershing's Mission in Mexico.* El Paso: Texas Western Press, 1978.

Bolton, Herbert Eugene, ed. *Spanish Exploration In The Southwest: 1542-1706,* New York: Scribner's Sons, 1916.

Carranza, Alberto Salinas. Mexico, D.F.: *La Expedicion Punitiva,* 1936.

Casey, Clifford B. *Mirages, Mysteries and Reality: Brewster County, Texas The Big Bend of the Rio Grande.* Seagraves, Pioneer Book Publishers, Inc., 1972.

Carlson, Paul. "The Discovery of Silver in West Texas", *West Texas Historical Association Yearbook,* LIV, 1978.

__________. *Pecos Bill: A Military Biography of William R. Shafter,* College Station, Texas A & M University Press, 1989.

Castaneda, Carlos E. *Our Catholic Heritage in Texas, 1519-1936,* Austin: Von Boeckmann-Jones, 1936.

Chambers, Boyd. "Taped Interviews to Glenn Justice" December, 1994.

Chipman, Donald E. "In Search of Cabeza De Vaca's Route Across Texas: An Historiographical Survey" *Southwestern Historical Quarterly* 91(October 1987)

Clark, John, Jr. *Archaelogical Investigations At The Ramon Castelo Outbuilding, Shafter, Presidio County, Texas,* 37, Austin: Texas Department of Highways and Public Transportation, 1988.

Clendenen, Clarence. *The United States and Pancho Villa: A Study in Unconventional Diplomacy.* Ithaca: Cornell University Press, 1961.

________________. *Blood on the Border: The United States Army and the Mexican Irregulars.* New York: Macmillan, 1969.

Coerver, Don M., and Linda B. Hall. *Texas and the Mexican Revolution: A Study in State and National Border Policy 1910-1920.* San Antonio: Trinity University Press, 1984.

Covey, Cyclone ed. *Cabeza De Vaca's Adventures in the Unknown Interior of America,* Albuquerque: University of New Mexico Press, 1987.

Cumberland, Charles C. *Mexican Revolution: Genesis Under Madero.* Austin & London: University of Texas Press, 1952.

________________. *Mexican Revolution: The Constitutionalist Years:* Austin & London: University of Texas Press, 1972.

Deaton, Charles. *Texas Postal History Handbook,* Houston: 1981.

Dooley, Claude and Betty Dooley and the Texas Historical Commission, *Why Stop? A Guide to Texas Historical Roadside Markers,* (Houston: Gulf Publishing Company, 1978.

Eckhart, George B. "Spanish Missions of Texas: 1680-1800", *Journal of the Arizona Archaeological & Historical Society* 3 (1967).

Gilderhus, Mark T. *Diplomacy and Revolution: U.S.-Mexican Relations Under Wilson and Carranza.* Tucson: University of Arizona Press, 1977.

James B. Gillett, *Six Years With The Texas Rangers1877-1881*, Lincoln: University of Nebraska Press, 1976.

Gregg, J. E. "Additional History of Presidio County" *Voice of the Mexican Border,* (1934).

________. "The History of Presidio County" MA Thesis, Austin, University of Texas, (1933).

Greene, Pat. "Taped Interviews to Glenn Justice 7-28-84, 8-5-84, 10-13-84."

Gomez, Arthur. "The Glenn Springs-Boquillas Raid Reconsidered: Diplomatic Intrigue on the Rio Grande." *The Journal of Big Bend Studies* 4 (1992).

Guzman, Martin Luis. *Memoirs of Pancho Villa,* trans. by Virginia H. Taylor, Austin: University of Texas Press, 1973.

Hackett, Charles Wilson, ed. *Historical Documents Relating to New Mexico, Nueva Vizcaya and Approaches There to 1773,* Washington: Carnegie Institution of Washington, 1926.

Haley, J. Evetts. *Charles Goodnight: Cowman and Plainsman,* Norman: University of Oklahoma Press, 1983.

__________. *Jeff Milton: A Good Man With a Gun* , Norman: University of Oklahoma Press, 1982.

Harris, Charles III, and Louis R. Sadler, "The Plan of San Diego and the Mexican United States War Crisis of 1916: a Reexamination." *Hispanic American Historical Review 58* (August 1978).

___________, "The Underside of the Mexican Revolution." *The Americas 39* (1982).

___________, "Pancho Villa and the Columbus Raid: The Missing Documents." *New Mexico Historical Review* 50 (1975).

Harris, Jodie P. "Protecting the Big Bend: a Guardsman's View." *Southwestern Historical Quarterly* 78 (1975).

Harrison, Irene. "Spear-Cross Lawman" undated notes.

Hart, John Mason. *Revolutionary Mexico: The Coming and Process of the Mexican Revolution.* Berkeley: University of California Press, 1987.

Hill, Larry D. *Emissaries to a Revolution: Woodrow Wilson's Executive Agents in Mexico.* Batton Rouge: Louisiana State University Press, 1974.

Hill, Jim Dan. *Minutemen in Peace and War: History of the National Guard.* Harrisburg: Stackkpole Co., 1964.

Hinkle, Stacy C. "Wings and Saddles: The Air and Cavalry Punitive Expedition of 1919" *Southwestern Studies*, No. 19. El Paso: Texas Western Press, 1967.

Hickerson, Nancy P. "The Visits Of the Lady In Blue: An Episode In the History of the South Plains, 1629 ", *Journal of Anthropological Research* (1990).

Hobsbawm, Eric. *Bandits.* New York: Pantheon Books, 1981.

Hodge, Fredrick Webb, ed. *Handbook of American Indians North of Mexico*, Rowman and Littlefield, 1971.

May, Irwin, Jr. "Welfare And Ranchers: The Emergency Cattle Purchase Program and Emergency Work Relief Program in Texas: 1934-1935" *West Texas Historical Association Year Book*, XLVII, Abilene, 1971.

John, Elizabeth A. "Spanish-Indian Relations in the Big Bend Region" *Journal of Big Bend Studies* 3 (1991).

Johnson, Robert Bruce. "The Punitive Expedition: A Military Diplomatic and Political History of Pershing's Chase After Pancho Villa, 1916-1917." Ph.D. diss., University of Southern California, 1964.

Katz, Friedrich. "Pancho Villa and the Attack on Columbus, New Mexico." *American Historical Review* 83 (1978).

___________. *The Secret War in Mexico: The United States and the Mexican Revolution.* Chicago: University of Chicago Press, 1981.

___________. *Villa: El Gobernador Revolucionario De Chihuahua.* Mexico: Talleries Graficos Del Estado De Chihuahua, 1984.

Kelly, J. Charles. "Juan Sabeata and Diffusion in Aboriginal Texas", *American Anthropologist* 57 (1955).

Kelly, J. Charles. "Jumano and Patarabueye Relations at La Junta de los Rios," *Museum of Anthropology, University of Michigan*, 1986.

__________. "The Historic Indian Pueblos of La Junta De Los Rios", *New Mexico Historical Review* XXVII (1952)

Keil, Bob. "Personal Correspondence to Mrs. J. E. Walker 1961-1969."

Keith, Noel L. *The Brites of Capote.* Fort Worth: Texas Christian University Press, 1952.

Kilpatrick, J.J. "Personal Papers and Unpublished Manuscript 1857-1935. "Barker Texas History Center, Austin.

Knight, Alan. *The Mexican Revolution.* 2 vols. Cambridge: Cambridge University Press, 1986.

Knight, Bill. "Interview With Glenn Justice" August 2000.

Lay, Shawn. *War, Revolution and the Klu Klux Klan: A Study of Intolerance in a Border City.* El Paso: Texas Western Press, 1985.

Leavitt, Corning, Jr. *Baronial Forts of the Big Bend: Ben Leaton, Milton Faver and Their Private Forts in Presidio County*, Austin: Trinity University Press, 1969.

Leckie, William H. *The Buffalo Soldiers: A Narrative of the Negro Cavalry in the West*, Norman: University of Oklahoma Press, 1978.

Leckie, William H. and Shirley A. Leckie. *Unlikely Warriors: General benjamin grierson and His Family*, Norman: University of Oklahoma Press, 1984.

Lewis, Tracy Hammond. *Along the Rio Grande.* New York: Lewis Publishing Co., 1916.

Madison, Virginia. *The Big Bend Country of Texas.* New York: October House, Inc., 1969.

Madrid, Enrique, trans. *Captain Commander Joesph de Ydoiaga's Report to the Viceroy of New Spain*, Austin: Texas Historical Commission, 1992.

Mason, Herbert Mulloy, Jr. *The Great Pursuit* New York: Random House, 1970.

Means, Joyce E. *Pancho Villa Days at Pilares.*. Tuscon, 1985.

Mecham, J. Lloyd. "The Second Spanish Expedition To New Mexico", *New Mexico Historical Review* 1 (1926).

__________. "Antonio De Espejo And His Journey To New Mexico" *Southwestern Historical Quarterly* 30 (1927).

Metz, Leon C. *Fort bliss: An Illustrated History.* El Paso: Mangan Books, 1981.

Meyer, Michael C. *Mexican Rebal: Pasquel Orozco and the Mexican Revolution.* Lincoln: University of Nebraska Press, 1972.

Mitchell, F. A. "The Stampede At Robbers' Roost", *Voice of the Mexican Border*, Marfa, 1933.

Mitchell, William Burton. "My First Trip To The Big Bend 1885", MS in the W. B. Mitchell Collection, Archives of the Big Bend, Sul Ross State University, Alpine.

Munch, Francis J. *"Villa's Columbus Raid: Practical Politics or German Design?"* New Mexico Historical Review 44 (1969): 189-214.

Newcomb, W.W. *The Indians of Texas: From Prehistoric to Modern Times*, Austin, University of Texas Press, 1984.

Polese, Richard, ed. *"Assignment: Villa Raid, Exerpts From the Journal of Harold Palmer Brown."* El Palacio: Magazine of the Museum of New Mexico (Fall 1980): 2-14.

Pratt, Walter Merriman. "On the Border With Our Army." New England Magazine 46 (July-August 1911).

Pruett, Jessie A. "Life of Philip Halker Pruett Written From the Memories of Jessie A. Pruett" unpublised manuscript.

Raht, Carlysle Graham. *The Romance of Davis Mountains and Big Bend Country*. Rahtbooks Co., 1963.

Randolf, J. Ralph. "Border Reaction to the Villa Raids." *West Texas Historical Association Yearbook* vol. 49 (1973).

Raun, G. G. "The National Guard on the Border and One Soldier's Viewpoint." *The Journal of Big Bend Studies* 6 (1994).

Reed, John. *Insurgent Mexico*. New York: 1917.

Richmond, Douglas W. *Venustiano Carranza's Nationalist Struggle*, 1893-1920. Lincoln: University of Nebraska Press, 1983.

Russell, Francis. *The Shadow of Blooming Grove: Warren G. Harding in His Times*. New York: McGraw-Hill Book Co., 1968.

Samora, Julian, Joe Bernal, and Albert Pena. *Gunpowder Justice*. London: University of Notre Dame Press, 1979.

Sandos, James A. "German Involvement in Northern Mexico, 1915-1916: A New Look at the Columbus Raid." *Hispanic American Historical Review*. 50 (February 1970).

Scobee, Barry. "Don Milton Faver: Founder of a Kingdom", *True West* (1962).

Scott, Hugh L. *Some Memories of A Soldier*. New York Century Co., 1928.

Smithers, W. D. *Bandit Raids in the Big Bend Country*. Alpine: Sul Ross State College, 1964.

Smith, Ralph A. "Bounty Power Against The West Texas Indians", West Texas Historical Association

___________. *Chronicles of the Big Bend*. Austin: Madrona Press, Inc., 1979.

Swift, Roy L. and Leavitt Corning, Jr. *Three Roads to Chihuahua: The Great Wagon Roads That Opened the Southwest: 1823-1883*, Austin: Eakin Press, 1988.

Tate, Michael L. "Pershing's Punitive Expedition: Pursuer of Bandits or Presidental Panacea?" *The Americas* 32 (1975): 46-72.

Texas State Archives. Austin. *Proceedings of the Joint Committee of the Senate and the House in the Investigation of the Texas State Ranger Force.* January 13, 1919.

__________. *Biennial Reports of the Adjutant General of Texas 1911-1918.*

__________. *Governors' Papers: William P. Hobby.*

__________. *Governors' Papers: James E. Ferguson.*

__________. *Ranger Papers.*

Thompson, Cecilia. *History of Marfa and Presidio County, Texas 1535-1946,* Austin: Nortex Press, 1985.

Tompkins, Col. Frank. *Chasing Villa: The Story Behind the Story of Pershing's Expedition Into Mexico.* Harrisburg, Pa.: Military Service Publishing Co., 1934.

Toulmin, Harry A. *With Pershing in Mexico.* Harrisburg, Pa.: Military Service Publishing Co., 1935.

Tyler, Ronnie C. *The Big Bend: A History of the Last Texas Frontier.* Washington, D.C.: National Park Service, 1975.

__________. "Notes and Documents: The Little Punitive Expedition in the Big Bend." *Southwestern Historical Quarterly,* 78 (January 1975): 271-91.

Unites States Army, *Records of the United States Army Continental Commands, 1821-1920.* Record Group 393, National Archives Annex, Suitland, Md.

__________. *Records of the United States Army Mobile Units 1821-1942,* Record Group 391, National Archives, Washington, D. C.

__________. Department of Justice. *Investigative Case Files of the Bureau of Investigation,* 1908-1922, Records of the Federal Bureau of Investigation, Record Group, 65.

__________.Department of State. *Papers Relating to the Foreign Relations of the United States,* 1910-1920.

__________. Department of State. *Records of the Department of State Relating to the Internal Affairs of Mexico* 1910-1929.

United States Senate. *Investigation of Mexican Affairs.* Senate Document 285, 66th Congress, vols. 1 and 2.

__________. WarDepartment. *Annual Report, 1910-1920,* Washington: Government Printing Office, 1910-1921.

Utley, Robert M. *Fort Davis National Historic Site, Texas,* Washington: United States Department of the Interior National Park Service, 1965.

Utley, Robert M. *Frontier Regulars: The United States Army and the Indian: 1866-1891,* New York: Macmillian Publishing Co. Inc.

Warren, Harry. "Harry Warren Papers 1835-1932," Archives of the Big Bend, Sul Ross State University, Alpine.

Wasserman, Mark. *Capitalists, Caciques and Revolution: The Native Elite and Foreign Enterprise in Chihuahua, Mexico* 1854-1911. Chapel Hill: University of North Carolina Press, 198

Webb, Walter Prescott. *The Texas Rangers: A Century of Frontier Defense.* Austin: University Press, 1935.

White, E. Bruce. "The Muddied Waters of Columbus, New Mexico." *The Americas* 32 (1975).

Willeford, Glenn P. "American Red Cross Activities at the Battle of Ojinaga, December 1913-January 1914" *Journal of Big Bend Studies* 12 (2000).

Williams, Clayton. "The Pontoon Bridge of the Pecos, 1869-1886", *The Permian Historical Society Annual* XVII, 1978.

Wolfskill, George and Douglas W. Richmond, eds. *Essay on the Mexican Revolution: Revisionist Views of the Leaders.* Austin: University of Texas Press, 1979.

Wood, Tommy D. "Interview With Glenn Justice" October, 1994.

Wooster, Robert. *History of Fort Davis,* Santa Fe: Southwest Cultural Resources Center National Park Service, 1990.

Young, Danny Martin. "Identification of the Jumano Indians" MA Thesis, Sul Ross State University, Alpine (1970).

Candelaria army camp about 1918.
Courtesy Johnnie Chambers.

Captain Leonard F. Matlack, center, at Camp Kenney in Candelaria in 1917. According to a caption written on the back of the photo, the man on the left is described as the "leader of the Brite ranch raid." On the right stands the Presidente or mayor of San Antonio del Bravo
Courtesy Johnnie Chambers.

Lacking explosives, the Brite raiders attempted to batter open a safe with axes taken from the store's merchandise. Atop the safe is a broken axe used by the raiders.
Photo by Glenn Justice.

1919 view of Candelaria with army camp in the foreground.
San Antonio del Bravo, Mexico lies in the distance.
Photo from Marian Walker collection.

Interior of the Brite store as it appeared in 1986.
Photo by Glenn Justice.

'he Brite Ranch store in 1986. On Christmas Day 1917, Mexican bandits robbed
e store and hanged mailman Mickey Welch from the rafters in a back room.
'hoto by Glenn Justice.

James Judson Kilpatrick, the "King of Candelaria" poses in this undated photo.
Photo from Marian Walker collection.

Front view of Kilpatrick store, adobe structure on the right is one of the cotton gins.
Courtesy Johnnie Chambers.

◄ *The Eighth Cavalry band plays in front of Kilpatrick's store.*
Courtesy Burton McKenzie.

Kilpatrick's store in Candelaria. Note the "sleeping tower" above the porch on the left where the King of Candelaria is said to have mounted a .30 caliber machine gun to defend his town from Mexican raiders.
Photo from Marian Walker collection.

Darwin Dawkins Kilpatrick is shown in front of Kilpatrick store in Candelaria.
Photo from Marian Walker collection.

Dawkins Kilpatrick sits on his 1913 Indian 61 twin cylinder motorcycle at Candelaria. J.J. Kilpatrick stands at the far left.
Courtesy Marilyn Kilpatrick.

Dawkins Kilpatrick demonstrates his riding skill in Candelaria.
Photo from Marian Walker Collection.

Jesus Renteria with his wife and child in an undated photo.Renteria was also known as "Mocho" or "Corkleg" because of his missing right arm and leg. Although the U. S. Army claimed that Renteria was killed in 1919, there is some evidence that he lived until the 1970's.
Photo from Marian Walker collection.

Kilpatrick cotton shown after being hauled over the Candelaria Rimrock by mule team to Marfa.
Photo from Marian Walker collection.

Chico Cano and his men in Candelaria about 1917.
Photo from Marian Walker collection.

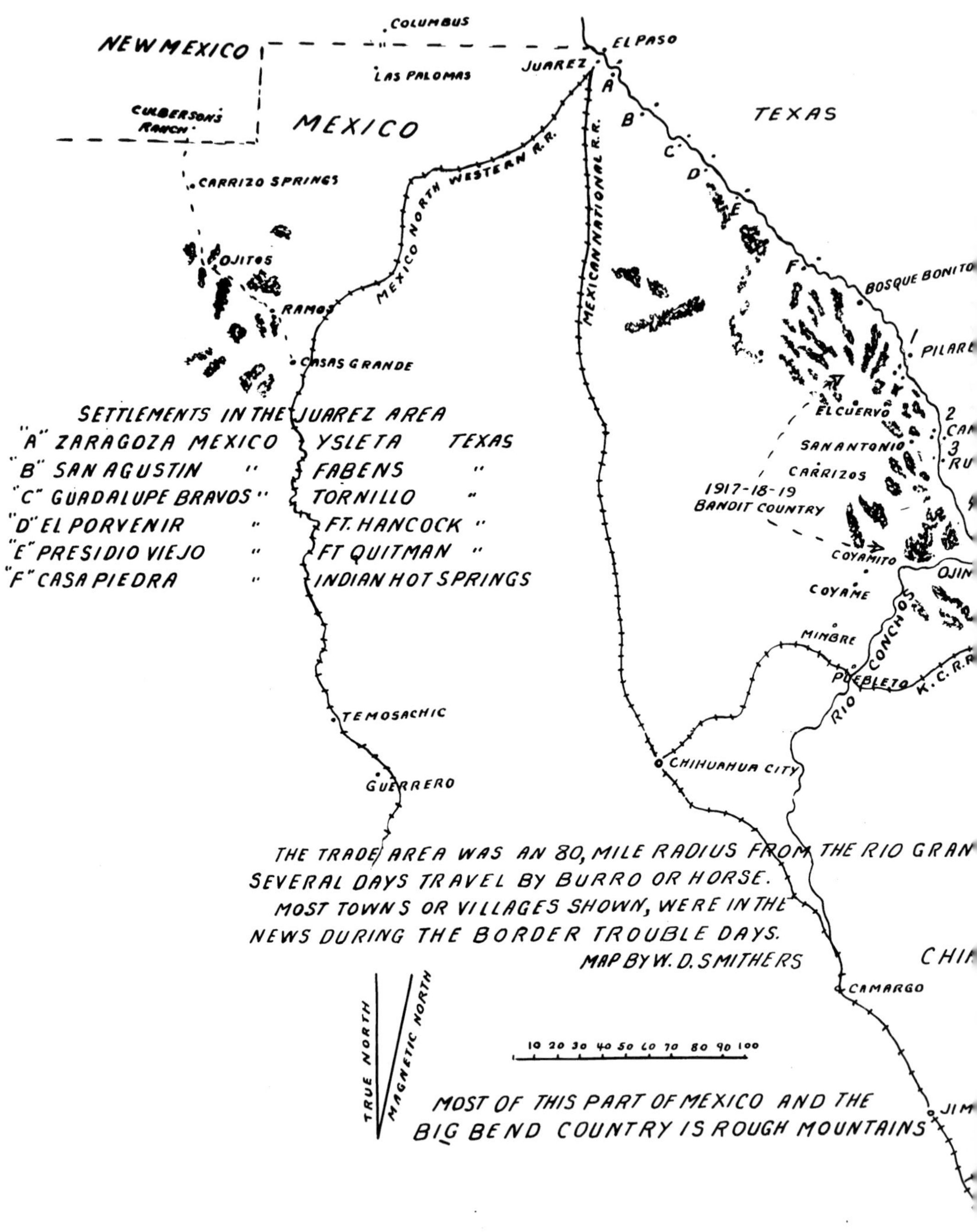

"Trading Posts on the Texas Side of the Big Bend In 1916-30"
Map by W. D. Smithers.
Archives of the Big Bend, Bryan Wildenthal Library, Sul Ross State University, Alpine, Texas.

ODING POSTS ON THE TEXA'S SIDE OF THE BIG BEND IN 1916~30.

ILARES,	OPPOSITE	PILARES	MEXICO
ANDELARIA	"	SAN ANTONIO	"
UIDOSA	"	BARRANCA	"
NDIO (LOS ADOBES)	"	BUENA VISTA	"
RESIDIO	"	OJINAGA	"
OLVO (REDFORD)	"	MULATO	"
AJITAS	"	LAJITAS	"
ASTOLON	"	SANTA HELENA	"
OHNSON'S	"	SIERRO CHINO	"
IOT SPRINGS			
DEEMERS	"	BOQUILLAS	"
CHATA'S	"	"	"

OSE NEAR THE RIO GRANDE WERE HANOLD'S,
NN SPRINGS, LA NORIA AND TERLINGUA. 15
(13) (14)

LANGTRY.
JUZGADO
RIO GRANDE
PORTATES
LESS INHABITED
PART OF THE BORDER
DEL RIO
VILLA ACUANA
15
14
7 LAJITAS
13
12
11
8
10
BOQUILLAS
9
EAGLE PASS
PIEDRAS NEGRAS
GLENN'S SPRINGS
RAIDERS HIDE OUT
ELPINO
STILLON
MEXICAN NATIONAL
COAHUILA
MUZQUIZ
SABINAS
OCAMPO
SIERRA MOJADA
NORTE
CUATRO CIENEGAS
MONCLOVA
SABINAS HIDALGO
MONTERREY
SALTILLO

Chico and his men in Candelaria.
Photo from Marian Walker collection.

"Army Supply Routes to Border Outposts in the Upper Part of Presidio County 1916-21." Map by W. D. Smithers, master photographer, map-maker and illustrator. ▶
Archives of the Big Bend, Bryan Wildenthal Library, Sul Ross State University, Alpine, Texas.

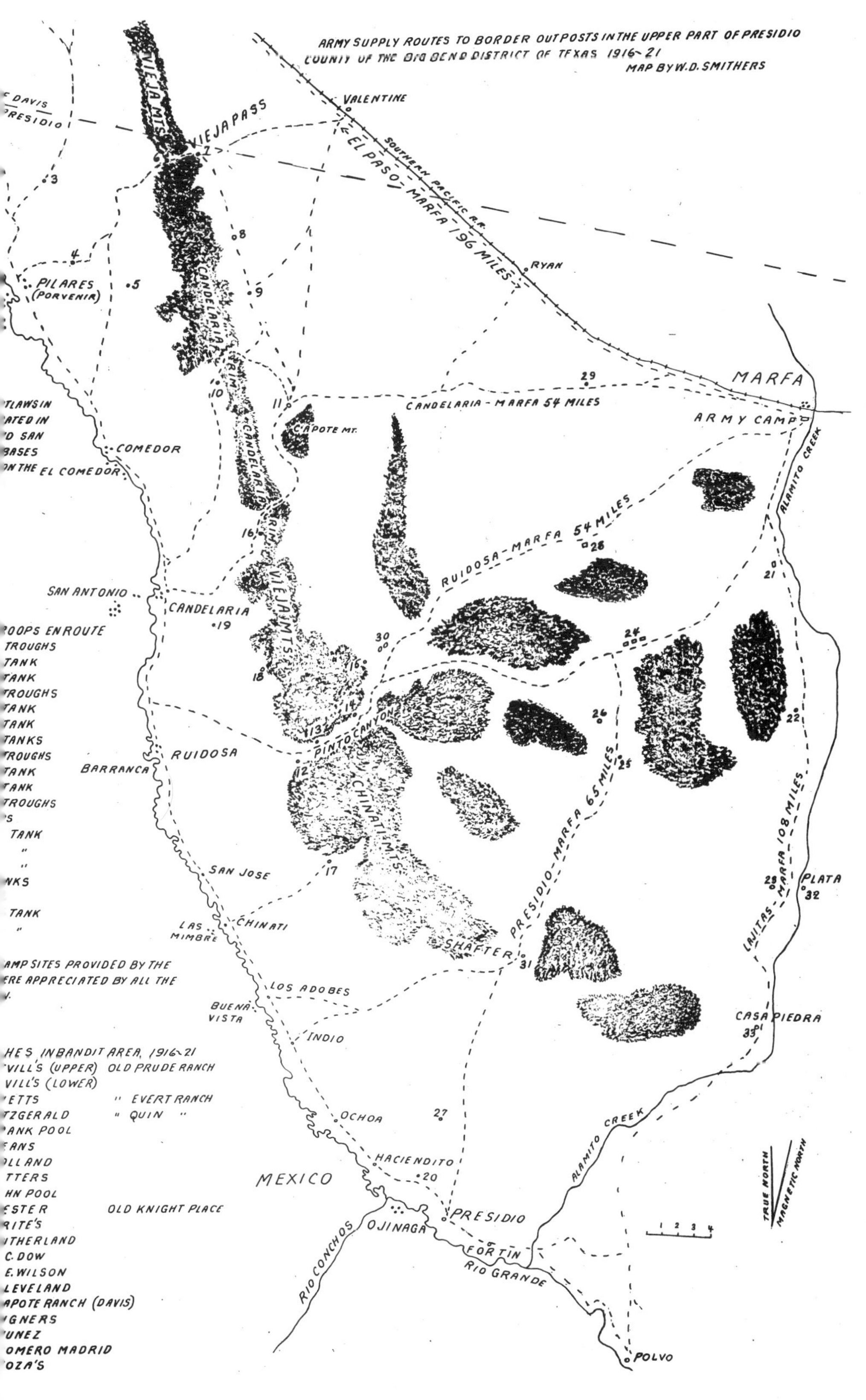
ARMY SUPPLY ROUTES TO BORDER OUTPOSTS IN THE UPPER PART OF PRESIDIO COUNTY OF THE BIG BEND DISTRICT OF TEXAS 1916-21
MAP BY W. D. SMITHERS
VALENTINE
VIEJA PASS
VIEJA MTS
SOUTHERN PACIFIC R.R.
EL PASO - MARFA 196 MILES
RYAN
PILARES (PORVENIR)
CANDELARIA RIM
CAPOTE MT.
CANDELARIA - MARFA 54 MILES
MARFA
ARMY CAMP
ALAMITO CREEK
COMEDOR
RUIDOSA - MARFA 54 MILES
SAN ANTONIO
CANDELARIA
VIEJA MTS
PINTO CANYON
RUIDOSA
BARRANCA
CHINATI MTS
PRESIDIO - MARFA 65 MILES
SAN JOSE
LAS MIMBRE
CHINATI
SHAFTER
LAJITAS - MARFA 108 MILES
PLATA
CASA PIEDRA
LOS ADOBES
BUENA VISTA
INDIO
OCHOA
HACIENDITO
MEXICO
PRESIDIO
OJINAGA
RIO CONCHOS
FORTIN
RIO GRANDE
POLVO
TRUE NORTH
MAGNETIC NORTH
1 2 3 4
OLD PRUDE RANCH
" EVERT RANCH
" QUIN "
OLD KNIGHT PLACE

Sam H. Neill was wounded slightly as he fought off Mexican attackers during the Brite Ranch Raid. He is standing in front of a window shot out during the raid.
Archives of the Big Bend, Bryan Wildenthal Library, Sul Ross State University, Alpine, Texas.